Consumer Protection

Consumer Protection

Edited by Lester A. Sobel

Contributing editors: Joseph Fickes, Mary Elizabeth Clifford, Stephen Orlofsky

Indexer: Grace M. Ferrara

FACTS ON FILE, INC. NEW YORK, N.Y.

Consumer Protection

© Copyright, 1976, by Facts on File, Inc.

All rights reserved. No part of this book may be reproduced in any form without the permission of the publisher except for reasonably brief extracts used in reviews or scholarly works. Published by Facts on File, Inc.,
119 West 57th Street, New York, N.Y. 10019.

Library of Congress Catalog Card Number 75-20836
ISBN 9-87196-287-X

9 8 7 6 5 4 3 2 1
PRINTED IN
THE UNITED STATES OF AMERICA

Contents

	Page
INTRODUCTION	1
GOVERNMENT POLICY	5
Kennedy Administration	5
Johnson Administration	7
Nixon Administration	11
Party Platforms	14
Consumer Agencies Under Fire	15
AUTOMOBILE INDUSTRY UNDER ATTACK	25
Nader Vs. the Auto Giants	25
Safety & Other Problems	29
Auto Defects & Recalls	32
Federal Regulation, Industry & the Critics	40
Action on Tires	44
DRUGS, MEDICAL DEVICES & HEALTH	47
Government Regulation	47
Advertising Transgressions Attacked	50
Overcharging Assailed	52
Government Powers & Action	55
Useless & Unsafe Drugs, Under Continuing Attack	59
Medical Practices Criticized, Industry-Physician Tie Seen	66
Health Devices	68
Birth Control Aids	70
Smoking & Health	74

FOOD 79
Standards & Inspection; Filth & Laxity Charged 79
Action Vs. 'Dangerous' Foods 82
Additives, Sweeteners, Food Colors & Animal Feeds 88
Nutrition, Labeling & Advertising Deception 94
Price Gouging Charged 99

HAZARDOUS PRODUCTS 103
Government Action & Inaction 103
Dangerous Toys 104
Sleep Products 105
Chemicals & Poisons 105
Other Products 111

OTHER CONSUMER ISSUES 113
Advertising & Selling Practices Under Scrutiny 114
Promotional Contests 120
Credit Practices 121
Price Manipulation 124
Other Developments 131

CONSUMERISM 139
Previous Periods of Consumer Unrest 141
Consumerism Enters a New Phase 142
Complaints of Consumers 144
Choices for Business & Government 149
Summary 152

GUIDE AGAINST DECEPTIVE ADVERTISING 155
Price Comparisons 156
Bait Advertising 157
Warranties 157
Miscellaneous 159

ABBREVIATIONS 161

INDEX 163

Introduction

DISHONEST, DECEPTIVE AND OTHERWISE unprincipled business practices victimize American consumers in many ways. Consumers are hurt in the pocket by overcharging, by the purchase of inferior merchandise and by extortionate credit policies. Their health is endangered by impure foods and drugs or by valueless medical devices. They or their children are often injured by poorly made appliances, unsafe vehicles, combustible toys and other defective items.

"Consumers, by definition, include us all," the late President John F. Kennedy noted March 15, 1962 in his special message on protecting the consumer interest. "They are the largest economic group in the economy, affecting and affected by almost every public and private economic decision. Two-thirds of all spending in the economy is by consumers."

Deception of consumers by vendors is a practice that, it is thought, developed almost simultaneously with the appearance of commerce. The biblical prophets assailed it. In Scythia, in the 5th century B.C., the philosopher Anacharis asserted that "the market is the place where men may deceive each other." And the medieval proverb *caveat emptor* (let the buyer beware) seems to be still good advice today.

Data produced by Senate inquiries indicate that overpricing, deceptive advertising, and services that are either unneeded or performed improperly combine to waste perhaps 30% to 40% of all the money consumers spend. It was estimated in 1970 that consumers spent $1 billion annually on useless or misrepresented medical devices and drugs. Consumers were reported to be paying $1 billion to $3 billion a year for unnecessary insurance—such as coverage of the same risk by more than one policy. A Senate subcommittee was told in 1970 that consumers were then overpaying about $45 billion a year because of monopolistic pricing. And the costs of these malpractices are said to have increased each year since then.

The National Commission on Product Safety reported in June 1970 that every year, in incidents related to consumer products, 20 million Americans suffered injuries in their homes that were serious enough to require medical attention or to disable them for a day or more.

Sen. Birch Bayh (D, Ind.) cited additional statistics Jan. 23, 1975: "Ten to 15 percent of the consumer's purchasing power is said to be wasted because consumers are unable to get the information they need. . . . An estimated $14 billion annually is wasted in supermarkets alone through deceptive and confusing packaging and labeling practices. . . . About 20% of [accidental] deaths and injuries throughout the country during the last year are said to have been related to household consumer products. . . . The National Commission on Product Safety reports that 60,000 people annually are injured by cosmetics severely enough to restrict normal activity or require medical attention. Approximately 1,500 recall campaigns involving 45,453,823 motor vehicles were initiated by the Department of Transportation over the last 7½ years."

According to documented claims, the nation's poor are the chief victims of overcharging, deceptive advertising, the sale of inferior and dangerous merchandise, costly credit and other shady or dishonest business tactics. The sociologist David Caplovitz called attention to these practices in 1963 in his descriptively titled book *The Poor Pay More*. Inquiries by Congressional investigators and journalists have amplified his charges considerably since then.

Government officials, legislators, journalists, honest businessmen and individual citizens had started attacking consumer abuses well before the end of the 19th century. Their efforts led to the enactment of many laws to protect consumers and the establishment of many municipal, state, federal and non-governmental bureaus dedicated to various consumer causes. More recently, in the 1960s, an upsurge of consumer activity took place as part of the growth of the public-advocacy movement.

"Modern day consumer impetus" in the U.S. "has had three major periods of thrust," according to Dr. Mary Jane Bostick of Wayne State University. In a June 1970 speech, Dr. Bostick reported that "the consumer movement began modestly in New York City with the Consumers' League of 1891, which expanded into the National Consumers' League in 1898. . . . The late 1890s and early 1900s had Upton Sinclair's book *The Jungle* to nauseate the public and motivate Congress. It brought about the Pure Food & Drug Act of 1906." In the 1930s, Dr. Bostick continued, "the public's concern [was] activated through Kallent and Schlinck's book *100,-000,000 Guinea Pigs* and resulted in the Federal Food, Drug & Cosmetic Act of 1938, replacing the less inclusive law of 1906." "Today's spokesman" is Ralph Nader, Dr. Bostick said, and Nader's book *Unsafe at Any Speed* "keyed the issues."

Some people consider the late Sen. Estes Kefauver (D, Tenn.) to be the initiator of the current consumer-protection movement. Kefauver was a major investigator of consumer abuses, and in 1959 he proposed unifying the various federal consumer-related programs within a single agency. During the next decade Congress spent considerable time studying the possible creation of a Cabinet-level Department of Consumer Affairs. Mrs. Virginia Knauer, then Special Assistant to the President for Consumer Affairs, noted in 1969 that such a department might be expected to take over 413 existing federal units administering 938 consumer-related programs. Many of these activities, however, are essential elements of technically complicated functions administered by a variety of federal agencies. Congress members and federal officials, therefore, concluded that it would be impractical to extract these duties from the existing bureaus solely for the purpose of unifying consumer-protection services. As a result, consumer activities remain scattered among an assortment of agencies.

This book is a record of the efforts made to curb consumer abuses during the final years of the 1960s and the first half of the 1970s. The material that follows consists largely of the developments chronicled by FACTS ON FILE in its weekly reports on current history. As in all FACTS ON FILE works, a conscientious attempt was made to keep this volume free of bias and to make it a balanced and reliable reference tool.

LESTER A. SOBEL

New York, N.Y.
December, 1975

Government Policy

Kennedy Administration

President John F. Kennedy had proposed a comprehensive consumer-protection program in 1962, and a drug-control bill was passed by Congress after the sedative thalidomide was reported to have resulted in the birth of thousands of deformed babies.

Kennedy program. A broad program of executive and legislative action to enable the government to "meet its responsibility to consumers in the exercise of their rights" was proposed by Kennedy in a special message to Congress Mar. 14, 1962. While two-thirds of all spending was by consumers, the President said, consumers formed the only major group in the economy that was not effectively organized. The government, the "highest spokesman for all the people," should be "alert to the consumer's needs" and advance his interests, Kennedy said.

The President said consumers had the right (a) to be protected against the marketing of unsafe goods and against fraudulent or misleading advertising, (b) to be assured, wherever possible, that a variety of competitive products and services would be available and that consumers' interests would get full consideration in the formulation of government policy and in administrative tribunals.

Kennedy said he had ordered: (1) the creation of a Consumers' Advisory Council to represent consumer interests; (2) agencies to appoint special advisers on consumer needs; (3) a pilot project to display in post offices publications useful to consumers.

Among the message's recommendations:

Food & drugs—Congress should enact legislation for the purpose of providing better, safer and less expensive drugs. Such legislation should: (a) require that drugs, therapeutic devices and cosmetics be safe, effective and reliable; (b) establish an enforceable system of preventing the illicit distribution of habit-forming barbiturates and amphetamines; (c) require that advertising of prescription drugs directed to physicians disclose ingredients, efficacy and adverse effects. The Meat Inspection Act should be broadened to promote adequate inspection of all meat slaughtered in the U.S.

Credit abuses—Legislation should be enacted to require lenders and vendors to disclose to borrowers in advance the actual amounts and rates they would pay for credit. The FTC would be responsible for enforcement.

All-channel TV sets—Legislation was needed to require that all sets manufactured receive both very-high-frequency (VHF) and ultra-high-frequency (UHF) channels.

Competition & monopoly—To promote competition and prohibit monopoly, legislation should be passed to: (1) empower the Federal Trade Commission (FTC) to issue temporary "cease and desist" orders against unfair competitive practices while cases involving permanent relief were pending before the agency; (2) require that federal anti-trust enforcement agencies be given reasonable advance notification concerning mergers into substantial-sized firms; (3) require publication of terms of all settlement agreements between persons applying for patent rights on the same invention; (4) authorize the cancellation of any trademarks that were common descriptive names of articles.

The President said that recommendations for legislation to establish packaging standards would be submitted after the Administration completed a survey of packaging and labeling abuses.

Packaging-labeling probe. Sen. Philip A. Hart (D, Mich.) called April 3, 1962 for "appropriate ground rules" to bar many deceptive packaging and labeling practices such as short-weighting and unsatisfactory contents designation. While packaging and labeling laws governing distilled spirits were adequate, Hart said, those governing basic grocery items were inadequate. He made the statements at the conclusion of a series of hearings, of which he had been moderator, held by the Senate Antitrust & Monopoly Subcommittee.

At the March 28 hearing, FTC Chairman Paul Rand Dixon had said that current law restricted the FTC to prosecution on a case-by-case basis. He urged enactment of broad legislation to "clarify business responsibility for fair packaging and accurate and complete labeling." Food & Drug Commissioner George P. Larrick had testified Mar. 20 that 132 food packages had been seized in 1961 for short weight or improper labels. He urged enlargement of Food & Drug Administration (FDA) staffs to achieve better enforcement.

Testimony in favor of new legislation on packaging and labeling was given by Mrs. Helen Ewing Nelson, consumer counsel to California Gov. Edmund G. Brown (D.); Carla S. Williams, the FDA's director of consumer programming, and Dr. Ruby Turner Morris, chairman of Connecticut College's Economics Department. Albert N. Halverstandt, general advertising manager of Procter & Gamble Co., and C. L. Rumberger, vice president of the H. J. Heinz Co., gave testimony opposing new labeling and packaging legislation.

Thalidomide tragedy. Phocomelia (literally, "seal limbs"), a very rare condition, had suddenly began to appear in almost epidemic proportions in 1958. Starting in West Germany and spreading to other parts of Europe and elsewhere, first dozens, then hundreds of cases were reported of babies being born with arms missing, shortened or otherwise deformed, with deformed legs or with other defects.

It took about three years before a Hamburg University pediatrician, Dr. Widukind Lenz, found the cause—thalidomide, a sedative developed in West Germany and marketed there starting in 1957. Lenz discovered that thalidomide prevented the proper development of the fetus when taken by the mother in early pregnancy.

Thalidomide was taken off the German market Nov. 26, 1961 as a result of Lenz' findings. But the drug had been sold extensively in other countries (and it was estimated that the number of deformed babies traceable to thalidomide ultimately exceeded 12,000).

An application to market the drug in the U.S. had been submitted to the Food & Drug Administration (FDA) by the William S. Merrell Co. of Cincinnati Sept. 12, 1960 after 20 months of research by the company. The application was denied by Dr. Frances Oldham Kelsey, 47, Canadian-born FDA medical officer, despite frequent, almost harassing appeals from the company for some 14 months. She held that the company had not given adequate proof of the drug's safety. Merrell's application was withdrawn and the Canadian sale of the drug was halted by the firm Mar. 20, 1962 after investigation of the reports that thalidomide caused phocomelia.

President Kennedy Aug. 17 awarded Dr. Kelsey the gold medal for distinguished federal civilian service—the highest honor for government workers—for her resistance to the "very rigorous" attempt to market thalidomide in the U.S.

The Health, Education & Welfare (HEW) Department reported Aug. 7 that 1,248 doctors in 39 states and Canada had received thalidomide to test on their patients. 15,904 U.S. patients, including 3,272 women of childbearing age, had taken the drug, the HEW reported. At least 207 pregnant women had taken it.

The need for stronger drug legislation was stressed by Kennedy at his press conference Aug. 1, 1962 and in a letter to Sen. James O. Eastland (D, Miss.) Aug. 3. Kennedy said the thalidomide incident showed the urgency of providing additional

GOVERNMENT POLICY

protection to American consumers from harmful or worthless drug products.

A proposed ruling requiring adequate preclinical research on new drugs before testing on human beings was announced by HEW Secretary Anthony J. Celebrezze Aug. 9. The ruling would: (a) permit the HEW Department to halt a drug's testing if doubt of safety arose; (b) require that the FDA be notified and given details when drugs were distributed to doctors; (c) require that clinical investigations be based on pre-clinical studies and planned and executed by qualified investigators; (d) require that the FDA and all doctors testing a drug be notified immediately if doubt arose as to its safety.

Dr. Kelsey's appointment as director of a new investigational drug branch of the Food & Drug Administration was announced by Celebrezze Dec. 28. The new office was to evaluate proposed tests of new drugs on people.

Drug control bill enacted. A compromise bill to safeguard the public against harmful and ineffective drugs was passed by Senate voice vote Oct. 3, 1962 and by 347-0 House vote Oct. 4. The bill, described as a "strong" one, was signed by Kennedy Oct. 10. Passage of the first version of the bill in the Senate had been by 78-0 vote Aug. 23 whereas first passage in the House had been by voice vote Sept. 27.

The enacted version, described as good by Sen. Estes Kefauver (D, Tenn.), principal sponsor of the Senate version, required that drugs be proven effective and be given affirmative approval of the government before they could be marketed. It also required: (a) certification by batch-by-batch testing of all antibiotics for human use; (b) registration with the government of drug manufacturers; (c) drug labels to show contents of bottles, with the generic name in type at least one-half as large as the manufacturer's trade or brand name; (d) prescription drug advertisements to give the generic names of drugs and brief summaries of side effects and effectiveness.

The Health, Education & Welfare Secretary was authorized under the bill to (1) withdraw a drug from the market if it were an "imminent" public health hazard, (2) establish simple generic names for new drugs when requested and review existing generic names with a view to simplifying them, (3) prevent testing of drugs on humans if he deemed pre-clinical testing inadequate.

The final version contained a compromise, agreed upon by conferees Oct. 2, that permitted physicians to waive a provision (included in the House bill but not in the Senate bill) requiring them to obtain the consent of patients or their relatives before dispensing experimental drugs.

Opposition to the bill had been expressed Aug. 21 by James F. Hoge, representing the Proprietary Association, and by D. L. Bruner of the Animal Health Institute during House Commerce Committee hearings.

Johnson Administration

Lyndon B. Johnson, who became President on John F. Kennedy's assassination, proposed a consumer-protection program similar to the Kennedy one.

Johnson program. A special message on consumer interests was sent to Congress by Johnson Feb. 5, 1964. The President made nine legislative recommendations. Eight of them had been proposed by the late Kennedy. The 9th would extend meat and poultry inspection to products produced and consumed within one state as well as to those crossing state lines.

The message also outlined a plan to help low-income urban families avoid swindles and learn family budgeting. It suggested adapting the agricultural extension service concept for urban consumer education. Consumer education programs in schools were also recommended. Johnson said his Special Assistant for Consumer Affairs, Mrs. Esther Peterson, would initiate a series of regional conferences to investigate "the problems of adequate consumer information."

Johnson strongly endorsed truth-in-packaging and truth-in-lending bills, the latter to require advance disclosure of the total amount of interest and annual rate of interest. He also asked for legislation: (a) requiring proof of safety before cosmetics could be marketed; (b) expanding government inspection authority (similar to that exercised over prescription drugs) to over-the-counter drugs, food, cosmetics and medical devices; (c) granting subpoena authority in administrative hearings on food, drugs and cosmetics; (d) requiring hazard warnings on labels for drugs, cosmetics and pressurized containers; (e) requiring safety certification for pesticides before marketing; (f) granting the FTC authority to ban, subject to court review, alleged false advertising or dangerous practices that might cause "irreparable injury to the public"; (g) extend to over-the-counter stocks and bonds the full disclosure requirements currently applicable to stock exchange securities.

In a special health message to Congress Jan. 7, 1975, Johnson repeated a call for modernization of the Federal Food, Drug & Cosmetic Act (a) to bring the production and distribution of barbiturates, amphetamines and their psychotoxic drugs under "more effective" control, (b) to require adequate labeling of hazardous substances and safety regulation of cosmetics and therapeutic devices by premarketing examination by the FDA and (c) to provide authority to seize counterfeit drugs at their source.

An Administration-backed bill expanding federal controls on distribution of amphetamines and barbiturates was approved by the Senate June 23, 1965 and House July 8 and was signed by Johnson July 15. The bill was designed to reduce illicit use and distribution of such drugs. The bill: authorized the HEW Secretary to designate for similar control other drugs which he determined to have potential for abuse; covered the drugs whether or not they had moved in interstate commerce; required manufacturers and distributors to register with HEW; made possession of these drugs illegal for persons other than doctors or those specifically authorized to handle them, unless the drugs were for use of the possessor or a member of his family.

In his 1966 State-of-the Union message, Johnson Jan. 12 again called for legislation "requiring all packages to state clearly and truthfully their contents, all interest and credit charges to be fully revealed, and keeping harmful drugs and cosmetics away from our stores."

1966 consumer message. Johnson March 21, 1966 sent to Congress a message requesting "comprehensive measures" to protect consumers. His proposals included a Child Safety Act to protect children from harmful drugs and toys. Johnson also renewed his appeals for legislation to require fair packaging, labeling and finance charges. "Free consumer choice—indeed, our free enterprise system—must rest on a firm foundation of reliable information on the costs and contents of the products we buy," the President said.

The packaging and labeling legislation, Johnson said, should: "(1) Require that each package provide simple, direct, accurate and visible information as to the nature and quantity of its contents, including ingredients where this is important. (2) Keep off the shelves packages with deceptively shaped boxes, misleading pictures, confusing or meaningless adjectives, inappropriate size or quantity markings, and promotional gimmicks that promise nonexistent savings. (3) Provide for the establishment of reasonable and appropriate weight standards to facilitate comparative shopping."

The "truth-in-lending" bill would require "lenders to state the full cost of credit, simply and clearly, and to state it before any credit contract is signed."

The proposed Child Safety Act would: (a) "Limit the amount of children's aspirin available in retail packages"; (b) "require certain patent drugs attractive to children to have safety-closure caps"; (c) "ban the ale of toys and other children's articles containing hazardous substances."

Johnson also asked for legislation to require certification "of all drugs whose potency and purity can mean life or death to a patient" and legislation to "control the unsolicited distribution of drug samples."

Opposition to the packaging and lending requests was expressed by Republican leaders Everett M. Dirksen (Ill.) of the Senate and Gerald R. Ford (Mich.) of the House.

In his 1967 State-of-the-Union message, Johnson Jan. 10 again proposed legislation to require honest and easily understood expressions of the cost of credit and to protect consumers against "hazardous household products."

'Truth-in-packaging' act passed. A "truth-in-packaging" bill was passed by the House Oct. 17, 1966 and Senate Oct. 19 and was signed by Johnson Nov. 3. The bill required that household products generally sold in supermarkets and drug stores be labeled clearly and accurately as to contents, net quantity, manufacturer and, if a number of servings was claimed, the weight of a serving. It barred use of qualifying words such as "jumbo ounces" or "giant half-quart."

The bill did not authorize mandatory standard package sizes. Federal officials could ask manufacturers to develop voluntary weight and measure standards; and if they failed to do so after one year, further legislation could be requested.

Federal officials were granted discretionary authority to establish standards for package sizes, to control use of such phrases on labels as "cents-off" and "economy size," to require common names of ingredients on nonfood items and to bar unnecessary "slack-filling" practices.

The discretionary provisions were to help the consumer make "value comparisons."

Transportation message. In a special message on transportation, submitted to Congress March 2, 1966, Johnson urged the creation of a Cabinet-level Department of Transportation and the enactment of a Traffic Safety Act.

The proposed Transportation Department, which would bring together about 94,000 federal employes and spend about $6 billion yearly, was needed, the President said, because "America today lacks a coordinated transportation system that permits travelers and goods to move conveniently and efficiently from one means of transportation to another, using the best characteristics of each." He said the new department would coordinate existing transportation programs, "bring new technology to a total transportation system," "improve safety in every means of transportation" and "encourage high quality, low cost service to the public."

The proposed Traffic Safety Act would establish a 6-year $700-million program that would: (a) Provide for construction of "a national highway safety research and test center." (b) Grant the Commerce Secretary authority to establish "safety performance criteria for all vehicles and their components" and to prescribe "nationwide mandatory safety standards" if manufacturers failed during a 2-year period to establish "adequate voluntary standards."

In urging passage of the act, the President cited the "truly unbelievable" facts that 1½ million Americans had died in traffic accidents since the introduction of the auto and that 50,000 traffic deaths were expected in 1966.

Other Congressional action requested by the President in his transportation message: (a) Passage of a bill to establish federal safety standards for tires sold in interstate commerce. (b) Enactment of legislation to tighten safety requirements of passenger ships and to establish financial responsibility on the part of their owners and operators.

Congressional plans. Sen. Warren G. Magnuson (D, Wash.), chairman of the Senate Commerce Committee and of its subcommittee on consumer matters, promised Jan. 16, 1967 to work for the enactment of consumer legislation providing for: (1) disclosure of tar and nicotine content on cigarette packages and in advertisements; (2) "truth-in-lending" advertising; (3) a 24-hour period during which purchasers would have the right to rescind contracts signed with door-to-door salesmen; (4) a commission on hazardous household products; (5) stricter rules on flammable fabrics; (6) a ban on deceptive warranties and guarantees.

Rep. Benjamin S. Rosenthal (D, N.Y.) Jan. 16 introduced legislation (a) to create a cabinet-level Consumers Department and (b) to begin an "Info-tag" system under which products would carry information, checked by a nonprofit national consumers foundation, on their contents and effectiveness.

1967 consumer message. Johnson Feb. 16, 1967 sent Congress a special message in which he proposed consumer protections covering credit, investing, medical devices, clinical laboratories, meat inspection, flammable fabrics and fire safety, electric-power reliability and natural-gas pipeline safety.

The investment proposals dealt with interstate land sales, pension and welfare plans and mutual funds. He asked for legislation to require developers engaged in interstate commerce to disclose all facts "needed for informed choice" in offerings of unimproved subdivided lots; such activity was to be subject to Securities & Exchange Commission registration procedure similar to the technique used for public offerings of corporate stock.

Johnson renewed his request for "truth-in-lending" legislation that should assure "full and accurate information to the borrower." He pointed out that "outstanding consumer credit today totals $95 billion" and that "the interest costs on consumer credit . . . amounted to nearly $13 billion in 1966." "When the consumer shops for credit," the President said, he should be told "the percentage rate per year that is being charged on his borrowing."

In the message, entitled "To Protect the American Consumer," the President requested legislation that would: (a) authorize the Transportation Secretary to establish minimum safety standards for natural gas pipelines; (b) "strengthen coordination among the electric power utilities"; (c) have the Food & Drug Administration "pre-clear certain therapeutic materials—such as artificial organ transplants—used mainly on or in the body" and establish standards for "certain classes of widely used devices—bone pins, catheters, X-ray equipment and diathermy machines"; (d) require clinical laboratories engaged in interstate commerce to be licensed by the Surgeon General and to comply with federal performance standards; provide grants to help state and city agencies strengthen regulations over clinical laboratories not in interstate commerce; (e) modernize the Federal Meat Inspection Act, which failed to cover "nearly 15% of the fresh meat supply and almost 25% of processed meat products [that] do not enter into interstate commerce"; encourage states to cooperate in raising the standard of meat inspection by recompensating them for up to half of the administrative cost of the inspection program; (f) extend the Flammable Fabrics Act to cover baby blankets, drapes, carpets and upholstery; (g) set up a research and education program in fire safety; (h) create a National Commission on Product Safety.

Product Safety Commission created. A bill establishing a National Commission on Product Safety was passed by 206-102 House vote Nov. 6, 1967 and Senate voice vote Nov. 7 and was signed by Johnson Nov. 20.

The President Nov. 20 noted that the resolution was the first major consumer legislation passed by Congress in 1967 and that "we need many others." "We ought to have had them already," he said. Johnson specifically called for action on "the strongest possible" meat inspection bill and on legislation for pipe-line safety, truth in lending and protection against flammable fabrics and the sale of worthless land.

The commission was to identify categories of potentially harmful household products, study existing state and federal controls over such products and report to Congress. Its 7 members, no more than 4 to be from the same political party, were to be appointed by the President.

Flammable fabrics ban. A bill strengthening the 1953 Flammable Fabrics Act was passed by 345-0 House vote Nov. 27, 1967 and Senate voice vote Dec. 1 and was signed by Johnson Dec. 14.

The 1953 act, confined to certain clothing articles, was extended to all clothing and to household and office interior furnishings made of fabric or fabric-like material. Mandatory flammability standards were to be issued by the Commerce Department, and a national advisory committee was to be established.

1968 consumer message. In a special message to Congress Feb. 6, 1968, Johnson proposed a program to "protect the consumer—and the honest businessman alike—against fraud and indifference." The President also recommended that the FTC be empowered to obtain federal court orders to "stop fraudulent and deceptive practices immediately" while cases were before the commission or the courts.

The requested program included proposals to: (1) "crack down on fraud and deception in sales," (2) "launch a major study of automobile insurance," (3) "protect Americans against hazardous radiation from television sets and other electronic equipment," (4) "close gaps in our system of poultry inspection," (5) "Guard the consumer's health against unwholesome fish," (6) "move now to prevent death and accidents on our waterways," (7) "add new meaning to warranties and guarantees and seek ways to improve repair work and servicing," (8) "appoint a government lawyer to represent the consumer."

The President said he would appoint a "consumer counsel at the Justice Department to work directly under the Attorney General and to serve the Special Assistant to the President for Consumer Affairs," Betty Furness. He said the counsel would "seek better representation for consumer interests before administrative agencies and courts" and "will be concerned with the widest range of consumer matters—from quality standards to frauds."

'Truth-in-Lending' bill enacted. A "truth-in-lending" bill was passed by voice votes of the House and Senate May 22, 1968 and signed by Johnson May 29. The bill was a compromise between a Senate bill passed July 11, 1967 and a much stricter House bill passed Feb. 1, 1968.

The House-Senate conference committee

GOVERNMENT POLICY

did not reach agreement on the compromise until May 15, mainly because of disagreement on a provision to require disclosure of interest rates on revolving charge accounts, used by many department stores and catalogue houses. The Senate version required such disclosure on a monthly basis, the House bill on an annual basis. The conferees settled on a requirement for disclosure on both annual and monthly bases. Disclosure of the "effective" interest rate (total annual income from revolving credit divided by annual earnings from interest rates on revolving accounts) was made optional.

Revolving credit transactions with finance charges of 50¢ per month or less were exempted.

The final bill also retained a garnishment restriction, a provision of the House bill but not the Senate bill. The accepted provision, to supersede all less restrictive state laws, provided an exemption from garnishment for 75% of a worker's take-home pay after all legally required deductions (such as taxes) had been made, or $48 a week (30 times the $1.60 federal minimum wage), whichever was greater. This provision took effect by July 1, 1970 (all other provisions took effect by July 1, 1969).

The major requirement of the bill was that consumers be informed of the cost of credit and that the information be completed, true and comparable—calculated at an annual rate under the same specifications by all lenders.

Disclosure of the annual interest rate was also required in all credit advertising that gave terms in figures.

If the cost of credit life insurance were included in the finance charge of a loan and if the loan were conditioned on purchase of the insurance, the bill required disclosure of the cost of the required insurance.

"Extortionate extension of credit" was barred under the bill. This provision applied whenever both parties understood that force or harassment were to be used to collect the debt. Charging a 45% annual interest rate, where illegal under a state law, would fall under this category automatically as an offense subject to punishment by imprisonment for 5 years and a $5,000 fine.

A provision required disclosure of the "true" annual interest rate of first mortgages on houses. This was a softening of the original House provision, which required disclosure of the total finance costs over the life of a first mortgage.

An exemption was provided in the bill for small finance charges—interest rates on all loans of $25 or less, loans of $25 to $75 with charges of $5 or less, and all loans over $75 with charges of $7.50 or less.

The bill also provided authorization for a bipartisan commission, operating until 1971, to make a study of consumer finance and to report its findings to Congress.

Nixon Administration

Richard M. Nixon was elected President in November 1968 to succeed Lyndon B. Johnson. His first message on consumer protection went to Congress the following fall.

1969 consumer message. The 1969 message on consumer protection was sent to Congress by Nixon Oct. 30. Nixon said in his message that the American consumer had a right to have accurate information on which to make a free choice among products and services, a right "to expect that his health and safety is taken into account by those who seek his patronage," and a right to "register his dissatisfaction and have his complaint heard and weighed when his interests are badly served."

Nixon proposed in his message: (a) A statutory office of consumer affairs in the White House (the current office, headed by Mrs. Virginia H. Knauer, was established by executive order) with authority to "resolve conflicts" among government agencies having differing approaches to consumer issues; (b) a new division of consumer protection in the Justice Department, headed by an assistant attorney general; (c) a new consumer protection law that would permit consumers either as individuals or as a class (a group) to seek redress in court; the latter would be permissible for 11 specified types of fraud or unfair trade practices but only after the Justice Department had successfully completed an action in the case, such as a consent or settlement agreement; (d) expanded powers for a "revitalized" Federal Trade Commission, including power to seek preliminary injunctions against unfair or deceptive business practices; (e) a "newly activated" national commission on consumer finance to investigate and report on the state of consumer credit; (f) expanded consumer education activities, including federal review of product-testing processes, a consumer bulletin and dissemination of product information; (g) stronger efforts for food and drug safety, an examination of the operations of the Food & Drug Administration and a review of products on the "generally regarded as safe" (GRAS) list, a full review of food additives; (h) creation of a consumer affairs unit in the antipoverty agency "for poorer Americans."

Warranty curbs. The Nixon Administration failed during 1970 and again in 1971 and 1973 in efforts to enact legislation to regulate warranties covering automobiles, appliances and all other consumer goods valued at $25 or more. It took until late 1974, after Gerald R. Ford had succeeded Nixon as President, for such a bill to win Congressional approval.

The Nixon Administration proposal had been submitted March 11, 1970 to the Consumer Affairs subcommittee of the Senate Commerce Committee by Mrs. Virginia H. Knauer, President Nixon's consumer affairs assistant; Richard W. McLaren, assistant attorney general for antitrust matters; and James T. Lynn, general counsel of the Commerce Department.

A major purpose of the proposed bill was to curb the use of written warranties with disclaimers that deprived consumers of free repairs or replacement parts unless conditions stated in the warranties were met. The effect of the disclaimer was to nullify the implied warranty of fitness, recognized by law in nearly all states, that assured the consumer a product would carry out its expected function reasonably well. The Administration bill would establish a new federal implied warranty of fitness that would prohibit the use of the words "warranty" or "guarantee" in connection with a disclaimer. Furthermore, the bill would require the manufacturer or merchant to state the disclaimer clearly and prominently.

The proposal would also authorize the Federal Trade Commission (FTC) and Justice Department to seek injunctions and bring suits for violation of FTC regulations and failure to complete terms of the warranties. It would permit individual consumers to sue a company for damages in federal or state courts after the government had successfully prosecuted a firm or merchant.

(The New Hampshire Supreme Court ruled that auto dealers were liable for defective cars, even without proof of negligence, it was reported Jan. 27.)

A bill considered broader than the Administration's proposals was passed by Senate voice vote July 1, 1970, but it died in House committee. Another bill to regulate warranties and expand FTC powers in the consumer area was passed by 76–2 Senate vote Nov. 8, 1971, but it also died in the House. A third bill to regulate warranties and increase FTC powers was passed by Senate voice vote Sept. 12, 1973, and it, too, died in the House.

A bill setting federal standards for product warranties and expanding FTC authority was finally passed by 75–0 Senate vote Dec. 18, 1974 and by House voice vote Dec. 19. Ford signed it Jan. 4, 1975.

Under the terms of the new law, sellers who offered such warranties would be required to specify whether they were "full" or "limited" and explain any limitations in writing. Full warranties would entail total replacement or refund for defective products in the period covered.

The FTC would be empowered for the first time to seek court redress for buyers and civil penalties of up to $10,000 against repeated offenders.

Justice unit formed. The Justice Department announced Dec. 15, 1970 that a consumer affairs section had been set up in the department's antitrust division to centralize functions performed by several departmental units, as well as coordinate and strengthen enforcement of consumer protection laws.

White House consumer office. President Nixon Feb. 24, 1971 issued an executive order creating a White House Office of Consumer Affairs to coordinate federal consumer activities. Mrs. Virginia H. Knauer, special Presidential assistant for consumer affairs, was ap-

GOVERNMENT POLICY

pointed by the President to assume the additional responsibility of director of the new office.

1971 consumer message. Nixon sent to Congress Feb. 24, 1971 a special consumer-affairs message framing a legislative program designed as "a Buyer's Bill of Rights." He asked Congress to authorize mandatory federal safety standards for consumer products not already regulated by federal law.

The President proposed that the secretary of health, education and welfare be given authority to set minimum safety standards for products, following hearings by the Food and Drug Administration. The secretary would also be empowered to ban from the market products that failed to meet federal safety standards. Civil penalties of $10,000 would be levied for each violation of the standards. Violators would also be subject to unspecified criminal penalties.

The President's consumer package, which was similar to a program he had proposed in 1969, would also (1) authorize the Justice Department to prosecute for 14 specific fraudulent advertising and selling practices, (2) empower the FTC to seek injunctions against unfair practices (but not to impose criminal penalties for frauds or compel restitution to consumers), (3) call for a study of class-action suits that would permit consumers to seek damages in federal courts but only after successful prosecution by the Justice Department, (4) bar deceptive warranties, and (5) set up a National Business Council in the Commerce Department to assist business in meeting its obligations to consumers.

The President rejected an earlier proposal for legislation to set up an independent consumer protection agency to represent the consumer before federal courts and regulatory agencies as merely adding to "the proliferation of agencies." Instead, he suggested the appointment of a "consumer advocate" within a federal trade practices agency proposed by his Advisory Council on Executive Reorganization.

Product safety agency created. The compromise Consumer Product Safety Act, establishing an independent consumer product safety commission, was approved by voice votes of the House Oct. 13 and Senate Oct. 14 and was signed by Nixon Oct. 28.

Nixon noted that he had opposed creation of an independent commission, preferring to give the new power to the Food and Drug Administration, an agency of the Department of Health, Education and Welfare, but he said it was "high time that the government provided for comprehensive regulation" in the consumer product field.

The Senate-House conference committee had approved the bill Oct. 11 after Senate conferees abandoned a Senate proposal to transfer the FDA's functions to the new agency.

The new commission, with five members named by the President and confirmed by the Senate, would set and enforce safety standards for thousands of household, school and recreation products, including some formerly regulated by other agencies, including toys, flammable fabrics, poisons and hazardous substances, but excluding tobacco, automobiles, pesticides, weapons, food, drugs and cosmetics.

The new commission would have power to ban the sale, order the recall or seek court seizures of unsafe products, and could inspect factories, conduct tests and subpoena records. The commission would regulate safety aspects of performance, composition, design and packaging of the products.

Violators would face criminal or civil penalties, and some private suits to require the commission to enforce standards or to seek damages from manufacturers would be allowed. Individuals could sue the commission to begin developing standards on a product, although no such suits would be permitted in the first three years.

Business-consumer council. Nixon Aug. 5, 1971 established the 80-member National Business Council for Consumer Affairs and named Robert E. Brooker, executive committee chairman of Marcor Inc., as council chairman. The council, appointed by the secretary of commerce, would serve as a forum to deal with valid consumer complaints and recommend solutions for "current and potential consumer problems."

Rep. John E. Moss (D, Calif.), chairman of a House Commerce subcommittee overseeing consumer legislation, noted Aug. 7 that several council members represented manufacturing firms whose products had been categorized as hazardous by the National Commission on Product Safety. He accused Nixon of "complete insensitivity" to consumer needs in his creation of a council that would "further blunt existing feeble consumer protection efforts."

Toxic chemical curb dies. A Senate-House impasse resulted in the death in 1972–73 of legislation to impose federal controls over the use of possibly toxic chemicals in consumer goods.

Such a measure had originally been passed by 77–0 Senate vote May 30, 1972.

Under the bill, manufacturers would have to pretest the several hundred new compounds planned for commercial use each year and not already covered by food, drug and pesticide laws, to determine possible damage to health or the environment. The Environmental Protection Agency (EPA) would have 180 days to decide whether to ban or limit distribution of each product.

EPA could also order testing for any currently used compound, or waive tests for any new substance "generally regarded as safe."

The Senate proposals, which exceeded Administration and industry suggestions, had been prompted by disclosures of the harmful effects of such widely used substances as mercury, PCBs, lead and phosphates.

The House, on receiving the bill, sought to exempt pretesting of new chemicals with no known hazards, and it sought to bar the EPA administrator from taking action under the bill if health or environmental hazards could be prevented under other laws. The bill, with these changes, was passed by 240–61 House vote Oct. 13.

The Senate, by 29–22 vote Oct. 14, revised the measure to make it conform more closely to its original version, but Congress adjourned before the House could take further action.

Rival versions of a similar bill were again passed by both houses in 1973, but once more Congress adjourned before the measure could be cleared.

Party Platforms

During the 1972 election campaign, both parties adopted platforms promising aid to consumers.

Democratic plank. The Democratic Party adopted its platform in Miami Beach, Fla. July 12, 1972. This is the text of its plank on consumer protection:

Rights of Consumers

Consumers need to be assured of a renewed commitment to basic rights and freedoms. They must have the mechanisms available to allow self-protection against the abuses that the Kennedy and Johnson programs were designed to eliminate. We propose a new consumer program:

In the Executive Branch. The executive branch must use its power to expand consumer information and protection:

■ Ensure that every policy-making level of government concerned with economic or procurement decisions should have a consumer input either through a consumer advisory committee or through consumer members on policy advisory committees;

■ Support the development of an independent consumer agency providing a focal point on consumer matters with the right to intervene as amicus curiae on behalf of the consumer before all agencies and regulatory bodies; and

■ Expand all economic policy-making mechanisms to include as assessment of social as well as economic indicators of human well-being.

In the Legislative Branch. We support legislation which will expand the ability of consumers to defend themselves:

■ Ensure an extensive campaign to get food, drugs and all other consumer products to carry complete informative labeling about safety, quality and cost. Such labeling is the first step in ensuring the economic and physical health of the consumer. In the food area, it should include nutritional unit pricing, full ingredients by percentage, grade, quality and drained weight information. For drugs, it should include safety, quality, price and operation data, either on the label or in an enclosed manual;

■ Support a national program to encourage the development of consumer cooperatives, patterned after the rural electric cooperatives in areas where they might help eliminate inflation and restore consumer rights; and

■ Support federal initiatives and federal standards to reform automobile insurance and assure coverage as first part, on a no fault basis.

GOVERNMENT POLICY

In the Judicial Branch. The Courts should become an effective forum to hear well-founded consumer grievances.

■ Consumer class action: Consumers should be given access to the federal courts in a way that allows them to initiate group action against fraudulent, deceitful, or misleading or dangerous business practices.

■ Small Claims Court: A national program should be undertaken to improve the workings of small claims courts and spread their use so that consumers injured in economically small, though individually significant amounts (e.g. $500), can bring their complaints to the attention of a court and collect their damages without self-defeating legal fees.

Republican plank. The Republican Party adopted its platform in Miami Beach Aug. 22. Its plank on consumer protection said:

The American consumer has a right to product safety, clearly specified qualities and values, honest descriptions and guarantees, fair credit procedures, and due recourse for fraud and deception. We are addressing these concerns forcefully, with executive action and legislative and legal initiatives.

The issues involved in this accelerating awareness on the part of consumers lie close to the heart of the dynamic American market: Good products at fair prices made it great; the same things will keep it great.

Enlightened business management is as interested in consumer protection and consumer education as are consumers themselves. In a market place as competitive and diverse as ours, a company's future depends on the reputation of its products. One safety error can wipe out an established firm overnight.

Unavoidably, the remoteness of business management from the retail counter tends to hamper consumers in resolving quality and performance questions. Technical innovations make it harder for the consumer to evaluate new products. Legal complexities often deny efficient remedies for deception or product failure.

To assist consumers and business, President Nixon established the first Office of Consumer Affairs in the White House and made its director a member of his personal staff and of the Cost of Living Council. We have also proposed a Buyer's Bill of Rights, including:

■ Federal authority for the regulation of hazardous consumer products;

■ Requirement of full disclosure of the terms of warranties and guarantees in language all can understand.

We support the establishment of an independent Consumer Protection Agency to present the consumer's case in proceedings before Federal agencies and also a consumer product safety agency in the Department of Health, Education and Welfare. We oppose punitive proposals which are more antibusiness than pro-consumer.

We pledge vigorous enforcement of all consumer protection laws and to foster more consumer education as a vital necessity in a marketplace ever increasing in variety and complexity.

Consumer Agencies Under Fire

The Federal Trade Administration, the Food & Drug Administration and other consumer-protection units came under repeated attack for alleged failures in defending consumer interests.

FTC criticized. Appearing before a Senate Government Operations subcommittee March 18, 1969, Prof. John E. Schulz of the University of Southern California asserted that the Federal Trade Commission should be abolished unless it received more money and authority and a new chairman willing to "galvanize the consumer forces behind him." Schultz had led a team of Yale and Harvard law students in an investigation of the FTC in the summer of 1968. In a report issued in January, the investigators had assailed the FTC and FTC Chairman Paul Rand Dixon.

A study group of the American Bar Association (ABA) said Sept. 15, 1969 that the effectiveness of the FTC was largely sapped by ineffectual and divided leadership, a staff characterized by "incompetence," misallocation of funds to "trivial matters" and a failure to establish goals and priorities. Many of the charges were similar to those leveled Jan. 5 by a group of student investigators organized by Ralph Nader.

William T. Gossett, past president of the ABA, had appointed the panel in May, at President Nixon's request, to assess FTC performance in areas of consumer protection and enforcement of antitrust laws. In a summary of an 84-page report, the panel concluded: "Notwithstanding the great potential of the FTC in the field of antitrust and consumer protection, if change does not occur, there will be no substantial purpose to be served by its continued existence."

The commission—composed of seven lawyers in private practice and two employed by non-profit groups, five law professors and two economists—was headed by Miles W. Kirkpatrick, a Philadelphia lawyer. The report was signed by every member of the panel except Richard A. Posner, a Stanford University

Law School professor, who was even more critical of the FTC than were his colleagues. Posner suggested that FTC funds be frozen at the current level so that "the forces of inflation and economic growth would gradually effect a practical repeal of the regulatory scheme."

The ABA panel said its study had shown that although the FTC had been armed with a rising budget and increased staff, "both the volume and force of FTC law enforcement have declined during this decade." The study group said that FTC enforcement activity rested "heavily on a voluntary compliance program devoid of effective surveillance or sanctions" and that its consumer protection efforts relied "almost exclusively on the receipt of outside complaints" rather than on any detection force of its own.

The report charged the FTC leadership with primary responsibility for FTC failures. It said that "bitter public displays of dissension among commissioners have confused and demoralized the FTC staff." Excessive delays and conflicts could be avoided by delegation of more authority to the staff, it said. But the panel also charged "insufficient competence" among higher staff members due to "an inadequate system of recruitment and promotion."

In the field of consumer protection, the report criticized FTC preoccupation "with technical labeling and advertising practices of the most inconsequential sort." The panel recommended "a new and vigorous approach to consumer fraud" through the establishment of task forces in major cities. The panel suggested that in addition to effecting improved enforcement, the task forces could be innovative and that such an approach "would establish new lines for communication and cooperation with state and local agencies."

The ABA group, in its summary, backed the retention of "concurrent jurisdiction of the FTC and the Department of Justice in antitrust enforcement" but urged that FTC antitrust resources be "re-examined and realigned." The group noted that FTC commissioners had been criticized for making themselves available to respondents of enforcement actions "on an ex parte, off-the-record basis" and suggested that FTC policy concerning such contacts should be defined.

The panel conceded that Congress was partly responsible for FTC failures because insufficient funds had been budgeted to the agency. The study group said that if its proposals were to be implemented, the FTC "must have the continuous vigorous support of the President and Congress."

A Senate Judiciary subcommittee held hearings Sept. 12, 1969 on complaints against the FTC.

In a 70-page reply (released Sept. 10) to a Senate questionnaire on the responsiveness of agencies to the public, FTC Commissioner Philip Elman had said the FTC was characterized by "waste, inefficiency and indifference to public interest." He charged FTC Chairman Paul Rand Dixon with preventing the reform of the agency staff, which, he said, was marked by "laziness, passivity and sluggishness." He added that "friendship or cronyism, political affiliation, and sheer longevity have been the dominant qualifications for advancement" on the commission staff.

In the subcommittee hearing, headed by Sen. Edward M. Kennedy (D, Mass.), Dixon Sept. 12 defended his agency and denounced Ralph Nader as a publicity seeker. He said the FTC would not ignore complaints by critics and argued that more funds could relieve the pressure on the staff. Dixon said staff appointments had been governed by merit and not politics.

Elman had charged the same day that pressure from congressmen "corrupts the atmosphere" in which the FTC worked, but Commissioner Mary Gardiner Jones denied knowledge of any such pressure.

FTC rules backed. The Nixon Administration Jan. 21, 1970 endorsed current FTC regulations and urged it to use its authority to file promptly complaints against retailers engaged in "bait" (or deceptive) advertising. At a hearing of the FTC division of trade rules and regulations on a proposed FTC rule prohibiting supermarkets from advertising items not available in all stores or priced higher than advertised, presidential assistant for consumer affairs Virginia Knauer said such a rule was unnecessary. Mrs. Knauer suggested that the FTC not only examine food retailers but also stores selling drugs, furniture, clothing, appliances and other products.

FTC revamped. FTC Chairman Casper W. Weinberger announced a major reorganization of the FTC June 9, 1970. Weinberger said that the object of the changes was to "increase the consumer's faith in the market place."

Under the reorganization, which was to take effect July 1, the commission would have two operating bureaus instead of the present six. The plan would abolish the present Bureaus of Field Operations, Textiles and Furs, and Industry Guidance and their functions would shift to other bureaus. The Bureaus of Restraint of Trade and Deceptive Practices would be replaced respectively by a new Bureau of Competition with seven divisions and a Bureau of Consumer Protection with nine divisions.

The new plan called for expanded field offices outside Washington and the elimination of the central Bureau of Field Offices—a reorganization that Weinberger said should speed the processing of complaints by making it possible to initiate cases in the field without going through a complicated bureaucracy.

The FTC chairman said the changes were not a direct result of the charges made against the agency in recent years but that President Nixon "may have had some of the criticisms in mind" when he spoke of revitalizing the FTC. Weinberger said the criticisms helped promote "examination of the existing structure."

The new plan would also create an Office of Policy Planning and Evaluation and an office of Congressional relations and would provide a new economics adviser for the commission. Weinberger said the changes were based on recommendations prepared by the Budget Bureau at his request.

FTC critic named to board. Miles W. Kirkpatrick, 52, a partner in the Philadelphia law firm of Morgan, Lewis and Bockius, was confirmed by the Senate Aug. 24, 1970 as an FTC member. President Nixon had announced Aug. 11 that Kirkpatrick, who had headed the ABA study of the FTC, was his choice to be FTC chairman. Kirkpatrick replaced Weinberger, who became deputy director of the new Office of Budget & Management.

In a related development hours after the announcement of Kirkpatrick's appointment, Philip Elman, an outgoing FTC commissioner, gave a speech before a group of St. Louis lawyers proposing that all independent government agencies directly regulating business should be revamped. Elman, who served on the FTC for 9½ years, suggested that the group of commissioners and chairman directing each of the agencies be replaced by a director who would be removable either by Congress or the President; this would make the latter directly responsible for an agency's failure and act as a check on the growth of partisan or special interests within the agencies. Elman also recommended that the adjudicatory function of the agencies be transferred to a trade court which would hear suits against business brought by the agencies, consumers and competitors, leaving the agencies free to develop up-to-date policies.

FTC lets public intervene. The FTC Oct. 26, 1970 announced a decision to allow, on a trial basis, consumer groups to intervene in an agency proceeding on behalf of the public. In a case involving the Firestone Tire & Rubber Co., the commission said the decision to allow intervention was a "delicate experiment" that should not be "construed as a permanent or irreversible policy decision."

The agency had charged Firestone with deceptive advertising misrepresenting tire prices and safety. In an FTC hearing tentatively scheduled for early in 1971, a George Washington University law student group planned to present evidence to force Firestone to disclose in future ads that its past advertising was deceptive, if so decided by the commission. The law students, Students Opposed to Unfair Practices, argued that the residual effect of advertising could still bring a company profit from a deceptive ad even if it were forced to discontinue the misleading promotion.

FTC power broadened. The Supreme Court ruled unanimously March 1, 1972 that the FTC's authority to protect consumers went beyond its power to enforce antitrust laws.

In a 7-0 decision written by Justice Byron R. White, the court said the FTC could go beyond the letter or even the spirit of the nation's antitrust laws and combat what could be immoral or unfair trade practices.

FTC officials had sought the broadened powers to help them fight unfair schemes against consumers. With the court's decision, the FTC would apparently have the authority to investigate such practices as the mailing of unsolicited credit cards and the high-pressure tactics of some door-to-door sales firms.

In the past, these practices did not clearly fall within FTC jurisdiction.

The case in which the decision was handed down involved the Sperry and Hutchinson Co., the largest and oldest trading stamp concern.

The company had been charged by the FTC in 1968 with violating antitrust laws in the way it restricted the redemption and exchange of the trading stamps, some 1,000 billion of which had been sold to retailers, who had been giving them to consumers as bonuses for their purchases.

A lower U.S. court had held that Sperry and Hutchinson had not violated any antitrust law. Subsequently, the Supreme Court upheld that ruling because the FTC did not challenge that specific point. The court sent the Sperry case back to the FTC for further proceedings.

FTC powers upheld. The FTC won a test of its regulatory authority June 27, 1973 when a three-judge panel of the U.S. Court of Appeals in Washington upheld the commission's power to issue broad regulations on unfair trade practices. The decision overturned a lower court ruling in 1972 that the FTC lacked the statutory authority to set trade rules having the force of law.

The appeals court conceded that the legislative history of the issue had been "ambiguous," but concluded that the FTC Act of 1914 had clearly sanctioned broad rule-making powers.

While the gasoline octane rating case involved in the 1972 decision was sent back to the lower court for further hearings, the FTC was ruled free to proceed with regulations for other industries.

Responding to the latest decision, FTC Chairman Lewis A. Engman announced July 17 that the commission's Bureau of Consumer Protection was being reorganized to give rule-making authority to all seven of the bureau's divisions. The commission had prepared several rules which were suspended pending the result of the appeal, it was reported July 18. These included rules on door-to-door sales, mail-order merchandise, franchising operations and unfair credit practices.

Court blocks FTC inquiry. A federal judge in U.S. District Court in Wilmington, Dela. Feb. 24, 1975 that the FTC had acted improperly in adopting its controversial line-of-business inquiry. The court issued a temporary restraining order blocking the agency from seeking reports from seven companies on sales and profits in their lines of business.

According to the court, the FTC violated the Administrative Procedures Act in trying to collect detailed reports from the companies without giving them adequate opportunity to comment on the line-of-business questionnaires.

The ruling, the court said, applied only to the seven companies which had filed suit opposing the inquiry and did not affect the 197 other companies that already had complied with the FTC's request for information. Another 338 companies had refused the agency's request for information, prompting the FTC to seek court action to compel their compliance.

The form requested data on a product-by-product basis for profits, sales, promotion, direct costs and research and development expenditures.

According to the FTC, the survey was designed to provide a better picture of business competition than the current company-wide reporting system. Under the line-of-business system, data would have to be provided under 219 product categories instead of the current 31.

Business organizations, led by the U.S. Chamber of Commerce, had opposed the survey for various reasons, including the expressed fear that confidential data might go to competitors. Business spokesmen had also objected to the cost and format of the questionnaire, and some had reportedly been concerned that the FTC might use the data for other than "statistical" purposes—such as development of antitrust suits.

Criticism by Nader teams. In 1970 two student task forces working under consumer advocate Ralph Nader issued two separate reports (1) March 16, urging the abolition of the Interstate Commerce Commission (ICC) and (2) April 8, calling for an overhaul of procedures and new regulations at the Food and Drug Administration (FDA).

The March 16 study was headed and partly financed by Robert Fellmeth, a student at Harvard Law School. The report advocated that the ICC be abolished on grounds that it was designed and administered to protect the transportation industry from consumers. Among other charges leveled against the federal agency: (1) appointees to the ICC were almost always "political payoffs," who had no experience or interest in transportation; (2) it had become normal practice for industry to offer "deferred payoffs" in the form of high-paying jobs after the commissioners retired from public office; (3) commissioners almost never met with consumer organizations, had made 220 trips in three years to industry meetings and none to consumer groups, and had declined to appoint a consumer counsel; and (4) internal procedures were costly, slow and controlled by a tired and unprogressive staff.

In denying the report's charges, acting Vice Chairman Dale W. Hardin noted that over 84% of ICC decisions before the courts in 1968 and 1969 had been sustained and that the Supreme Court's rate of sustaining ICC action was 92% in 1968-1969.

The FDA study described the federal agency as a tool of the food industry that was controlled by political pressures from the higher levels of government and therefore was unwilling and unable to protect the consumer. The Nader group charged that the safety, purity and nutrition of the food supply had deteriorated to the point of endangering the health of the population. Among various reforms proposed by the study was a demand for legislation making consumer protection actions compulsory rather than discretionary.

Panel criticizes FDA scientific work. An advisory panel criticized the Food and Drug Administration (FDA) May 27, 1971 for "poorly managed laboratories" and other inadequacies in the agency's scientific effort. The panel of five professors from leading medical schools, in a report based on a one-year survey requested by FDA Commissioner Dr. Charles C. Edwards, said, however, that the agency "does an extraordinary job in many ways" to protect the public, given budget and manpower limitations.

The report said some of the agency's laboratories were excellent, but it said facilities in Chicago and Philadelphia were antiquated, crowded and unsafe and labs in Denver were only barely adequate. The panel said, "one can also find laboratories so poorly managed that scientists seem to be unable to describe their work coherently or to produce interpretable data books containing their findings." The commission also complained of lack of sound data, "a curious aura of secrecy" and an "unhurried atmosphere."

The panel said the responsibilities of FDA laboratories "are literally overwhelming" and that the agency had "limited resources." Edwards, in a news conference announcing the report, said much had been done to implement many of the panel's 50 recommendations but that the FDA's $85 million budget would have to be dramatically increased to allow complete reform.

Specifically, the panel urged "overall surveillance at the source" of food and drug products to insure quality and safety. The report said the panel members were "dismayed to learn" that the FDA had no continuously up-to-date data on the identity and amount manufactured of all drugs on the U.S. market. The report pointed to one area of "possible danger to the public" in the wide use of antibiotics in livestock and poultry feed despite "the fact that the public health significance of drug residues in meat and poultry is not well understood."

The panel asked that sound science be the basis of the agency's decisions rather than "economic or political factors."

■ Consumer advocate Ralph Nader testified Aug. 14 before the House Public Health and Welfare Subcommittee that the FDA and the Agriculture Department were "eroding public confidence" by their failure to disclose possible health hazards. He asked for an independent food inspection agency that would be free of "agonizing conflicts of constituencies."

■ The National Canners Association, representing producers of 90% of the nation's canned foods, submitted a 48-page proposal to the FDA Oct. 25, suggesting registration of canners, stricter processing rules, more thorough reporting to the agency, and FDA embargo powers.

FDA to open files. The FDA proposed May 4, 1972 to open as much as 90% of its records and correspondence to public scrutiny. Under former rules, which would remain in effect for 60 days to allow for public comment, about 90% of the FDA's documents had confidential status, according to general counsel Peter Hutt, who made the announcement.

The public would have access to most information on the safety and usefulness of thousands of drugs and food additives. Letters and any recorded summaries of phone calls to the agency from businessmen and congressmen would also be available, as well as internal operating manuals, informal enforcement actions, reports of factory investigations, and the results of the FDA's own research.

Trade secrets, such as manufacturing processes and commercial and financial information, would be kept confidential. So would information on new drugs still being tested and files of active law enforcement probes.

FDA to get vaccine unit. Secretary of Health, Education and Welfare (HEW) Elliot Richardson said May 25, 1972 that the entire Division of Biologics Standards (DBS), which regulates and supervises research in vaccines and other biologic products, would be transferred July 1 from the National Institutes of Health (NIH) to the FDA.

HEW had previously announced a transfer only of DBS regulatory functions, but Richardson said a breakup of DBS functions would "require Solomon-like division of the effort of individuals."

Both transfer moves came after the DBS was criticized for inadequate and inconsistent actions by the General Accounting Office, Sen. Abraham Ribicoff (D, Conn.) and an internal NIH study, and after the Senate Commerce Committee had voted 17-1 March 21 to dismantle the FDA and DBS in favor of an independent consumer agency, over Administration opposition.

Under the new setup, the FDA would have jurisdiction over all vaccines, blood products, human organs and other biological drugs.

IRS OKs tax-free law firms. Commissioner Randolph W. Thrower of the Internal Revenue Service (IRS) resolved a five-week dispute Nov. 12, 1970 by issuing guidelines under which the IRS would continue to grant tax exemptions to public-interest law firms. An Oct. 9 announcement that the IRS was reconsidering the tax-free status of such firms had brought considerable protest from environmental and consumer groups, congressmen and members of the Nixon Administration.

Sen. Gaylord Nelson (D, Wis.), chairman of a Senate subcommittee that had scheduled hearings on the IRS Oct. 9 proposal, said Nov. 12 that Thrower's statement "indicates that the IRS has backed down and restored without qualification the right of charitable organizations to engage in litigation."

Thrower, in announcing the new guidelines, said the IRS had originally been "somewhat diverted by looking at

GOVERNMENT POLICY

causes" to decide which were "charitable" under the tax laws. He said the agency had later decided it "could not pick and choose among causes." In testimony before Sen. Nelson's subcommittee Nov. 16, Thrower explained further that under the new guidelines, the public-interest litigation itself was eligible for tax-exempt status "rather than the particular cause being served."

The guidelines provided that an organization could receive tax-exempt status if the litigation involved "can reasonably be said to be in representation of a broad public interest rather than a private interest." Another provision stated that a tax-free law firm could "not attempt to achieve its objectives through a program of disruption of the judicial system, illegal activity, or violation of applicable canons of ethics." Thrower said Nov. 12 that he knew of no organization that could not retain its tax-exempt status under the new guidelines. He said there were about 50 public-interest law firms, some with tax exemption and some without, and that they were "proliferating."

ABA offers consumer aid plan. An alternative plan to consumer class action suits was presented to the Senate and House Commerce Committees by a special committee of the American Bar Association (reported April 12, 1970).

The plan, submitted without public notice, proposed that the Federal Trade Commission (FTC) award damages to individual consumers for fraudulent, deceptive or unfair trade practices after the commission or the Justice Department had successfully prosecuted an offender for one of 11 types of offenses. The FTC would also appoint a hearing examiner to insure that injured consumers were afforded relief.

The committee opposed class action suits as cumbersome and expensive because of the court costs and lawyers' fees involved. However, Reps. Bob Eckhardt (D, Tex.) and Benjamin S. Rosenthal (D, N.Y.) sternly protested the report, noting that all nine members of the committee were lawyers with large corporate clients.

■ New York State's Court of Appeals unanimously rejected a class-action test case May 13 in which consumer advocates sought to establish the right of one person to sue a company on behalf of all persons similarly injured by the company. The court upheld a previous decision in favor of Coburn Corp. of America. The case concerned the type size in Coburn's retail installment loan contracts. The suit was brought by two consumers on behalf of all customers who had signed similar contracts.

The plaintiffs, joined in the suit by the NAACP Legal Defense and Educational Fund, Inc., the New York attorney general's office, the New York City Bar Association, Consumers Union and New York City's Community Action for Legal Services Inc., said the poor would be denied access to the courts if they could not band together against a company by means of a class-action suit.

Their plea was denied, however, by the court, which said the consumers in the test case did not qualify as a "class" under New York law. The ruling said: "There must be more of a common interest than the fact that a number of persons made a number of quite different and unrelated contracts with a number of different and unrelated sellers using the same written form, which is claimed to be illegal."

Greater access to courts urged. The National Institute for Consumer Justice, a study panel established at President Nixon's request in 1971, recommended Sept. 28, 1973 that consumers get increased rights to take grievances to the federal courts in class action lawsuits.

The key proposal was to allow consumers to pool complaints against the same defendant to reach the $10,000 minimum claim required by federal court rules. Under current law, each of the individual claims in a group action had to be at least $10,000.

The panel rejected restrictions proposed by the Administration which would have allowed class action suits only after federal agencies had completed administrative action in a dispute and which would have limited such suits to specified offenses involving fraud and deception.

The report suggested, however, that judges determine—after preliminary hearings—whether a trial would be "in the public interest."

Among other recommendations, the panel urged expansion and upgrading of small claims courts and establishment by all states of legally binding arbitration procedures for buyer-seller disputes.

Court curbs class action lawsuits. The Supreme Court ruled unanimously May 28, 1974 that plaintiffs in class-action suits had to bear all costs of notifying all those in the class on whose behalf they were suing. Conceived as an inexpensive means for consumers to press separate small claims in court, a class action involved pooling all claims into one suit, which was then brought by a group of individuals purporting to represent the whole group.

The ruling came in a suit brought against the New York Stock Exchange and two of its member firms (since merged) by a New York investor, Morton Eisen, on behalf of himself and other purchasers of odd lots—trades involving less than 100 shares of stock. The suit charged that the defendants had conspired to monopolize odd-lot trading, and had imposed excessive surcharges in violation of antitrust law.

Justices William O. Douglas, William J. Brennan Jr. and Thurgood Marshall dissented in part. Douglas argued against outright dismissal, suggesting that the case be returned to the district court and the class of plaintiffs divided into a smaller, more manageable group.

Writing for the majority, Justice Lewis F. Powell Jr. said the "express language and intent" of the applicable federal rule of procedure "leave no doubt that individual notice must be provided to those class members who are identifiable through reasonable effort." Eisen also had to bear, Powell wrote, the full cost of the notice, as nothing in the federal rules suggested "that the notice requirements can be tailored to fit the pocketbooks of particular plaintiffs." The court estimated that Eisen would have to spend $315,000 to notify all members of the action, from which he stood to recover $70 at most.

Powell, who conceded that the decision might make such suits impractical or even impossible, pointed out that federal court rules required notification to all identifiable parties, so that each could bring his own attorney or drop out of the suit if he preferred not be bound by its outcome.

Chamber of Commerce sets code. The U.S. Chamber of Commerce issued a 10-point consumer relations code March 8, 1970 to improve "consumer satisfaction." The CoC's board of directors had approved the code the previous week. Compliance with the code would be voluntary. The code included recommendations to provide consumers with information to make "sound value comparisons," seek a goal higher than strict legality by honesty in all transactions, meet high quality standards at the lowest reasonable price, simplify and clarify product warranties and guarantees, and provide effective channels to receive and act upon consumer complaints and suggestions.

Nader vs. unit's demise. Consumer advocate Ralph Nader March 20, 1971 protested the abolition of the Special Consumer Inquiry of the House Government Operations Committee. Nader asked the committee chairman, Rep. Chet Holifield (D, Calif.), to revive the unit that had been active in consumer affairs since 1966. Rep. Benjamin S. Rosenthal (D, N.Y.) had chaired the unit since its founding by the full committee's former chairman, the late Rep. William Dawson (D, Ill.).

Holifield explained that he was forced to abolish the unit under a new House rule that prohibited any House member to chair more than one subcommittee. However, Rosenthal, who was also chairman of a House Foreign Affairs subcommittee, said he had told Holifield he would have given up the foreign-affairs chairmanship in order to keep the consumer unit intact. Holifield denied that Rosenthal had made the offer.

The functions of the former Rosenthal unit were to be carried out by the newly

GOVERNMENT POLICY

created Subcommittee on Military Operations and Executive and Legislative Reorganizations.

Betty Furness out. Betty Furness resigned July 12, 1971 as chairman of the New York State Consumer Protection Board, charging that the state legislature "established this office and then made it impossible to run."

She said budget cuts had forced her to dismiss seven of her 19 staff members. She also noted that of the 19 bills in Gov. Nelson Rockefeller's consumer legislation package, three were passed.

Automobile Industry Under Attack

Nader Vs. the Auto Giants

As a crusader for consumer interests, Ralph Nader has no rivals. The youthful lawyer and his dedicated young followers—the widely admired (or detested) "Nader's Raiders"—have investigated almost every aspect of American life in which "public-interest advocacy" can play a role. Their interests range from product safety and environmental concern to the performance of members of Congress. But it is as "consumer advocates" that Nader and his colleagues are best known.

Crusade for auto safety. Nader first erupted into public consciousness in 1965 with an attack on some of the biggest giants of American industry—the automobile manufacturers. In his book "Unsafe at Any Speed," which quickly became a best-seller, Nader assailed "The Designed-In Dangers of the American Automobile." He charged that mayhem and massacre on U.S. roads were largely the fault of auto makers, who sacrificed safety to styling in the interests of higher profits. (The General Motors Corp., biggest of the auto makers, announced Jan. 31, 1966 that its net income had risen from the record $1.735 billion of 1964 to $2.126 billion in 1965. This was the largest profit ever reported by an American firm.)

Nader, born Feb. 27, 1934 in Winsted, Conn. to immigrant Lebanese parents, attended Princeton University's Woodrow Wilson School of Public & International Affairs on scholarship. Elected to Phi Beta Kappa, he graduated magna cum laude in 1955. At Harvard Law School, Nader supported himself with a part-time job, edited the Harvard Law Record and graduated with distinction in 1958. Nader's interest in auto safety started at Harvard when he studied auto-injury cases. He investigated automobile technology, and this study resulted in an article, "American Cars: Designed for Death," published in the Harvard Law Record in 1958.

After working for auto safety on the local and state level, Nader served as a consultant to the U.S. Labor Department, for which he produced a 200-page study on the subject. His own book was published shortly thereafter and was considered a major influence in the adoption of auto safety legislation that followed.

A frugal life has enabled Nader to plow back most of the money from his writing and public appearances into public-interest causes. With his own money (and in some instances funds from foundations), Nader has created such organizations as the Center for the Study of Responsive Law, Public Citizen, Inc., the Center for Auto Safety, Professionals for Auto Safety and the Public Interest Research Group, which form part of a growing network of Nader-inspired public-interest groups.

Nader's early successes include various laws that were passed at least partly because of his crusading zeal. These are the National Traffic & Motor Vehicle Safety Act of 1966, the Wholesome Meat Act of 1967, the Natural Gas Pipeline Safety Act of 1968, the Radiation Control Act of 1968, the Coal Mine Health & Safety Act of 1969 and the Comprehensive Occupational Safety & Health Act of 1970.

In the meantime, other critics of the automobile industry had been attacking alleged malpractices of the auto makers with varying degrees of success.

Iowa state officials attending a car-safety hearing called by State Attorney General Lawrence F. Scalise in Des Moines Jan. 10, 1966 had heard Dr. Paul W. Gikas, consultant to the U.S. General Services Administration, testify that government control was necessary "because the manufacturers have not done it on their own." Gikas, a pathologist, and Donald F. Huelke, an anatomist, had made a four-year study for the U.S. Public Health Service of 139 accidents in which 177 persons were killed in the Ann Arbor, Mich. area. They said April 4 that 71 (40%) of the 177 killed "would have lived if they had been wearing a simple lap seat belt" and that 35 others (another 20%) "would have been saved by . . . shoulder harnesses and belts."

A report of the New York State Motor Vehicles Department Jan. 31 had said the number of highway deaths and injuries could be halved if car manufacturers installed available safety devices. The report was prepared by the Republic Aviation Division of Fairchild Hiller Corp., working under a $100,000 appropriation from the state legislature.

The American Trial Lawyers Association opened a campaign in New York Feb. 2 against "murder by motor." President Lyndon B. Johnson helped launch the campaign with a telegram calling highway accidents the "gravest problem before this nation" after Vietnam. The 1965 auto accident toll: 49,000 persons killed, 3½ million maimed and injured, $8 billion property damage. (Johnson said April 22 that it was time to establish "strict safety standards for automobiles" and that the industry should stop raising "picayunish" objections to federal standards. "We can no longer tolerate unsafe automobiles," he said. "The alternative to federal standards is unthinkable: 50 different sets of standards for 50 different states." He made the remarks as he designated the week of May 15 as National Transportation Week.)

Nader investigated by GM. General Motors Corp. (GM) acknowledged March 9, 1966 that it had ordered an investigation of Nader. Nader had appeared as an opening-day witness at a Senate Commerce subcommittee hearing Feb. 10 to accuse the automobile industry of ignoring safety while engaging in "stylistic orgies." Subcommittee Chairman Abraham Ribicoff (D, Conn.), referring to the not-yet-admitted GM investigation, said March 8 that incidents involving Nader were "an apparent attempt to harass and intimidate a subcommittee witness."

In its March 9 statement, GM denied that its investigation of Nader involved "harassment or intimidation." It said it had asked "a reputable law firm" (Alvord & Alvord of Washington) to undertake "a routine investigation" to determine whether Nader "was acting on behalf of litigants or their attorneys in Corvair design cases against General Motors." (GM reportedly was the defendant in 106 suits charging that the 1960–63 Corvairs had unsafe rear suspension systems.) Nader March 10 denied representing Corvair plaintiffs and said he had suspended his law practice during his campaign for auto safety.

GM President James M. Roche faced the Ribicoff panel March 22 and heard Ribicoff assert that the "right to testify freely without fear or intimidation is one of the cornerstones of a free and democratic society." Roche apologized to Nader, and Nader accepted the apology. Roche said he had been unaware of the investigation until its public disclosure and had innocently ordered a denial. Then, he said, "I discovered to my dismay that we were indeed involved." He agreed with Ribicoff's comment that the probe was "most unworthy of American business."

Nader told the Senators that GM's investigators had sought "to obtain lurid details and grist for invidious use." It was revealed that 50 to 60 of Nader's friends and family members had been quizzed by private investigators about Nader's sex habits, political beliefs and attitude toward Jews. Nader had also revealed two separate encounters with young women who had invited him to their apartments (he had declined).

The investigation was disclosed to have been conducted by private detectives hired through the law firm retained by GM. Vincent Gillen, who had handled the detective work, said at the hearing that surveillance of Nader had been ended "because it was not being very productive." Ribicoff said he had read all the detective reports on Nader and that they had uncovered nothing "detrimental" to Nader.

(Nader later filed an invasion-of-privacy suit against GM, and the company settled out of court Aug. 13, 1970 for $425,000. Nader said he would use the money to

AUTOMOBILE INDUSTRY UNDER ATTACK

monitor GM's activities in the safety, pollution and consumer-relations areas.)

Nader's testimony on car safety. Nader, testifying before the Senate Commerce Committee April 4, 1966, urged public disclosure of car-safety data by the manufacturers. He said: "If 20 years ago the public knew that the so-called safety windshield in their cars could be penetrated at an impact as low as 12 miles an hour, which was true through 1965, it might not have taken 2 decades for improvements to be made."

Appearing before the Senate Public Works subcommittee April 14 (the committee handled all highway-aid bills), Nader reported three unpublicized instances in which cars had been recalled by the manufacturers for mechanical corrections. He said that GM's Chevrolet Division paid only $2 each plus delivery costs for tires and that "it is hard to find a more dangerous car than the [German-made] Volkswagen." Nader said later that his main criticisms of the Volkswagen were of allegedly unsafe door latches (changed to safety latches in 1965), alleged instability in high-speed traffic and an alleged tendency to "over-steer" caused by the two-part rear axle.

Nader testified before the House Commerce Committee May 4 that the English-built Rolls-Royce was "overrated and overpriced . . . [and] has poor door latches." He cited research evidence that "the Rolls-Royce's doors, hood and trunk will come open" in a 20-mph. impact. Nader said he had cited the Rolls only to stress his point that indifference to safety was "endemic to the automobile industry." Nader renewed his criticism of Volkswagen as lacking safety features and criticized the insurance industry for not adding to its accident statistics data on "vehicle differences." Such data should be made public "for use in prevention programs," he said. Committee member Glenn Cunningham (R, Neb.) suggested May 5 that Nader might in a "clever" way . . . [be] representing trial lawyers, so-called ambulance chasers, by picking on big industry." Nader replied: "I am not concerned with ambulance chasers. I am concerned with people in the ambulances."

Industry proposes standards. The four major U.S. auto manufacturers April 5, 1966 proposed the establishment of an industry safety board to set safety standards for new cars. The proposal was made in a statement submitted to the Senate Commerce Committee, which had begun hearings March 16 on the Administration's proposed Highway Safety Act of 1966. The bill would give the government discretionary authority for establishing and enforcing safety minimums for new cars. The industry plan, presented by Ford Motor Co. Vice President John S. Bugas, chairman of the Automobile Manufacturers Association's Safety Administrative Committee, was offered as an alternative to the Administration bill.

Bugas was accompanied before the committee by Executive Vice President Bernard A. Chapman of the American Motors Corp., Chrysler Corp. Vice President Harry Chesebrough and Executive Vice President George Russell of the General Motors Corp. (GM). The joint safety board they proposed would promote the exchange of safety data among the companies and report to "appropriate" federal agencies. It would consist of the presidents of their companies plus "a person of national stature from outside the industry" as chairman.

Bugas requested that the proposed board be granted an exemption from federal anti-trust laws. He said the Justice Department was subjecting the industry to anti-trust investigation on charges of collusion in designing devices to eliminate air pollutants from auto exhausts. In reply to Sen. Vance Hartke (D, Ind.), who asked why the joint safety effort had not been initiated long ago, Bugas cited the anti-trust problem. In a letter to the committee April 6, Assistant Attorney General Donald F. Turner, in charge of the Justice Department's Anti-Trust Division, said the Justice Department was investigating "charges . . . of cooperative efforts to suppress—not promote—the utilization of auto emission devices." He opposed a grant of anti-trust immunity for the joint development of auto safety devices. "The anti-trust laws do not prohibit such arrangements where joint efforts seem necessary and constructive and are not accompanied by unduly restrictive collateral agreements," he said. The exemption, he said, "seems to be not only unnecessary to desirable cooperation but could, indeed, provide a broad umbrella against anti-trust that shelters suppression and delay in the development and incorporation of safety devices."

The Administration bill had been supported by Commerce Secretary John T.

Connor in testimony before the committee March 16. He defended in particular a proposal not to impose safety standards before the 1970 model year. Although the General Services Administration (GSA) had set safety standards for 1967 model cars bought by the government and stricter standards for 1968 models, Connor said March 17, at a House Commerce Committee hearing on the same subject, that the GSA standards "have not yet been thoroughly evaluated" for cars bought by the public.

(New standards for 1968 model cars were published by the GSA March 8. Two GSA standards for the 1967 models, a dual-brake system and a collapsible steering column, were made standard items on 1967 GM cars, GM had announced Feb. 9. American Motors, which had equipped its cars with dual brakes since 1962, also announced that its 1967 models would have collapsible steering wheels. This latter standard was tightened by the March 8 GSA action; the 5-inch allowable displacement toward the driver was shifted from the maximum for a 20-mph. crash to the maximum in a 30-mph. crash.)

Senate Commerce Committee Chairman Warren G. Magnuson (D, Wash.) and Sen. Abraham A. Ribicoff (D, Conn.), chairman of the subcommittee that had held hearings on the subject, urged March 16 that the standards be imposed (for cars bought by the public) earlier than the date proposed in the Administration bill.

(GM and Chrysler announced April 7 that they would comply with Ribicoff's request for records of mechanical defects in their cars. Ford announced its compliance April 8. The recall of certain models for correction of faults was disclosed by GM April 4, Chrysler April 12 and Ford April 12. GM said about 1½ million Chevrolets were being recalled for free installation of a shield to prevent the throttle from sticking. A spokesman said there had been five instances where the throttle had jammed during operation at a steady speed in a heavy, wet snowstorm. Chrysler said some 17,500 of its 1966 Dodge models and an unspecified number of Chrysler and Plymouth models were being recalled for replacement of an improper throttle linkage that caused a too-high idling rate. The recalling of 16,000 1965-model cars because of faulty door latches was confirmed by GM's Chevrolet Division April 14. Ford announced that 25,000 1966 Fords and 5,000 Mercuries were being recalled for inspection of a brake line possibly damaged in rail transit.

(Ribicoff received from the companies May 5 the reports he had requested on their recall of cars for inspection and correction of suspected defects. The reports covered model years 1960-66. Ribicoff made the reports public May 6. They revealed that the companies had conducted 426 "recall campaigns" involving 8,700,225 passenger cars. GM had recalled 4,700,000 cars, Ford 2,100,000, Chrysler 1,100,000, American Motors 796,000. Ribicoff said: He had been "startled" by the large number of cars recalled—18½% of the more than 47 million cars produced in the past six years; it was his "guess" that more than half of the 426 recalls had involved obvious safety features; the data "shatters once and for all the myth that accidents are invariably caused by bad driving; from now on we must be concerned—not just with the 'nut behind the wheel' but with the nut in the wheel itself, with all the parts of the car and its design." The reports listed 66 defects involving brakes, 33 in suspension systems, 28 steering defects and 28 defects in hood and door latches, wheels, tires and gear-shifting controls.

(Industry sources stressed that the number of cars involved in the recalls was necessarily larger than the number of cars found defective.)

Immediate imposition of the standards was urged by the GSA's Federal Supply Service commissioner, Heinz A. Abersfeller, in testimony before the Senate committee March 17. Sen. Robert F. Kennedy (D, N.Y.) urged in March 30 testimony (a) that the standards be made effective within 2 years, (b) that manufacturers be required to give "adequate [post-sale] notice . . . to customers once a defect is discovered" and be required to remedy the defect, (c) that the industry put 5% of its profit toward safety research and testing by an independent agency. Dr. Seymour Charles, president of Physicians for Automotive Safety, told the committee March 30 that autos should be regulated by the federal government, as drugs were, in the interest of safety.

Henry Ford 2d, board chairman of the Ford Motor Co., said April 15 that the auto industry was "in trouble" over safety but that Congress should not "do something that is irrational" lest it "upset the

AUTOMOBILE INDUSTRY UNDER ATTACK

economy of this country very rapidly." Ford made the remarks in a speech dedicating a factory at Woodhaven, Mich., near Detroit. Safety was "on everybody's mind" and was "a harassment to the automobile industry," he said. "We are being attacked on all sides, and we feel that these attacks are unwarranted." The industry had always built safe cars, "but that is not to say we can't make them safer," he declared. "If these critics who don't really know anything about safety of an automobile will get out of our way, we can go ahead with our job—and we have a job to do. We have to make our cars safer."

The auto industry's opposition to federal standards for car safety was finally modified April 26 as car-safety hearings were resumed by the House Commerce Committee. Ford Vice President Bugas, speaking for the Automobile Manufacturers Association and accompanied by executives from GM, Chrysler and American Motors, told the committee that "appropriate guidelines and procedures should be set by Congress."

Bugas said the industry was abandoning its proposal that anti-trust exemption be granted to an industry safety board. He proposed that determinations be made (a) on whether a safety standard "is worth the cost that is required to put it into effect," (b) on whether the standard was "practicable" in engineering and manufacturing terms and (c) on whether there was "adequate time . . . allowed for meeting the standard in an efficient and economical manner." Bugas asked for provision for judicial review of standards. He said that the manufacturers should be authorized under the standards legislation to cooperate with one another and that the Commerce Secretary should be directed "to collaborate with state motor vehicle authorities in an effort to achieve a consensus that will result in federal and state standards being as uniform and complementary as practicable."

Safety & Other Problems

Safety laws enacted. In a White House ceremony Sept. 9, 1966, President Johnson signed the Administration's Traffic & Motor Vehicle Safety Act of 1966 (S3005) and the Administration's Highway Safety Act of 1966 (S3052). He also announced appointment of Dr. William Haddon Jr. as administrator of the National Traffic Safety Agency established under S3005. In his remarks before about 200 persons, including Ralph Nader, the President said safety was "no luxury item, no optional extra," and he cautioned the auto industry to "build in more safety without building on more costs."

S3005 had been passed Aug. 31 by 365–0 House vote and Senate voice vote. It provided for: (a) establishment by the Commerce Secretary of interim federal safety standards for new motor vehicles by Jan. 31, 1967 (to be effective within 180 days to one year after publication and thus applicable to 1968 models) and revised safety standards by Jan. 31, 1968; (b) applicability of the federal standards to trucks and buses; (c) establishment of safety standards for used cars by Sept. 9, 1968; (d) establishment of federal standards for tires, effective before Jan. 31, 1968, and of a grading system for tires, effective before Sept. 9, 1969; (e) notification by manufacturers to new-car buyers of safety defects discovered after sales, (f) penalties of $1,000 for each violation of the safety law, the maximum penalty being $400,000 for any series of related violations; (g) expansion of a national service listing the names of drivers with suspended or revoked licenses; (h) establishment of a National Motor Vehicle Safety Advisory Council to give advice on safety standards to the Commerce Secretary.

S3052 had been passed by 360–3 House vote Aug. 31 and Senate voice vote Sept. 1. It provided for a $322 million highway safety program through fiscal 1969. States were required to adopt a federally-approved highway safety program by Dec. 31, 1968 or lose 10% of federal-aid highway funds.

Johnson consolidated the federal motor vehicle safety and highway safety agencies June 6, 1967 into the National Highway Safety Bureau. Dr. Haddon, director of both agencies, was appointed to head the new bureau.

Safety standards proposed, then revised. The Commerce Department Dec. 1, 1966 published 23 car-safety standards to be set under the new safety act. In early 1967, however, the government started easing the standards after industry protests.

Dr. William Haddon Jr., head of the National Traffic Safety Agency, had disclosed the initial 23 regulations in a speech Nov. 29, 1966 at the Detroit Automobile Show, attended by the industry's leading officials. Haddon said "many of the standards" being proposed "are already met by most of the vehicles to which they would apply" but "others might be difficult to meet in some cases." "Today's cars, by and large, provide greater safety than ever before," he said. "But it still remains true that voluntary standards have failed to produce the degree of safety that could well be afforded through the more universal application of modern technology."

Among the standards: (a) more lights and reflective devices, some on the sides of cars, to make cars more visible at night; (b) head rests to guard against "whip-lash" injuries; (c) glazing materials to minimize cuts in crashes and prevent passengers from crashing through windows; (d) redesigning of instrument panels and interior projections for more cushioning in collisions or less chance of impact; (e) endurance and braking requirements for tires; (f) six lap belts for six-passenger cars; (g) elimination of wheel nuts, discs and hub caps that were hazardous to pedestrians and cyclists.

Haddon Dec. 5 announced nine safety requirements that a state would have to meet to qualify for its full share of federal highway aid. The requirements included periodic driver examinations and motor vehicle inspections, helmets for motorcyclists, different driver licenses for different types of vehicles, driver-training programs, checking of past driving records, alcohol examination of certain drivers and pedestrians killed, licensing recommendations by state health agencies.

GM informed Haddon Dec. 31 that, "given certain conditions," it could comply with 16 of the agency's proposed 23 safety standards for 1968 model passenger cars. But GM held that five standards would "require more research" and that two other standards could be met in part but also required "extensive additional tests and study." The latter standards dealt with reflecting surfaces and lighting. The five requiring more research involved new tires, occupant protection against interior impact, head restraints, seat anchorages and seat-belt anchorages.

Ford, Chrysler and American Motors notified the National Traffic Safety Agency Jan. 3, 1967 that they would be unable to meet six to 10 of the 23 proposed safety standards for 1968-model autos. All said they would be unable to meet (for 1968 models) standards for glare reduction, side-lighting, protection against interior impacts and stronger attachments for seats and seat-belts.

Three of the standards were withdrawn Jan. 31, 1967 on the ground that more technical information was needed. These would have required front-seat headrests and performance standards for tires and wheel rims. Eight of the standards were modified.

Twenty more federal safety standards for cars, trucks, buses and motorcycles sold in the U.S. were issued by the safety agency Jan. 31. Most of the standards were to become effective Jan. 1, 1968.

The new standards required: (a) Seat belts for all forward-facing seats in passenger cars and shoulder belts for the driver and the outside front-seat passenger; (b) energy-absorbing steering systems, (c) rupture-resistant fuel tanks; (d) shatter-resistant windshields; (e) crash-proof door latches; (f) padding of interior surfaces and protrusions; (g) windshield defrosters, washers and two-speed wipers; (h) outside rearview mirrors; (i) limited glare from metal surfaces; (j) parking brakes, warning lights to indicate brake failure, emergency brake systems; (k) a ban on "spinner" hub caps or "winged wheel projections"; (l) side marker lights or reflectors and increased visibility of vehicle for night driving; (m) easy access to and labeling of controls; (n) P–R–N–D–L sequence for all automatic transmission levers and "an engine-braking effect" in one of the lower gears.

The new standards were denounced as too lenient by Ralph Nader Feb. 1, and William I. Stieglitz, 55, resigned Feb. 2 as an engineering consultant to the safety agency in protest against the "totally inadequate" standards. Nader said the agency's leaders "did not compromise with the industry" but "surrendered to it."

The safety agency March 30, 1967 rejected auto industry requests for changes or delays in 19 of its safety standards, but it agreed to schedule hearings on the requirement for interior padding. Federal Highways Administrator Lowell K. Bridwell then announced Aug. 11 that the car-interior standard was being modified by the elimination of requirements for extra knee and leg impact protection and changes of interior handles and knobs. The standard still required more arm rests and more padding of interiors, such as energy-absorbing sunvisors, instrument panels and seat backs.

Bridwell had assured the manufacturers

AUTOMOBILE INDUSTRY UNDER ATTACK

May 26 that the standard would be modified and had announced plans for consultations between industry and federal officials to "draw up those specifications that we mutually agree will be necessary." He made the remarks during a meeting with about 50 representatives of domestic and foreign manufacturers in Washington. Bridwell also acknowledged the industry's complaint about lack of communications with the federal auto safety officials and said better liaison was "absolutely necessary."

Federal and industry officials had met in a closed-door session June 16, 1967 and agreed to hold regular meetings on the safety issue. This development was attacked by Nader as "outrageous," as "a way for the industry to get in on the ground floor and determine the timing and the scope of the new standards." Bridwell defended the procedure as "a device to obtain information, not write standards." He said the meeting was secret to facilitate a "complete, uninhibited exchange of views." A Nader charge that the industry was striving for collusion on safety standards was denied June 29 by Automobile Manufacturers Association President Thomas C. Mann, who contended that "the primary channel of communication concerning safety standards is between individual companies and the government."

Two new standards for safer tires and wheel rims were proposed July 19, 1967 by the FHA (Federal Highway Administration). One would require a tread-wear indicator and permanent labels for passenger car tires. The 2d would require that new cars be equipped with (a) tires capable of carrying the loaded weight of the vehicle and (b) tire rims capable of holding tires for safe stops from speeds of up to 60 miles an hour. New cars were also to have a permanent listing of seat capacity, fully-loaded weight and manufacturers' recommendations for tire sizes and inflation pressures for full loads.

Ten new safety standards for 1969-model autos were proposed Oct. 12 by the FHA. The new standards would require: (a) protective restraint of small children in crashes; (b) performance standards for brake linings; (c) elimination of damaging exterior protrusions; (d) protective features for motorcycles, such as roll bars; (e) warning devices for vehicles stopped in emergencies; (f) mounting of windshields to prevent dislodging in crashes; (g) standards to eliminate inadvertent opening of auto hoods; (h) safe-to-open pressure radiator caps; (i) "fail-safe" reliability of head-lamp covers; (j) accessible and visible identification numbers.

A previous requirement for shoulder harnesses as well as lap belts for front-seat occupants of 1968 models manufactured after Dec. 31 was reaffirmed Oct. 9 after a 7-week study by federal safety officials.

A final order on passive restraint devices for car interiors was issued Nov. 3, 1970. It postponed for six months (ending July 1, 1973) the deadline for car makers to install automatic crash-protection systems. An 18-month extension was granted for installation of the systems in rear passenger seats.

Ban on discounters invalid. The Supreme Court ruled unanimously April 28, 1966 that General Motors and 3 of its dealer associations in the Los Angeles area had conspired to prevent the sales of Chevrolets by discount houses. The ruling reversed the dismissal by a U.S. District Court in Los Angeles of a civil and antitrust suit filed by the Justice Department in 1962. (In a companion criminal suit, GM, four Chevrolet officials and four dealer associations had been acquitted.) According to Justice Abe Fortas April 28, the defendants had been engaged in "a classic conspiracy in restraint of trade" since 1960. The decision made it illegal for GM or any other manufacturer to engage in a "concerted effort" with its franchised dealers to bar discount houses from selling brand-name merchandise.

Auto-repair hearings. At a hearing into the quality and costs of auto repairs Dec. 5, 1968, Tom A. Williams, chairman of the National Automobile Dealers Association, told the Senate Antitrust & Monopoly Subcommittee that two-thirds of car-owners surveyed were satisfied with the cost and quality of repair work done. His report was based on a survey of 10,000 car owners. When asked about the "other 36%," Williams replied that "the chances are that a good part of that 36% did get good service."

Williams' testimony was in contradiction to that of other witnesses. Norman Bennett, a member of the Society of Automotive Engineers in Washington, said Dec. 4 that consumers were "really being taken for a ride by the manufacturers." He protested the "vulnerability to damage designed into vehicles by those in Detroit who dictate the rules to inspire the perpetuation of high profits after the initial profit is pocketed."

Statistical evidence, compiled by Glen F. Kriegel, operator of an automotive diagnostic plant in Denver, and presented to the Senate panel Dec. 3, indicated that of 5,000 cars tested, fewer than 1% had been repaired satisfactorily and in compliance with work specifications. In many cases, Kriegel said, the work had not been done at all.

Auto Defects & Recalls

Study cites new-car defects. The Automobile Club of Missouri revealed in a report to a Senate investigating subcommittee June 1, 1969 that new-model cars had a high rate of safety defects. The organization said that among 10,000 vehicles inspected by the club's diagnostic branch in St. Louis, safety defects were found in 45% of those driven no more than 500 miles. The study also revealed that 90% of vehicles five years old had safety defects. The auto club said half the 1968 models tested (the latest on the market at the time of the inspections) had defects.

The study, sponsored by the National Highway Safety Bureau, was made public by Senator Philip A. Hart (D, Mich.), who was investigating the auto-repair industry as chairman of the Senate Antitrust & Monopoly Subcommittee.

The St. Louis study reported that the most common defect was improper wheel alignment.

(The New York Times reported March 30, 1971 that 738,000 domestic cars and trucks had been recalled in 1970 because of safety defects; 503,000 imported cars, more than half of them made in Japan, were recalled. Thus, imports, accounting for 15% of the sales, made up 41% of the safety defect recalls.)

Brakes & tires fail tests. In auto-safety tests conducted by independent laboratories, 18% of the passenger cars tested failed to meet federal brake standards and 13% of the tire brands checked failed to meet at least one requirement (of 120 tire tests), the National Highway Safety Bureau said Nov. 24, 1969. Of the 360 tires checked, including several of each brand and size, 30 tires (8%) failed to meet some requirement involving endurance, strength and high-speed performance.

One group of tests, involving Goodyear, B.F. Goodrich, Armstrong and Firestone tires, showed a 25% failure rate.

Another set of reports issued by the Department of Transportation listed the separate sizes and brands of tires that had failed 14% of the safety tests, the Wall Street Journal reported Dec. 2. Two of five 1968 car models were cited for failing brake tests.

(The Federal Trade Commission informed the Firestone Tire & Rubber Co. Dec. 1 that it would issue a formal complaint against the company for false advertising, including the misrepresentation of the safety of some of its tires. It was reportedly the commission's first action against a tire company in connection with its 1964 guidelines for tire advertising. The commission said Firestone advertisements had failed to note such safety limitations as vehicle weight and inflation pressure.

(The General Tire & Rubber Co. had agreed to pay $50,000 for alleged violations of 1966 federal tire safety laws, according to a government report Oct. 28. Although the company insisted it had "in no way violated" safety laws, it agreed to pay the fine to avoid further litigation. General Tire had been cited in April for two separate violations in which 19 out of 21 Safety Jet tires and 17 General Jet tires failed safety tests. The company subsequently had recalled 70,000 tires.)

GM replaces truck wheels. General Motors Corp. agreed Oct. 9, 1969 to replace without cost the wheels of 40,000 1960–65 GMC and Chevrolet trucks in an attempt to end the threat of a $427.5 million suit and to avoid intervention by the Federal Highway Administration. GM said it considered itself under no obligation to replace the wheels but agreed to do so "in the interest of reducing the safety hazard resulting from overloading" and to terminate an FHA investigation.

In May 1969 GM had sent "advisory" letters to the owners of the 40,000 pickup trucks advising them that extreme overloads could lead to a disintegration of the trucks' wheels. GM suggested that owners replace the wheels at their own expense. In August a $427.5 million class-action suit was filed against GM in Los Angeles, Calif. on behalf of all owners of the trucks. The suit also asked for damages from the Kelsey-Hayes Co., which manufactured the truck wheels for GM.

AUTOMOBILE INDUSTRY UNDER ATTACK

GM had installed the three-part disc wheels on an estimated 200,000 Chevrolet and GMC three-quarter-ton trucks in the 1960–65 models. The 40,000 trucks whose wheels were repaired under the October agreement were mainly on those with camper or other special bodies.

Ralph Nader sued the Department of Transportation and FHA in U.S. district court in Washington March 31, 1970 in an effort to reverse the FHA decision on the remaining 160,000 vehicles, whose wheels, he contended, were unsafe. Nader asked the court to force the government to declare the wheels "inherently defective," thereby forcing GM to notify owners of the trucks and initiate a recall. The Nader suit claimed that the FHA, in ending its investigation, had ignored National Highway Safety Bureau engineers who had said a safety defect threatened all 200,000 GM trucks equipped with Kelsey-Hayes wheels.

The Transportation Department Sept. 15 reversed its decision on the 160,000 trucks by declaring them unsafe. The department held a hearing Sept. 30 to decide whether to conduct a formal inquiry and order GM to notify the trucks' owners. GM asked the government at the hearing to drop the inquiry, saying the safety bureau had "no evidence" of a defect that could cause some of the wheels to collapse without warning; however, the company did not present any engineering testimony.

The Transportation Department ordered GM Nov. 4 to notify owners of the 160,000 trucks that the wheels were subject to "sudden and catastrophic failure." It was the first formal order issued by the agency to a car manufacturer to inform customers of an auto safety defect.

GM countered by filing suit in Wilmington, Del. Nov. 4. The company asked for a temporary restraining order against the government ruling on grounds that "competent engineering evidence" had not turned up inherent defects in the wheels. The GM action represented the first case in which an auto maker had gone to court against the government over a safety issue. The court Nov. 9 rejected GM's request for a temporary injunction. Judge Caleb Wright said GM had not given evidence it would suffer "irreparable injury" in carrying out the order.

The U.S. Court of Appeals for the District of Columbia ruled Aug. 16, 1974 that GM must warn the truck owners that the wheels were a safety hazard. The ruling upheld a June 14 district court decision. GM had agreed that there were defects related to the wheels but contended that cracks were caused by overloading. The company said that its 1969 warning against overloading should have been sufficient. The government held, however, that the wheels could crack without overloading, a position accepted in the June decision by Judge Oliver Gasch. Gasch ruled that the occurrence of a large number of failures, regardless of the circumstances, established that a safety hazard existed.

Nader's charges. Ralph Nader charged Aug. 24, 1969 that the Ford Motor Co. was installing auto gasoline tanks that were potential safety hazards. Nader reported that the gas tank tops on several Ford models also served as the floor of the car trunk, increasing the possibility of an explosion in the trunk.

Nader used as evidence a circular printed by the Army Corps of Engineers that called the gas tanks hazardous. The circular reported that most of the potentially dangerous tank tops had been installed in 1968 Ford Fairlane models. Nader charged, however, that Ford had been using the same tank top as far back as 1963.

A spokesman for Ford said the firm had investigated the reports and "found absolutely no evidence of hazard."

Nader charged Aug. 30 that the Federal Trade Commission had ignored his warnings that unauthorized Volkswagen dealers had been selling used Volkswagens as new ones for years. Nader had first made the charge at an FTC hearing in February. Nader said he had asked FTC Chairman Paul Rand Dixon why the FTC had "remained silent" even after the FTC's Bureau of Deceptive Practices had issued a report supporting Nader's charge of fraud. Nader said two attorneys for the Volkswagen Co. had asked the FTC to "require the factory in West Germany [Hamburg] that does the cosmetic job on these used Volkswagens to affix a label indicating that those vehicles were reconditioned and not new."

Nader vs. Corvair. Ralph Nader, in a letter to Transportation Secretary John A. Volpe Sept. 4, 1970, accused GM executives of concealing test data that Chevrolet's Corvair car was unsafe.

Nader asked Volpe to require GM to notify owners of Corvairs still on the road that the cars were defective.

Nader also charged that GM (1) was suppressing reports, memos and films on proving ground tests in 1962–1963 in which Corvairs rolled over at speeds of 26, 28 and 30 miles per hour; (2) had never supplied the data in response to court orders and government inquiries; (3) had engaged in a policy of false statements in comparing the car with other American models; and (4) had "demanded or condoned unethical behavior by its lawyers and engineers."

In a letter to Volpe Sept. 8, GM President Edward N. Cole conceded that the Corvairs had overturned in secret tests, but he claimed the rollovers had been intentional. He said the tests had been made to evaluate experimental parts and their effect on the Corvair's handling features.

Cole noted that the company had won five damage suits in connection with Corvair crashes, but acknowledged that 50 cases were still pending.

Nader replied Sept. 8 that Cole had not mentioned more than 100 out-of-court settlements against the company, including a $200,000 settlement in Chicago. Nader also noted that Cole had not referred to his charge concerning the leakage of combustion gases into passenger compartments.

Sen. Abraham A. Ribicoff (D, Conn.) asked Nader and GM Sept. 12 to give his Senate Government Operations subcommittee data on Nader's charges.

In a letter to Ribicoff Oct. 24, Nader renewed his accusation that GM had engaged in a "massive conspiracy" to conceal detrimental evidence concerning 1960–63 model Corvairs. Nader's letter alleged that GM officials had testified falsely under oath about the stability and safety of the car and that their testimony conflicted with undisclosed data from company tests conducted from 1959 through May 1965. Nader quoted from a Washington Post interview Sept. 27 in which a former GM engineer, Carl Thelin, alleged that it was "a corporate policy to consciously withhold" damaging data and mislabel films to hamper their retrieval from company files. Nader said GM's "untruthful" testimony had led to "untold numbers of fraudulent judgments or settlements" in Corvair damage suits. Among several hundred suits, it was reported that all final judgments (5) had been in favor of GM.

GM, which turned over to Ribicoff the proving ground data in question, asserted that it had not misrepresented its testimony on the Corvair and said it was fully confident in the "veracity" and professional qualifications of its witnesses.

The National Highway Traffic Safety Administration (NHTSA) Jan. 14, 1971 warned owners of about 1.4 million 1961–69 Corvairs that their car heaters were safety and health hazards. The agency said tests had confirmed leakage of carbon monoxide and other fumes into the cars' compartments.

The agency issued the warning in the form of a special "consumer protection bulletin," used when evidence of "significant consumer risks" was insufficient to declare certain vehicle flaws full-fledged safety defects. The field tests, it was noted, had only covered a "limited sample" of Corvairs.

Transportation Secretary Volpe announced Nov. 16 that GM had agreed to send defect notices to warn owners of more than 750,000 Corvairs of possible heater system defects. The department had begun formal proceedings to force GM to issue the notices after it made a formal "preliminary finding" Oct. 29 that the heating systems created "unreasonable risk of accidents and injury."

The defect notices advised owners to have their cars inspected and repaired if necessary by a Chevrolet dealer, but GM did not offer—and the safety agency was not empowered to require it—to pay for the repairs.

A study of the Corvair by the NHTSA, released July 30, showed that the "handling and stability performance of the 1960–63 Corvair does not result in an abnormal potential for loss of control or rollover and it is as least as good as the performance of some contemporary vehicles both foreign and domestic." The study was prompted by Nader's charges.

Nader July 20 termed the government report "a shoddy, internally contradictory whitewash."

The report rejected two pieces of evidence submitted by Nader in support of his allegations. The government said that documents from three automotive engineers, whose data was based on a GM test of an experimental Corvair which was intentionally turned over, was unacceptable. A film produced by the Ford Motor Co. showing a Corvair spin out of control behind a Ford Falcon, which Nader had also submitted to the government agency, was rejected as biased.

Nader charged that the government used "biased testing procedures and model selection" in its study by its use of only well-maintained, 1963 model Corvairs fitted with late model tires. The cars were monitored by instruments rather than subjected to actual test driving.

Owners to get warning letters—Douglas Toms, administrator of the NHTSA, told the Senate Commerce Committee July 25 that the agency would send letters to 200,000 owners of 1960–63 Corvairs warning them of "special problems" in their cars.

Toms said the government, rather than GM, would alert car owners because the recent NHTSA study uncovered no safety defect in the car.

But an independent panel of engineers which certified the government report suggested that the government notify owners of an "oversteer phase" in which "these vehicles may exhibit unusual handling characteristics under conditions of hard cornerings."

GM recalls school buses. GM announced March 18, 1969 that it was recalling 10,400 school buses because of a potential brake defect. The action followed an accident Nov. 19, 1968 in which a school bus rolled down a mountain near Huntsville, Ala., killing one student and injuring 23 others.

GM moved to recall the buses after an investigation reported that the hydraulic braking systems might be faulty.

GM announced March 29 it was accelerating the pace of the recall after owners of the vehicles had complained that GM had recalled only a fraction of them.

GM reported April 17 that efforts to repair the brake defect in the 10,400 buses had created a second brake defect in 4,000 of them. GM said it had notified the owners and operators to take the buses off the road.

In a later action, GM said Feb. 19, 1970 that it was recalling 4,269 school buses and 21,681 trucks (1968 and 1969 models) to check (and repair) possible defects in brake hose retaining springs and rear steel brake lines. The recall was prompted by reports of five accidents, involving the truck models cited, and the findings of a company survey in December 1969 and January of its 1969 model, V-6 school buses.

The survey, requested by Presidential Consumer Adviser Virginia H. Knauer, grew out of complaints made in December 1969 by a Washington school-bus operator concerning exhaust-system problems and frequent brake and clutch repairs. Only one of the 850 buses checked turned up defective brakes. However, the survey disclosed problems with clutch durability and faulty front brake hoses. As a result of the survey, GM placed "resident inspectors" at plants which mounted buses on GM chassis; the buses themselves were not built by GM.

The Transportation Department's Safety Board warned Aug. 26, 1970 of potential danger to many children because of structural defects in school bus bodies. The board, an advisory arm of the department, offered its conclusion in a study that was an outgrowth of two 1968 school bus crashes in Huntsville and Decatur, Ala.

The board's study pinpointed "inadequate and inefficient" bolting and riveting of school bus bodies as a contributory factor in the deaths and injuries in the two Alabama crashes. The board reported that the circumstances surrounding the two crashes in Alabama and at least two other accidents in Waterloo, Neb. and Atlanta pointed up to the fact that "the problems of inadequate assembly are not restricted to any one type of bus, but are fairly widespread."

Bolts and rivets were used by welders to join both exterior and interior panels and to secure them to the framework of the bus bodies. According to the board's report, the failure of such fasteners to hold exterior panels together had contributed to "disintegration" of school bus bodies and "is an implied threat in future school bus crashes."

The National Highway Safety Bureau warned Nov. 2, 1970 that school buses manufactured by GM in 1959-62 had "potential safety problem" that could result in a loss of foot brakes. The bureau revealed that safety checks in connection with a 10-month investigation of the schoolbuses and GM truck chassis had turned up the danger. The problem was found to occur whenever the exhaust-system tail-pipe happened to touch and rupture the brake line below the tailpipe near the rear axle.

GM Jan. 22, 1971 issued a recall order for 9,600 S Model school buses and 44,000 E Model medium-duty trucks for chassis modifications to eliminate potentially faulty clutch linkage parts.

GM took the action despite its disagreement with the findings of a 10-month investigation by the National Highway Traffic Administration (formerly the National Highway Safety Bureau). From interviews with drivers in five states (Maryland, Virginia, New Jersey, Massachusetts and New Mexico), the agency said that reported failures of ball studs, cordon shafts and ball stud brackets indicated that all parts of the clutch control linkage system were subject to failure without advance warning.

Interstate buses inspected. Transportation Department officials reported Sept. 26, 1970 that half of the nation's interstate buses appeared to have defects in violation of federal safety standards. As a result of a government inspection program which began Aug. 18, at least one in 10 buses checked was barred from further travel until they were repaired.

(Transportation Secretary John A. Volpe, who announced the inspection program Aug. 17, said the government intended to inspect 5,000 scheduled and chartered buses in September and October. In 1969 less than 500 buses were checked for possible safety violations by government inspectors and mechanics.)

Volpe said Sept. 26 that the buses "ordered out of service were found to have hazardous defects which presented immediate dangers for passengers." Volpe added that "many other buses were cited for lesser safety violations as were a number of drivers."

According to Frank B. White Jr., the department's Bureau of Motor Carrier Safety field coordinator, of the 3,516 buses inspected since Aug. 18, more than half had at least one safety violation and 11.5% were removed from the road for immediate servicing. White said the results of the inspection appeared to be an accurate reflection of the safety condition of the 25,000 interstate buses.

Ford recalls police cars. Secretary of Transportation John A. Volpe announced Aug. 19, 1970 that Ford was recalling 85,000 police cars.

The department's National Highway Safety Bureau had found cracks in the lower control arms—a major part of the linkage between the front wheels of a car and its frame, serving to hold the wheels in place. Ford said it would replace at its own expense the lower control arms on the full-size Ford and Mercury Monterey police car models that were sold during 1965-1969.

In a letter to Volpe Sept. 21, auto safety critic Ralph Nader challenged the bureau's exclusion from the recall of four million regular passenger models that had been outfitted with the same control-arm designs. The bureau had cleared the control-arm mechanism as satisfactory for "normal passenger car use." Nader charged that the bureau's testing was inadequate and that Ford had cases on file where passenger models, not subject to rough police use, had also experienced mechanism failures.

Ford replied Sept. 22 that its tests had conclusively established that the four million cars were defect-free.

Safety warning on 4 million Fords—The National Highway Safety Bureau warned Oct. 14 that four million Ford and Mercury cars built between 1965 and 1969 might have defective and hazardous wheel control arms. The warning issued

AUTOMOBILE INDUSTRY UNDER ATTACK

in the bureau's first "Consumer Protection Bulletin," apparently was the result of Nader's challenge against the bureau's findings that the cars were safe. But the bureau did not order the cars' recall because the known failure rate was less than one in 100,000 cars.

Ford recalls Pintos. Ford Motor Co. Oct. 30, 1970 announced a recall of 26,000 early production 1971 Pinto model cars because of an accelerator linkage problem that might cause the accelerator to stick. The recalls represented 36.4% of the 73,350 Pintos then manufactured by Ford and about 80% of the cars already sold since introduction on the market in September.

Ford March 29, 1971 announced a recall of 220,000 Pintos built between August 1970 and March 19, 1971 to correct a defect that had caused about 90 to 100 engine-compartment fires.

A Ford spokesman said the new problem stemmed from the size, shape and design of the Pinto's air cleaner and its evaporative emissions control system required on all 1971 model cars by federal clean-air regulations.

Nader scores GM on Vegas. Ralph Nader accused GM's Chevrolet division May 19, 1971 of masking safety-related defects in an April 8 letter to 1971 Vega owners in which it suggested that they visit their dealers for "product improvements."

In a letter May 19 to Douglas W. Toms, acting head of the National Highway Traffic Safety Administration, Nader said the letter amounted to a violation of a 1966 law requiring car makers to send letters to customers informing them of safety defects. The letters usually resulted in the car's recall for repair.

The "product improvements" cited by Chevrolet in its letter to nearly 23,300 Vega owners included a loose carburetor choke lever, an incorrectly installed windshield wiper, spillage from the fuel tank, inadequate underbody clearance and a faulty rear seat. Nader claimed that all but the rear seat defect were safety hazards. He asked Toms to require GM to send out immediate safety-defect notifications to Vega owners.

In Detroit, GM replied that the purpose of the letter was to give early purchasers of the 1971 Vega an opportunity to take advantage of improvements made in later production. It said safety matters were not involved and therefore the notices demanded by Nader had not been required.

Vegas recalled—GM announced April 4, 1972 that it was recalling 130,000 1972-model Vegas to correct a possible fuel-and-exhaust-system fire hazard. It acted after Nader March 31 had charged the National Highway Traffic Safety Administration with a "painfully slow rate" of investigating fire hazards in the Vega, the Ford Motor Co.'s 1969-71 LTD, Torino and Cougar models, and in 1961-67 Volkswagens.

GM said "preparation for the recall was under way at the time GM was advised of Mr. Nader's letter," and denied Nader's assertion that the company had ordered dealers to conduct an "informal recall" of the cars.

Nader made his charges in a March 31 letter to Douglas Toms.

GM announced May 8 its recall of 350,000 1971 and 1972 model Vegas to correct a weak solenoid bracket that had, in six reported cases, broken off and jammed the throttle in an open position.

In its third 1972 recall of Chevrolet Vegas, GM disclosed July 3 that 500,000 cars built in 1971 and 1972 required correction for a safety defect that could lead to a rear axle and wheel falling off because of a manufacturing error involving short axles.

The Center for Auto Safety urged GM Sept. 5, 1972 to recall 250,000 1971 Vegas for numerous alleged defects, including faulty brake, transmission and electrical systems.

The group said the small car was a "sloppily crafted, unreliable and unsafe automobile," based on more than 500 complaints received from owners and reports from workers at GM's Lordstown, Ohio assembly plant where the Vega was manufactured. Employes there charged GM with "chaotically managed quality control on the assembly line."

GM recalls 11.6 million vehicles. GM Dec. 4, 1971 announced the largest voluntary recall in auto industry history. It disclosed in a letter to the Transportation Department's National Highway Traffic Safety Administration it would call in 6,682,000 1965–1969 Chevrolet cars and trucks and GMC trucks to secure their V-8 engines against mount breakage.

GM had been under pressure by the government for more than 18 months. The pressure had intensified after Ralph Nader Sept. 1 wrote a letter to Douglas Toms, head of the safety agency. In his letter, Nader listed safety problems of late-model cars and chastising the government for alleged laxity in pursuing the problems. Subsequently, the agency had issued a special consumer bulletin Oct. 15 warning Chevrolet owners of potentially defective front engine mounts, and the agency Dec. 1 had notified GM that it planned to rule that the engine mount was a safety hazard.

GM denied that the defects of the engine mounts were safety-related and blamed "publicity" for a "great deal of misinformation and misunderstanding on the part of Chevrolet owners." The company said it was preparing to notify owners that it would install a cable-like device to prevent hazards should the engine mounts fail; it did not say it would replace the defective parts.

Only 20% of the 6.7 million Chevrolets recalled in December 1971 for motor-mount problems and fewer than 12% of the Vegas recalled in April 1972 due to fire hazards were modified, the Wall Street Journal reported June 15.

The GM disclosures came in reply to Ralph Nader's charge that GM was footdragging in the repair of the cars. GM responded saying fewer than expected owners had been delivering their cars to dealers for the corrections.

GM Jan. 22, 1973 recalled 3.7 million 1971 and 1972 full-size Chevrolets, Buicks, Pontiacs and Oldsmobiles to correct a defective steering mechanism. It was said that the defect may have caused 96 incidents among which 12 persons were injured after stones lodged between coupling and car frame and jammed the steering.

GM recalled 1.2 million 1973- and 1974- model cars and trucks Feb. 15, 1974 because of a defective brake part.

GM wins on defect notice order—A U.S. district court in Detroit ruled April 29, 1975 that GM was not required to send defect notices to owners of 1959 and 1960 Cadillacs because a steering defect did not present an "unreasonable risk" of accident. The National Highway Traffic Safety Administration had ordered the notices sent but GM went to court, arguing that the defect could cause steering failure only in parking and other low-speed maneuvers when loss of control could be handled by braking. The court noted that there were no deaths or injuries involved in the case and only 33,000 of the 15- to 16-year-old cars were still on the road. The Center for Auto Safety had demanded the government action.

Nader scores Volkswagen. A 200-page report, compiled by Ralph Nader's Center for Auto Safety in Washington and released Sept. 11, 1971, called the West German Volkswagen "the most hazardous car currently in use in significant numbers" in the U.S. Nader urged Volkswagen to recall all 3.2 million cars to correct safety defects; the recall would cost the company $184 million.

Nader said the VW Microbus should be barred from the road entirely because of only six inches of "crush distance" protecting occupants from a head-on crash, its lack of power and susceptibility to high winds.

Nader said his conclusions were based on the following factors: the danger of injury from the windshield, weak seat backs and seat tracks, weak door latches and the likelihood of passenger ejection in a crash, the dangerously located gas tank, propensity of the gas cap and gas lines to come off during a crash, and doors vulnerable to side impacts.

Toyota Land Cruiser safety scored. Consumer Reports magazine charged

AUTOMOBILE INDUSTRY UNDER ATTACK

that the Toyota Land Cruiser could drench car occupants with gasoline and hot radiator fluid in the event of an accident, according to the Washington Post Aug. 27, 1972.

The article in the magazine's September issue said evaluators "seldom have seen a vehicle designed with such disregard for occupant safety," saying the car had "inadequate rollover protection," an interior which "bristles with sharp edges and hostile protrusions," and suffered from "treacherous handling on paved roads," in addition to having a fuel tank under the front passenger seat and an engine coolant system running under the front floor area.

The magazine, published by Consumers Union, attributed the safety defects to a "gaping loophole" in federal guidelines for multi-purpose vehicles.

Ford recalls Montegos & Torinos. Ford Motor Co. April 25, 1972 announced a new recall of its full 1972 run of 436,000 Mercury Montegos and Ford Torinos, after an earlier recall announcement April 17 for the same cars was denounced by consumer groups as inadequate.

The earlier announcement had warned that corrosion of a rear axle bearing had led to separation of the rear wheel assembly in 16 reported cases, with no confirmed personal injuries. Ford ordered dealers to install retainer plates to "insure audible warning in the event of bearing failure" before further damage occurred. Assembly line changes to take effect immediately would include heavier axles and premium bearings.

Ford's second announcement came after the Center for Auto Safety in Washington, a group associated with Ralph Nader, and about 500 customer letters opposed the approach of reliance on the driver's hearing. New rear axles and bearings would be installed on all the cars, Ford announced, at a cost to the company of $26 million. The retainer plates would also be installed, at a cost of $5 million, since about four months would be needed to produce the necessary axles.

In an action later in 1972, Ford June 29 recalled more than 4 million 1970 and 1971 model passenger cars and pickup trucks to correct a plastic locking device which would break with frequent use, preventing the attachment of front seat shoulder belts.

EPA orders Chrysler recall. The Environmental Protection Agency (EPA) March 6, 1974 ordered the Chrysler Corp. to recall 804,000 1973-model cars and light trucks and about 1,000 early production 1974-model light trucks because of a defect in the exhaust gas recirculation system designed to reduce nitrogen oxide pollution.

According to the EPA, a temperature sensor located in the radiator failed to activate the system until excessively high engine temperatures were reached. The defect caused the release of nitrogen oxides 15%-60% above federal standards.

Chrysler Jan. 16 had announced the recall of nearly 160,000 1974 model cars for repair of a defect in the suspension system that could result in loss of steering control.

GAO calls recalls ineffective. The General Accounting Office reported March 1, 1975 that the car recall program was not working effectively and recommended a major probe of the program by the Transportation Department. The GAO study indicated that not all owners of vehicles were notified of defects, that some owners did not seek remedy of the defects, that dealers were not always ready to service the vehicles and that some dealers were selling recalled vehicles without fixing them.

Secret Ford warranties. Ford Motor Co. confirmed July 9, 1975 that it had repaired rust damage on 69,000 1969-73 model vehicles under a warranty program that had not been publicly disclosed. The program was disclosed when the Center for Automotive Safety, founded by consumer advocate Ralph Nader, sent a copy of a confidential Ford bulletin on the program to the Federal Trade Commission. The group charged that the program was unfair to vehicle owners unaware of the program.

Federal Regulation, Industry & the Critics

Seatbelt lock made optional. A bill making optional the seatbelt ignition interlock system for automobiles was signed by President Gerald R. Ford Oct. 27, 1972. The rule that seatbelts be fastened before 1974 and 1975 model cars could be started had met with widespread public resistance.

The bill, passed by voice votes of the Senate Oct. 10 and House Oct. 15, also authorized federal safety standards for school buses. The secretary of transportation was to promulgate the standards within 15 months.

The bill added a number of other amendments to the National Traffic and Motor Vehicle Safety Act, which it extended for two years with authorizations of $55 million for fiscal 1975 and $60 million for fiscal 1976. One of the new requirements was submission to Congress of any proposed regulations requiring non-seatbelt safety restraint systems, such as airbags. If Congress did not disapprove the proposal within 60 days, it would take effect.

Another amendment required manufacturers to remedy safety-related auto and tire defects free of charge to the owners or provide reimbursement.

The bill also required stronger fuel tanks for passenger cars made on or after Sept. 1, 1975, approval by the Transportation Department for the sale of regrooved tires, and a demonstration project by the department to help states develop high-volume car-inspection facilities. The requirement for manufacturers to notify car owners of defects by certified mail was changed to first class mail.

The requirement for either a seatbelt ignition interlock or a sequential warning device on new cars was to be withdrawn within 120 days of enactment of the bill. The owners of cars with the equipment could have the systems dismantled.

Safety systems deadlines. The Department of Transportation March 5, 1971 set Aug. 15, 1973 as its deadline for installation of automatic crash protection systems in front seats of automobiles. Installation of full protection passive restraint systems for both front and rear seat passengers was delayed until Aug. 15, 1975.

The department order also called for an interim standard, effective Jan. 1, 1972, that provided for combination lap and shoulder belts with automatic retractors and warning devices for unbuckling, unless car makers chose to meet the 1973 or 1975 regulations at that time.

Cars built after the 1973 deadline would be equipped with passive restraints (devices preventing passengers from being tossed about in crashes without the aid of safety belts or other preventive action) that would protect front-seat occupants in head-on crashes at 30 miles an hour. Unless the passive system also provided protection in lateral collisions and rollovers, lap belts and buzzers and lights warning passengers to buckle up would also be required.

The Transportation Department Feb. 24, 1972 granted auto makers a two-year delay in mandatory installation of automatically inflatable air bags in all cars. The U.S. Court of Appeals in Washington had dismissed Ralph Nader's suit to enforce the department's original 1974 deadline.

The air bags, a "passive restraint" system designed to cushion passengers during head-on crashes of up to 60 m.p.h. impact, were originally to be required on 1974 model year cars. After the industry claimed it could not meet the deadline, the department in 1971 had granted a delay until the 1976 model year, provided that 1974 and 1975 model cars be equipped with systems preventing start-ups until front seat passengers fastened their seat belts.

In filing suit against the delay, Nader claimed that 8,600 lives could be saved each year by air bags.

Manufacturers were simultaneously challenging the 1976 deadline in federal court in Cincinnati.

The 6th Circuit Court of Appeals in Cincinnati Dec. 5, 1972 ordered the Transportation Department to postpone the August 1975 implementation date for auto safety standards requiring the use of airbags or other "passive restraint" devices. It acted on appeals by Ford, Chrysler, American Motors and the Automobile Importers of America.

In a 2-1 ruling, the court agreed that the federal testing procedures were inadequate and "could not produce consistent, reliable or repeatable test results."

As a consequence of the first legal challenge by the car manufacturers to the proliferating government safety standards, the court ordered a delay "until a reasonable time" after new test specifications were issued.

(The same court Feb. 6, 1973 upheld the department's order that interlocking seat-belt systems be installed in all new cars built after Aug. 15, 1973.)

Douglas N. Toms of the National Highway Traffic Safety Administration had told a House Commerce subcommittee June 14, 1972 that two recent air-bag test failures were attributable to faulty wiring.

The Transportation Department April 14, 1971 had made public a new, modified safety standard for protective bumpers on passenger cars. The new standard required front bumpers on 1973 models to be able to withstand crashes against fixed barriers at 5 mph without damage to specific safety-related parts. However, it cut the required rear-bumper strength level to 2½ mph. Slightly stiffer requirements for 1974 models called for additional absorption at various angles of 5 mph crashes by front bumpers and 2.81 mph blows by rear bumpers.

The department announced March 5, 1975 that it had canceled a plan to weaken the standard. Yielding to industry objections that the rule meant higher prices, more fuel usage and higher repair costs on cars crashed at more than five miles an hour, the department had proposed in January easing the standard to a 2½-mile-an-hour test. This was opposed by insurance companies and key members of Congress.

Truck brake rule canceled—The Transportation Department April 28, 1975 withdrew its new brake standard for trucks, most buses and multipurpose vehicles such as campers. The standard, due to go into effect Sept. 1, was retained for school buses. For the other vehicles named, the requirement for better hydraulic brakes was withdrawn because of the "substantial costs" involved in meeting the standard, and the modest "safety benefits" to be attained.

Federal safety rules scored. The Insurance Institute for Highway Safety said Aug. 23, 1972 that the Department of Transportation (DOT) exempted federal agencies from safety guidelines which must be met by states.

The private study group charged that of 18 DOT requirements, including blood-alcohol levels, vehicle inspection, hazardous material removal and consistent traffic codes, only one had been applied to federally administered areas. That rule required that stop signs and traffic signals be of uniform size and height.

According to the group, federal agencies were not eligible, unlike states, for matching funds from the DOT to meet the requirements.

DOT spokesmen said Aug. 22 that the department was drafting regulations to provide "varying safety requirements for all the different kinds of streets and highways [the government] administers."

Safety test coverup charged. Ralph Nader's Center for Auto Safety charged Aug. 22, 1972 that the National Highway Traffic Safety Administration (NHTSA) was guilty of suppressing test results of crash helmets in which only eight of 75 types complied with minimum safety standards.

The group, accusing NHTSA Administrator Douglas W. Toms of a "cowardly coverup" of the findings, said an estimated 3,000 motorcyclists would die in accidents during 1972. According to the center, 44 states and the District of Columbia required that crash helmets be worn.

Safety expert criticizes designs. Dr. William Haddon Jr., former director of the National Highway Safety Bureau, testified at hearings before a subcommittee of the Senate Commerce Committee March 10, 1971 that auto makers deliberately designed autos prone to costly damages. Haddon, currently president of the Insurance Institute for Highway Safety, supported his remarks with the results of low-speed crash tests of 1971 models conducted by the institute.

According to Haddon, the institute found that average estimated repair costs in four out of five test crashes were about 50% higher for 1971 models than for 1970 cars as a result of 5 mile-per-hour test crashes; in head-on crashes average damage for 1971 models cost $332, compared with $216 for 1970 cars; in rear-end crashes 1971 models averaged $329 compared with $219 for 1970 models. Haddon said the increases were caused chiefly by "designed-in delicateness" of the cars, rather than higher prices for labor or parts.

Haddon contended that the auto industry had not taken advantage of body design changes and use of energy-absorbing bumpers to cut down damage potential, because of "a highly remunerative market in replacement parts sales, most of which automobile design has made certain will be made by the maker of the automobile itself."

Chrysler names consumer unit. Chrysler Corp. created an Office of Public Responsibility in response to the growing consumer and environment movement in 1971 and named an ombudsman to handle complaints.

It was reported Feb. 20 that Virgil Boyd, vice president of the Chrysler board of directors, would head the new consumer unit. Byron J. Nichols, vice president-consumer affairs, took charge of the ombudsman program March 3.

In announcing the new consumer unit, Board Chairman Lynn Townsend said: "The increasing public demand for improvement of the environment and the quality of life places special demands on industry for continuous progress in matters of clean air and water, consumer protection, safety and equal opportunity."

Safety award criticized. Walker Sandbach, executive director of Consumers Union, resigned July 16, 1972 from the National Motor Vehicle Safety Advisory Council to protest the group's first award for auto safety to Edward N. Cole, president of General Motors Corp.

Sandbach said the naming of Cole, "the father of the Corvair, one of the most dangerous cars produced in recent years, makes a mockery of the council's efforts to stimulate the development of safer cars."

The award was presented July 17 at the First International Congress on Automotive Safety in San Francisco.

Car makers' ad evidence made public. The Federal Trade Commission July 13, 1971 ordered seven auto makers to substantiate 60 advertising claims. The FTC then made public Oct. 13 the data the companies had submitted to prove their claims.

Among the claims that fell under FTC scrutiny were the Ford Motor Co. ad that the LTD was "over 700% quieter" and the General Motors Corp. claim that the Chevrolet Chevelle had "109 advantages to keep it from getting old before its time." Also included were 24 other GM ads, five other Ford ads, eight claims by Chrysler Corp., three by American Motors Corp., 11 by Volkswagen of America Inc., four by Nissan Motor Corp. in U.S.A. and three by Toyota Motor Co. Ltd.

The auto industry was the first target of a new FTC policy announced June 10 ordering all major industries to document advertising claims involving safety, performance, quality and pricing.

The FTC June 17, 1974 announced an agreement under which Ford Motor Co. would cease making claims about its autos' strength and quietness without reliable supporting evidence. The FTC complaint involved ads for 1971 and 1973 models which Ford claimed had body reinforcements as strong as highway guard rails and ran as quietly "as a glider."

GM, Ford acquitted. General Motors Corp. (GM) and Ford Motor Co. were acquitted by a federal jury in Detroit Dec. 19, 1973 of charges of participating in a conspiracy calling for fixing of prices in the automobile fleet sales market. U.S. District Court Judge John Feikens Dec. 13 had found the automakers not guilty of charges they had plotted to monopolize the fleet sales market.

In his instructions to the jury Dec. 19, Feikens said no one had testified that Ford and GM had conspired to eliminate price competition. He pointed out that the firms had been within their rights to watch each other's pricing activities as well as change prices so long as there was no express agreement between them. Similarly, Feikens had ruled the automakers were not guilty of the monopoly charges because the government had failed to produce sufficient evidence.

The indictment alleged that in 1969 and 1970 the companies, supported by two co-conspirators, the National Automobile Dealers Association and Peterson, Howell & Heather, Inc., the nation's largest automobile leasing company, conspired through public statements and talks to third parties in the industry to end the practice of discount pricing on fleet cars. The Chrysler Corp. originated the discount policy in 1962, and only partially curtailed it when GM and Ford moved out of the discount market.

Toyota price suit. The Justice Department filed a civil antitrust suit March 12, 1975 against two U.S. units of Toyota Motor Co. Ltd. of Japan, charging that they had conspired to fix the prices of Toyota cars and trucks since 1969. Toyota Motor Sales U.S.A. Inc., the only importer of Toyota vehicles into the continental U.S., and Toyota Motor Distributors Inc., a distributor to 14 states, were accused of conspiring to fix prices charged by dealers, to prevent dealers from advertising discount prices and to prevent dealers from advertising or selling outside assigned market areas, with the effect of suppressing or eliminating sales competition and maintaining high, noncompetitive and artificial prices.

A proposed consent agreement, under which the defendants neither admitted nor denied the charges, was submitted with the civil complaint to U.S. District Court in San Francisco.

Also named in the suit as unindicted co-conspirators were Toyota Motor Sales of Japan, the firms's worldwide distributor, and five of Toyota's six U.S. regional distributors. The U.S. importer's sales in 1972 exceeded $712 million and 1972 sales by all U.S. distributors totaled more than $762 million.

Car exhaust standards delayed. Russell E. Train, administrator of the Environmental Protection Agency, announced March 5, 1975 a one-year delay to car manufacturers in meeting antipollution standards set for 1977-model cars. The one-year delay was the maximum allowed under current legislation.

Train said the action was not based on industry objections. Industry had maintained that the new standards would result in higher prices and more fuel consumption because of the installation on cars of catalytic converters—the antipollution devices to control two major pollutants, hydrocarbons and carbon monoxide. The delay, Train said, was based solely on the agency's recent discovery that catalytic converters produced sulphuric acid emissions that could accumulate, from mass use of the converters, to unacceptably high levels and be a serious health risk for asthmatic persons.

At the opening of hearings on the Big Three carmakers' request for a freeze on emission standards through 1977—the industry had received a one-year deferment in meeting 1976-model emissions standards and wanted to extend the deferment through the 1977-model year—Train told the industry representatives Jan. 21 that "the economic vitality of the auto industry is closely related to the economic health of our nation, but at the same time the continued reduction of pollution from autos is vital to the physical health of the American people and public health must be our highest priority."

Nader contests carmakers' stand— Ralph Nader Jan. 21 released a letter President Ford contesting the carmakers' contention they could not attain the 40% improvement in gasoline mileage requested by the President and still meet the

1977 emission standards. Accompanying the release of the letter was a previously undisclosed study by the Federal Energy Administration that the Big Three could attain the 40% fuel economy without any easing of pollution standards.

After the President had proposed in his State-of-the-Union message a five-year moratorium on standards to gain the 40% fuel improvement, Nader said Jan. 15 the President "appears to have been deceived by the auto industry. General Motors has already improved its fuel efficiency by 28% from its 1974 to 1975 model year."

Action on Tires

Tire price settlement. Fourteen tire and tube manufacturers and two trade associations, accused by the FTC in 1959 of conspiring to fix prices in the tire industry, had signed an FTC consent order Jan. 10, 1962 to settle the suit. They agreed to avoid uniform pricing, exchanging of price information and fixing of bids on government contracts. Among the manufacturers signing the order: Goodyear Tire & Rubber Co.; Firestone Tire & Rubber Co. and B. F. Goodrich Co., all of Akron; U.S. Rubber Co., New York. The trade associations: Rubber Manufacturers Association (N.Y.) and Tire & Rim Association, Inc. (Akron).

Dunlop rejects recall. The National Highway Safety Bureau in the Transportation Department said Feb. 5, 1970 that the Dunlop Tire & Rubber Corp. had declined to recall its CT, size 6.50X13 four-ply rayon tires, which the bureau said "could be hazardous under certain conditions."

The 90,000 tires, manufactured in France between Jan. 1 and Aug. 1, 1968, failed government tire safety tests. Nine of 48 tires had failed the endurance test and 30 of 56 tires had failed the strength test.

The Dunlop action marked the first time a company in the auto industry refused to recall a product when the bureau requested that owners be notified of a safety defect.

In a statement issued through the Tire Industry Safety Council in Washington, Dunlop said its own tests and customer performance records indicated that the tires were "safe and first-grade merchandise." The company, an American subsidiary of Dunlop Co. Ltd. in England, said it would replace tires on the usual basis of value adjustment according to amount of use.

FTC accuses Firestone. Following a breakdown in talks between the Federal Trade Commission (FTC) and the Firestone Tire & Rubber Co., the FTC filed a formal complaint July 10, 1970 against Firestone for allegedly deceptive advertising about the safety and price savings of its tires.

The deception charges referred in part to the use of the name Safety Champion for a particular line of tires. The commission also charged the company had not provided scientific proof that cars with Firestone's Super Sports Wide Oval tires could be stopped 25% faster than other tires, as advertised. The complaint thus marked a reversal in FTC procedures by transferring the burden of proof from the commission to the advertiser. Another accusation said Firestone had falsely advertised that its tires were greatly reduced from regular prices.

Firestone denied the allegations.

The Supreme Court ruled Dec. 17, 1973 that the FTC could prohibit Firestone from advertising that some of its tires stopped "25% quicker" unless Firestone conducted adequate scientific tests under proper conditions.

FTC vs. tire firms. The FTC and five major tire producers tentatively settled an antitrust complaint against certain tire-leasing agreements between producers and bus firms. The settlement March 12, 1971 with Goodyear Tire & Rubber Co., Firestone Tire & Rubber Co., Uniroyal Inc., B. F. Goodrich Co. and General Tire & Rubber Co. was reached out of court by means of a provisional consent order and represented a new antitrust approach for the agency against oligopolies. Under the new antitrust theory, parallel courses of business that enabled acquisition of 99% of the market would violate the Federal Trade Commission Act as "unfair methods of competition."

Tire firms' break-up sought. The Justice Department filed separate antitrust charges Aug. 9, 1973 against the nation's largest tire makers, Goodyear Tire & Rubber Co. and Firestone Tire & Rubber Co., charging that the firms had made independent attempts to monopolize the $2 billion market in replacement tires bought directly by consumers.

In a rare request, the government asked federal district court in Cleveland to order the breakup of Goodyear and Firestone in an effort to restore competition to the tire industry.

The companies were accused of making substantial price reductions, beginning in 1959 and continuing until 1966. During that period, they allegedly engaged in reciprocal trade agreements to restrict the market of its smaller competitors, which also were unable to match the lower tire prices. Subsequently, the weakened firms were acquired by Goodyear and Firestone during the 1959-1966 period, according to the government. It was alleged that the two large manufacturers maintained the artificially low prices until 1966, when it had eliminated its competitors.

The Justice Department claimed that as a result of monopolistic practices, Goodyear increased its share of the consumer tire market from 23% in 1959 to 28% in 1973; Firestone's share was reported to have increased from 15% to 25% during the same period.

Grading standards opposed. The Transportation Department May 21, 1975 issued final standards for grading new tires on tread wear, traction and temperature resistance. Six tire producers immediately challenged the regulations in a suit filed in the U.S. Court of Appeals in Cincinnati. The companies: Firestone Tire & Rubber Co.; B.F. Goodrich Co.; Goodyear Tire & Rubber Co.; General Tire & Rubber Co.; Cooper Tire & Rubber Co.; Mansfield Tire & Rubber Co.

Drugs, Medical Devices & Health

Government Regulation

Pharmaceutical manufacturers and other segments of the U.S. medical establishment have been accused repeatedly of foisting unsafe, impure or worthless drugs and medical devices on American consumers. The chief government agency charged with preventing such practices is the Food & Drug Administration (FDA), which under various titles and rules has been carrying out this function since Jan. 1, 1907, when the Food & Drug Act of 1906 took effect. But the FDA has sometimes been accused of being too solicitous of the interests of the pharmaceutical industry—even when such concern conflicts with consumer interests. The FDA currently is a unit of the Department of Health, Education & Welfare, which oversees most government activities in the health field.

Drug-test rules. The FDA Jan. 4, 1963 issued in final form its new drug-testing regulations, which became effective Feb. 7. The regulations included modifications of the first FDA rules, issued Aug. 9, 1962 following the thalidomide furor. (Thalidomide had been distributed to more than 1,000 U.S. physicians for human testing while the manufacturer unsuccessfully sought FDA approval for commercial U.S. marketing.)

The final FDA regulations maintained the basic original requirement of comprehensive records and reports by pharmaceutical companies on their drug-testing activities. They also required full FDA approval of the results of animal testing of drugs before allowing human trials; this was a major modification of the original proposal that authorized the FDA to halt tests on humans if there was doubt as to the drug's safety or if testing rules were disobeyed. Other revisions included authorization of FDA to halt tests on humans (1) if a drug was proven ineffective for the purposes for which it was being developed, (2) if a drug firm submitted false statements about the drug or if it failed to meet safety requirements for the drug's production, (3) or if the drug was being commercially dispensed before legitimate testing had been completed.

Safety & effectiveness. The FDA published regulations Feb. 28, 1964 as a new means of finding out whether drugs being sold to the public were safe and effective. The rules took effect after a 30-day period given interested parties for comment. Within 30 days thereafter, drug manufacturers were required to report whether drugs developed between 1938 and June 20, 1963 were still on the market, and they were to report within 60 days thereafter on the effectiveness, safety and side effects of the drugs. Any adverse side effects had to be reported immediately. Reports were already required on all drugs developed since June 20, 1963.

Chas. Pfizer & Co. of New York and Burroughs Wellcome & Co., Inc. of Tuckahoe, N.Y. were ordered by the FDA March 4, 1966 to change the labeling on drugs sold to control nausea and morning sickness to warn adequately that they might present a danger of birth deformity when taken by pregnant women. The affected drugs included the antihistamines meclizine, cyclinzine and chlorcyclizine, sold under the trade names Bonadoxine and Antivert.

The FDA March 8, 1966 banned the manufacture of antibiotic throat lozenges sold without prescription because, "despite up to 15 years' experience with [them]," the FDA had found "no substantial" medical evidence of effectiveness" in the treatment of sore throats. The ban, based on 1962 legislation requiring all antibiotic products to be FDA-approved for safety and efficacy and certified thereafter batch by batch, stressed that the lozenges were not found to be unsafe and that manufacturers could use up stocks on hand. The order affected 250 products manufactured by 70 companies and accounting for more than $25 million in retail sales annually.

The FDA Dec. 6, 1969 ordered eight manufacturers to recall about 40 million capsules of oxytetracycline, a widely used infection-fighting drug. The FDA action followed a complaint by Pfizer, original patent holder of the drug, that the products of other manufacturers, although containing equal doses of the drug, did not produce the same levels in the blood as its version. The FDA said its findings confirmed the complaint. The order affected the Pro-Ter Laboratory (Milan, Itlay), Bates Laboratories Inc. (Chicago), Atral Laboratories (Lisbon, Portugal), Davis-Edwards Pharmacal Corp. (New York), McKesson Laboratories (Bridgeport, Conn.), Richlyn Laboratories (Philadelphia), Rondex Laboratories (Guttenburg, N.J.) and Zenith Laboratories (Englewood, N.J.).

Krebiozen acquittal. A federal jury in Chicago Jan. 29 and 31, 1966 acquitted four men of charges of conspiracy and fraud in the promotion and sale of Krebiozen, an alleged anti-cancer medication.

Those cleared Jan. 29 were Dr. Andrew C. Ivy, 72, Roosevelt University physiologist and an ex-vice president of the University of Illinois, Marko Durovic, 64, brother of Dr. Stevan Durovic (developer of Krebiozen), and William F. P. Phillips, 52, a Chicago physician. The jury Jan. 31 acquitted Stevan Durovic, 60, and his Krebiozen Research Foundation.

A spokesman for the FDA, chief opponent of the drug, said in Washington Jan. 31: "The decision . . . was a disappointment. However, it does not alter the determination [of the FDA] to keep Krebiozen out of interstate commerce as a so-called anti-cancer agent." The agency announced plans for civil action against the defendants on the ground that they had violated the FDA's prohibition against "introduction or delivery for introduction into interstate commerce" of a drug that lacked FDA approval.

Controversy over the drug had started March 26, 1951, when its development as an "agent for the treatment of malignant tumors" was announced at a news conference in Chicago. Although Krebiozen was lauded by many persons who said that they or members of their families were cancer victims whose lives had been prolonged by the drug, Krebiozen was denounced by government and private medical authorities as ineffective against cancer.

A 49-count federal indictment was filed against the defendants Nov. 17, 1964. A federal court jury was sworn in April 30, 1965, and the trial that ensued was the longest in the history of the federal court in Chicago. The prosecution charged that Krebiozen was simply mineral oil with traces of a body substance called creatine, that it cost pennies to produce, that it was valueless in the treatment of any disease and that the defendants had made at least $500,000 annually from the sale of Krebiozen by collecting $9.50 to $95 per dose.

Although the efficacy of the drug as an anti-cancer agent was not at issue at the trial, several defense witnesses testified that the drug had arrested or cured their cancer. Ivy testified that he had received no compensation for his work with the drug, that his sole interest in Krebiozen was to bring about a fair clinical test of it by medical organizations but that the FDA, the AMA and cancer research groups had prevented such a test.

2 reports clear FDA. The Food & Drug Administration was cleared by two reports Oct. 6 and Nov. 1, 1960 of charges made during June hearings conducted by Sen. Estes Kefauver (D, Tenn.) and his Senate Anti-Trust & Monopoly Subcommittee in an investigation of the drug industry.

A National Academy of Sciences committee, established at the request of the Department of Health, Education & Welfare, reported Oct. 6 that it had uncovered no evidence that FDA decisions of the past decade on new drugs and antibiotics had disregarded public health.

The HEW Department announced Nov. 1 that a special three-man investigating unit established by HEW Secretary Arthur S. Flemming had reported that none of the 900 FDA employes to which it had sent detailed financial questionnaires had reported "sources of personal income . . . incompatible with their government employment."

(Dr. Henry A. Welch, ex-director of the FDA Antibiotics Division, had resigned after the Senate inquiry had revealed that he had worked on the side for two antibiotic magazines and had received $287,000 from them in 8 years.)

Adriani rejected for FDA post. Dr. John Adriani, a New Orleans physician and professor of surgery at Louisiana State and Tulane Universities, was informed Aug. 25, 1969 that officials "at the top" had vetoed the appointment he had accepted in July as director of the FDA's Bureau of Medicine. Adriani, who had been approached for the job by Food & Drug Commissioner Herbert L. Ley Jr., was told of the action by FDA Deputy Commissioner Winton B. Rankin. White House Press Secretary Ronald L. Ziegler said Aug. 26 that President Nixon had not been involved in the appointment.

In an interview with the New York Times Aug. 26, Adriani attributed the withdrawal of the job offer to drug industry pressure in reaction to his testimony before the Senate Monopoly Subcommittee May 20. Adriani had testified that brand names in prescriptions should be abolished because they were useless, "deceptive and confusing" aliases. Adriani favored the use of generic, or common chemical, names.

Withdrawal of the appointment drew fire from Sen. Gaylord Nelson (D, Wis.), chairman of the subcommittee before which Adriani had testified, and Sen. Russell B. Long (D, La.), who had sponsored 1967 and 1968 amendments to the Social Security Act requiring the government to favor generically-labeled drugs for medicare and medicaid programs. Both senators accused drug manufacturers of exerting influence to block the appointment.

Dr. Roger O. Egeberg, assistant HEW (health, education and welfare) secretary for health and scientific affairs, denied Aug. 29 that the "so-called pharmaceutical lobby" had influenced the decision against Adriani. In a statement, later modified, Egeberg charged that Adriani, who had confirmed reports of his candidacy to a newspaper, had showed "poor judgment" during an interview by "ascribing political connotations to the process of filling a career position." Egeberg was apparently referring to an Aug. 14 report in the New Orleans Times-Picayune that, the Egeberg statement said, quoted Adriani as "saying that he had a firm job offer which required White House approval because of its political sensitivity." Egeberg said that his deputy, Dr. Jesse Steinfeld, had decided on the basis of that statement to reject Adriani's candidacy. According to the New York Times Aug. 30, Steinfeld and Egeberg later reversed themselves and said Adriani had made no improper "political" comments. Egeberg said the main problem had been "premature disclosure."

FDA staff charges harassment. Eleven FDA staff scientists charged in Senate testimony Aug. 15, 1974 that their superiors had harassed, transferred and overruled them when they had produced adverse findings on drugs needing final FDA approval before being marketed.

Caspar W. Weinberger, secretary of health, education and welfare, Aug. 24 announced a "full review" of the procedures and practices by which the FDA evaluated the safety and effectiveness of new drugs for use in general medical practice. The review was being called, Weinberger said, at the request of the FDA commissioner, Dr. Alexander M. Schmidt.

The testimony, before the combined Health Subcommittee of the Labor & Public Welfare Committee and the Administrative Practice & Procedure Subcommittee of the Judiciary Committee, was backed by three outside consultants, who had been named to FDA panels created to review staff work. One consultant, Dr. Gerald Solomons of the University of Iowa, characterized his dealings with the agency as "one of the most frustrating, embarrassing and degrading experiences I've had in my medical career."

Solomons had been called in to review an FDA staff member's finding against Cylert, a drug made by Abbott Laboratories for use on hyperkinetic children. Noting that his review panel had also recommended against Cylert, Solomons testified that he had sensed "a lack of cooperation of not obstructionism" against the review committee's position. "It appeared that our deliberations were being relayed to the drug company after confrontation with administrative officers," he said. Solomons added that "professional personnel who had been involved and enthusiastically supported our findings were assigned to other projects."

Dr. Roger D. Freeman of the University of British Columbia, a member of the same reviewing team, testified that his findings had confirmed the original staff report that Abbott Laboratories had presented insufficient data to back its application for approval of Cylert. Freeman said that he had not been permitted to comment on a rebuttal from Abbott and that when a second medical review team was set up, "we were to have no contact with this new committee."

Dr. Carol Kennedy, the FDA staff member and psychiatrist who first recommended against Cylert, said she had been transferred later to the dental-surgical section to study soft contact lenses.

Schmidt appeared before the joint subcommittees Aug. 16. He rejected Sen. Edward Kennedy's (D, Mass.) assertion that FDA decisions often reflected the "power and influence of the drug companies." He said he had always emphasized "scientific integrity" and a need to explain the FDA's work "openly, honestly and well."

Kennedy challenged Schmidt on another assertion that his policy had been to keep records. Kennedy produced a Dec. 1, 1972 internal FDA memo ordering destruction of verbatim transcripts of advisory committee meetings as soon as summary transcripts had been approved by the committees. Under oath, Schmidt said that the memo was in error and that the policy had never been implemented. Schmidt conceded that a second memo correcting the error had never been sent.

Dr. Richard Crout of the FDA's Bureau of Drugs testified Aug. 16 there were "real misconceptions" among the 11 staff members and three consultants testifying Aug. 15. Disapproval of a drug "commonly [was] not a permanent turndown," as adverse reports were often reviewed in the light of new information, he said.

Advertising Transgressions Attacked

Arthritis drug ads 'false.' The FTC issued complaints against three national distributors of arthritis and rheumatism medicines March 31, 1957 on charges of "falsely advertising" that their products were "adequate, effective or reliable treatment for the aches and pains of arthritis, rheumatism and related diseases." The three companies accused were: Mentholatum Co., Inc. of Buffalo, N.Y., maker of Mentholatum Rub; Whitehall Pharmacal Co. of New York, maker of InfraRub and Heet; Omega Chemical Co., Inc. of Jersey City, maker of Omega Oil. The actions against them were the first in a new program that was started in October 1956, when the FTC set up a special unit under FTC lawyer T. Harold Scott to monitor radio and TV commercials.

Dolcin Corp. of New York had been found guilty of criminal contempt by the U.S. Court of Appeals in Washington Dec. 18, 1956 for continuing to advertise that its product gave relief from arthritis after the FTC had judged this claim false in 1949. Dolcin executives Victor van der Linde, George Shimmerlik and Albert T. Wantz also were found guilty.

Aspirin ad complaint. The FTC Jan. 17, 1963 charged Sterling Drug, Inc. (N.Y.), maker of Bayer Aspirin, and its advertising agency, Dancer-Fitzgerald-Sample, Inc., with falsely advertising that Bayer Aspirin was superior to other pain relievers.

An FTC-financed study of aspirin compounds at Baltimore hospitals had found no significant difference among the five leading non-prescription aspirin compounds—Bayer, St. Joseph's Aspirin (made by Plough, Inc. of Memphis, Tenn.), Anacin (made by American Home Products Corp. of New York), Bufferin and Excedrin (both made by Bristol-Myers Co. of New York). The research findings, published in the *Journal of the American Medical Association,* had indicated that aspirin and Bufferin caused fewer stomach upsets than Anacin or Excedrin.

The FTC said that, contrary to the Bayer advertising claims: (a) the Baltimore research was not indorsed by the government, the American Medical Association or the medical profession; (b) Bayer was not found to be gentler than other aspirin compounds.

As early as March 19, 1961, the FTC had accused the makers of Anacin, Bufferin, St. Joseph's Aspirin and Bayer Aspirin (see above for company names) of false advertising claims about the speed with which their products relieved pain.

DRUGS, MEDICAL DEVICES & HEALTH

The FTC Feb. 19, 1972 published complaints and consent orders charging the makers of Anacin, Bufferin, Excedrin and Bayer Aspirin with false and deceptive advertising. According to the FTC, the firms had misrepresented to consumers "that there are significant therapeutic differences among the products," and consumers therefore, had paid more for the products than for equally effective pain killers. In addition, the FTC challenged advertised claims that the products could relieve emotional stress and tension.

The cease-and-desist orders required the firms, which spent $80 million annually on advertising, to devote 25% of their promotion budgets on "corrective ads" for two years, separate from any sales-promoting advertising. In previous cases the FTC had ordered corrective ads for one year, and permitted their inclusion in normal commercial messages, but the large volume and extended duration of the companies' allegedly deceptive campaigns called for stricter countermeasures, according to Robert Pitofsky, director of the FTC consumer protection bureau. Two of the five FTC commissioners dissented from the corrective ad order.

The FDA April 19, 1972 published the results of a 1968 National Academy of Sciences study of the effectiveness of 14 analgesics and 18 antacid drugs. Of 51 claims, the study found only six definitely validated, and three were found invalid. The widely used over-the-counter drugs were either "possibly effective" or "probably effective" for the other claims, according to the study.

Fines for Regimen ads. The Drug Research Corp., producer of diet pills selling under the name Regimen Tablets, its president, John Andreadis, and the advertising agency of Kastor, Hilton, Chesley, Clifford & Atherton, Inc. (the sole advertisers) were fined a total of $8,500 in Manhattan (N.Y.) Criminal Court Feb. 15, 1965 on their plea of guilty to misdemeanor charges. They were accused of advertising falsely that the "useless" Regimen Tablet helped control weight.

A federal jury in Brooklyn May 6, following a 12-week trial, found the advertising agency, Drug Research and Andreadis guilty of fraud for falsely advertising that Regimen Tablets caused nutritional weight loss without dieting. Two women who appeared in TV commercials had been represented as losing 25 pounds in six weeks by use of the pills although both had undergone severe diets. The allegations covered the period 1956-63, when 4 million boxes of Regimen pills, costing 30¢ a box to manufacture, were sold at an average of $4 a box.

On the basis of the May 6 conviction, Drug Research, the advertising agency and Andreadis were fined an additional $50,000 each June 25, and Andreadis was given an 18-month jail sentence.

FTC guidelines. The FTC March 18, 1969, issued guidelines to control the advertising of over-the-counter drugs :those that could be bought without a prescription). The guidelines stated that the adververtising of over-the-counter drugs (those with drug labeling and must avoid untruthful claims that one product was superior to another. The proposals covered rules on the use of trademarks, drug guarantees, representations concerning the extent of drug testing and the responsibilities of advertising agencies in nonprescription drug ads.

AMA ads probed. As the Senate Monopoly Subcommittee took testimony on the honesty of drug advertising carried in the Journal of the American Medical Association, Dr. Edward R. Annis, an AMA trustee and former president, admitted March 18, 1969 that "some" misleading ads "have slipped through our screen." He insisted, however, that corrective letters sent by the drug companies, as ordered by the FDA, were "the proper action."

The case in point was advertising for Chloromycetin, the Parke, Davis & Co. brand of chloramphenicol, an antibiotic that some medical experts said had been greatly overused and could cause fatal anemia in occasional cases. Sen. Gaylord Nelson (D, Wis.), chairman of the subcommittee, denounced the AMA for its refusal to warn readers about Chloromycetin advertisements that were later labeled misleading by the FDA. After persistent questioning by Nelson, Annis promised that the AMA would take the matter "under advisement." Asked by Sen. Robert Dole (R, Kan.) to comment on "the feeling there is some sort of conspiracy" between the AMA and drug companies, Annis denied any "alliance with the industry."

Geritol sued by government. The Justice Department filed a $1 million suit April 20, 1970 against the makers and advertisers of Geritol, an iron and vitamin preparation, on the ground that they had violated FTC orders to stop deceptive advertising.

The federal action called for penalties of $500,000 each against the J. B. Williams Co., Inc., makers of Geritol, and the Parkson Advertising Agency, Inc.

The action came after more than 10 years of investigation, complaints and orders challenging the claim that Geritol was an effective remedy for "tiredness, loss of strength, run-down feeling, nervousness or irritability." The government charged that as late as October 1969, Geritol advertisements did not make clear that the majority of people experiencing tiredness did not suffer from iron deficiency anemia—the condition that Geritol and a companion product, FemIron, were designed to combat.

FTC sues for substantiation. In 1970 the FTC began action to halt the advertising of unsubstantiated claims.

The FTC filed a complaint against Charles Pfizer & Co. Inc. April 16 in an attempt to establish the concept that companies violate federal statutes against "unfair, misleading and deceptive" advertising when they make unsubstantiated but not necessarily false representations about products. The FTC said the company advertised a sunburn product, UnBurn, with claims that it "anesthetizes nerves in sensitive sunburned skin" and "relieves pain fast." Without challenging the truth of the claim, the FTC said the product's pain-relieving properties had not been substantiated "by adequate and well-controlled scientific studies or tests."

■ Sandoz Pharmaceuticals (Hanover, N.J.) agreed Oct. 2 to halt an advertising campaign promoting Serentil, an antialcoholism prescription medicine. The FDA, in a letter to the company Sept. 24, had charged that the promotion was "false and misleading" in that it claimed the drug was "useful in the prevention and treatment of alcoholism" when, in fact, it was only proved useful in relieving side effects of alcoholism such as depression and nausea.

In a similar development reported by the Washington Post Dec. 3, the CIBA Pharmaceutical Co. (Summit, N.J.) agreed to withdraw an advertising claim that Ritalin, an amphetamine-type prescription medication, "helps relieve chronic fatigue due to mild depression." The FDA had said in an Oct. 27 letter to the company that a review of the drug by the National Research Council did not support the claim.

FDA orders ads warning of adverse drug findings. The FDA announced June 7, 1971 that labels and advertisements for prescription drugs would have to include adverse findings on their effectiveness by the National Academy of Sciences-National Research Council. The ruling, to take effect in October, applied only to prescription drugs, usually advertised only in medical journals.

TV to curb drug ads. The nine-member National Association of Broadcasters (NAB) code review board voted unanimously Feb. 22, 1973 to impose limitations on nonprescription drug commercials beginning Sept. 1, in a move apparently designed to ward off consumer and Congressional criticism.

The rules would be obligatory, although not legally enforceable, for all stations subscribing to the NAB code, including the networks. The rules would bar on-camera pill-taking, advertising during or adjacent to children's programs, the use of children in commercials for adult drugs, personal endorsements by "authority figures or celebrities" and commercials which presented drugs as everyday or casual products.

Overcharging Assailed

Prescription prices 'unreasonable.' U.S. prescription-drug prices were described as "unreasonable" compared with industry costs and profits and prices charged for U.S. drugs sold overseas. The charge was made in a report issued June 27, 1961 by Chairman Estes Kefauver (D, Tenn.) of the Senate Monopoly Subcommittee.

The report, based on a 1960 inquiry, blamed the high prices on the large firms' control of the drug market through the use of patents, trade names and sales specialization with a resultant high cost of advertising and drug promotion. It criticized the practice, required in many states, under which a pharmacist filled prescriptions according to brands ordered by a doctor.

The report was signed by Sens. John A. Carroll (D, Colo.), Philip A. Hart (D, Mich.) and Thomas J. Dodd (D, Conn.). Sens. Everett M. Dirksen (R, Ill.) and Roman L. Hruska (R, Neb.) issued minority views scoring the report as a "monstrosity."

(Dr. Austin Smith, president of the Pharmaceutical Manufacturers Association, assailed the report June 28 as an "unjustified attack" on the drug industry.)

Drug ads proposed. The FTC June 2, 1975 proposed regulations that would permit druggists to advertise the retail prices of prescription drugs. The proposed regulations would supersede any state and local laws to the contrary and bar any private attempts, such as by pharmacists' associations, to restrict a druggist from disclosing or advertising prescription drug prices.

Pharmacists would not be required to advertise drug prices, but if they did the commission was considering formulating guidelines for such ads.

Currently, such advertising was prohibited by laws and regulations in 33 states and codes of ethics of at least three dozen state pharmaceutical associations.

The commission's staff report said consumers were "woefully uninformed" about prescription drug prices, that they could vary widely. FTC Chairman Lewis A. Engman, in a speech before the American Advertising Federation June 2, said the consumer was "ignorant" about such pricing and "I have reason to believe that he is ignorant because advertising bans keep him that way." Engman cited a survey in the San Francisco area showing that 100 tablets of a high-blood-pressure drug were for sale at 38 different prices ranging from $2.50 to $11.75.

Consumer spending on prescription drugs totaled nearly $7 billion a year and potential savings through awareness of the availability of lower-priced drugs were estimated at $130 to $200 million a year.

A three-judge federal court had voided, as an infringement of the First Amendment, a Virginia law prohibiting drugstores from advertising the prices of prescription drugs, it was reported March 25, 1975. The court agreed that the elderly, the infirm and others who spent large parts of their incomes on medicine, had the right to know prescription prices so they could shop for bargains.

U.S. suit vs. pharmacists—The Department of Justice filed a civil antitrust suit in federal district court in Grand Rapids, Mich. Nov. 24 alleging that the 50,000-member American Pharmaceutical Association and the Michigan State Pharmaceutical Association had conspired to prohibit advertising by their members of retail prices for prescription drugs.

Assistant Attorney General Thomas A. Kauper said this was the first antitrust suit in which the government had ever challenged advertising restrictions practiced by a national association. The suit charged the two groups with "adopting, publishing and distributing a code of ethics containing a provision which prohibited pharmacist members of associations from advertising the retail prices of prescription drugs." The court was asked to order the defendants to cancel such prohibitions from their codes of ethics.

HEW acts on drug costs. In a move designed to save state and federal governments up to $75 million on drug costs, the Department of Health Education and Welfare (HEW) gave final approval to a plan known as Maximum Allowable Costs. The plan provided that the government would not pay for high-priced medicines for Medicare and Medicaid patients if less expensive ones, readily available, would do as well.

The plan, which took effect July 25, 1975, gave the FDA power to declare that no difference existed in biological effects of different brands of the same drug. HEW would then set the price it would reimburse pharmacists for each drug based on the lowest cost at which it was available to the druggists.

Doctors would then be given a list, published and continually updated by HEW, which would catalogue the most frequently prescribed drugs and the price the area druggists paid for them. This list would help doctors become aware of which drugs were covered by the federal program. The list would also be made available to the general public to allow them to know of the least expensive drugs.

HEW officials said that less than a fourth of commonly prescribed drugs were sold under more than one brand name. Sources estimated that only about a dozen of the best-selling drugs would ultimately be included in the program in its first year.

The new regulations still gave doctors the right to prescribe any drug they wanted to Medicare and Medicaid patients regardless of cost. But they had to certify in writing on the prescription that they believed there was a "medical necessity" for that brand."

The provision was included in the regulations in an attempt to appease American Medical Association (AMA) objections, according to an HEW official. Nevertheless, the AMA sued to halt implementation of the plan.

According to the suit, filed in Chicago federal court July 29, the AMA contended that doctors would be forced to prescribe only the cheapest drugs, when they otherwise would prescribe a drug "which they believe to be safer, more reliable, or more effective."

Wonder-drug acquittal. A Supreme Court tie vote Jan. 24, 1972 automatically affirmed an appellate court ruling overturning a 1967 criminal antitrust verdict against Chas. Pfizer & Co., American Cyanamid Co. and Bristol Myers Co. Upjohn Co. and the Squibb unit of Squibb Beech-Nut Inc. had been named as co-conspirators but not as defendants in the case.

A New York federal jury in 1967 had found the three major drug companies guilty of conspiring to fix prices and monopolize production and distribution of broad-spectrum antibiotics, principally tetracycline. The conviction followed a 1961 indictment that charged the defendants with illegally grossing $655 million in profits during the period 1953–61. According to the prosecution, it cost $1.59 to $3.87 to manufacture 100 capsules of tetracycline, which were then sold at $30.60 a hundred to druggists and $51 a hundred to consumers. (The other antibiotics involved: aureomycin and terramycin.)

The 2nd Circuit Court of Appeals had reversed the conviction on grounds that U.S. District Court Judge Marvin E. Frankel had misinformed the jury on the law applicable to the case. The court also held, in effect, that the companies could not be convicted solely on the circumstantial evidence which was the basis of the Justice Department's case.

In arguments before the Supreme Court, the department contended that Frankel's jury instructions had been "exemplary" and asked the court to reinstate the convictions with an accompanying declaration that reviewing courts should treat trial judges in complex cases more generously. It also said the appeals court decision had placed a "serious burden" on the government's prosecution of antitrust cases because there was rarely "direct proof of the conspiracy and the government almost invariably has to rely upon circumstantial evidence."

Aspirin findings. The Senate Monopoly Subcommittee heard testimony in 1971 on the effectiveness and price of such over-the-counter (OTC) drugs as aspirin.

An FDA official testified June 17 that "nothing" in the OTC market had been shown to be more effective than aspirin in relieving pain or lowering fever. Dr. Henry E. Simmons, director of the FDA Bureau of Drugs, said two products, Anacin (American Home Products) and Excedrin (Bristol-Myers), both advertised as "stronger than aspirin," simply "provide more aspirin . . . and are combined with other ingredients that contribute little or nothing."

Price comparison studies prepared by the subcommittee staff showed a supermarket brand of 100 aspirin tablets selling for 19¢, compared to 73¢ for Bayer aspirin (Sterling Drugs), $1.17 for Anacin and $1.19 for Excedrin. Simmons also said "timed-release" or "long-acting" painkillers "have no real advantage over an equivalent dose of regular aspirin." The price study listed the price of 72 tablets of Bayer Timed Release aspirin at $1.69.

Government Powers & Action

FDA power upheld. The Supreme Court June 18, 1973 unanimously upheld the FDA's power to remove ineffective drugs from the market.

The court upheld 1962 Congressional legislation authorizing the FDA to require prescription drug manufacturers to prove their products' effectiveness as well as their safety. The decision was also extended to uphold a part of the 1962 law that gave the FDA power to regulate drugs that previously had been cleared for safety but not for effectiveness.

Reversing an appellate court ruling, the Supreme Court said the FDA could, without going to court, remove "me too" drugs from the market. "Me too" drugs were never approved by the FDA on the grounds they contained the same ingredients as other prescription preparations already being marketed.

The FDA was also held to have the jurisdiction to decide administratively, subject to judicial review, whether a product had to be cleared as a "new drug" before marketing.

The court ruled the FDA could deny a hearing to a drug manufacturer when it failed to provide evidence its product met requirements.

Justice Douglas wrote: "If the FDA were required automatically to hold a hearing for each product whose efficacy was questioned . . . even though many hearings would be an exercise in futility, we have no doubt that it could not fulfill its statutory mandate to remove from the market all those drugs which do not meet effectiveness requirements."

Non-prescription drugs sold over the counter were not affected by the rulings.

FDA defends rules—The FDA commissioner, Charles C. Edwards, and the FDA drug bureau director, Dr. Henry E. Simmons, had told the Senate Monopoly Subcommittee Feb. 5, 1973 that their caution in licensing new drugs had probably prevented thousands of deaths and deformities among Americans. They cited some 25 harmful drugs that had been marketed abroad but never reached the U.S. public because of the policy.

The agency was responding to criticism that amendments to the Pure Food and Drug Act in 1962 had decreased the number of beneficial new drugs appearing on the market. Subcommittee Chairman Sen. Gaylord Nelson (D, Wis.) cited a Jan. 8 Newsweek magazine column by economist Milton Friedman charging that the amendments "condemn innocent people to death." Nelson expressed his "dismay" at attacks on the FDA by "certain elements of the medical profession."

Simmons cited the well-known case of thalidomide, in which over 10,000 babies were born deformed in European countries to mothers who had used the drug during pregnancy in the early 1960s.

"Of even more concern," he said, was a report that an aerosol spray for bronchial asthma had probably led to the death of 3,500 children in England and Wales alone in the mid 1960s. The drug, Simmons claimed, could not have been licensed in the U.S. without extensive animal and human testing. In another case, an appetite suppressant called aminorex, which the FDA had barred from further human tests in 1968 because of safety problems, might have caused an "epidemic" of a type of fatal high blood pressure of the lungs among German, Austrian and Swiss citizens in the late 1960s.

The amendments required evidence of effectiveness before a drug could be marketed, informed consent from participants in new drug tests and generally stronger safety measures.

Panalba barred—A federal court of appeals in Cincinnati, Ohio Feb. 27, 1970 had upheld an FDA order to Upjohn Co. to recall Panalba, a widely prescribed combination of antibiotics. The FDA and the National Academy of Sciences-National Research Council had found the product ineffective because the combination proved to be no more efficacious than its ingredients used singly.

(The FDA commissioner, Charles C. Edwards, announced June 24 that the FDA had completed legal actions to remove from the market 48 combination antibiotic drugs that were ruled ineffective more than a year earlier. The action—affecting all fixed combinations of penicillin and various sulfa drugs and penicillin with streptomycin—was in line with previous steps the agency had taken against combination drugs, following results of a study conducted by the National Academy of Sciences-National Research Council.

(In a ruling reported July 25, the FDA said that after July 31, it would no longer certify Signemycin—an antibiotic combination manufactured by Pfizer Co.—as safe and effective. The agency said the company had failed to produce studies supporting use of the drug, which had been prescribed for severe, acute infections.

(According to an Aug. 24 report, the FDA ordered 13 nasal sprays and drops removed from the market within 30 days. Commissioner Edwards said there was no reason to believe that the preparations—combination products mostly sold by prescriptions—could produce the results claimed. He said the preparations included antibiotics combined with steroids, vaso-constrictors, decongestants and antihistamines. The order applied to products of the Upjohn Co., Kalamazoo, Mich.; Merck & Co., West Point, Pa.; Smith, Kline & French Laboratories, Philadelphia; Warner-Lambert Pharmaceutical Co., Morris Plains, N.J.; and Lemon Pharmacal Co., Sellersville, Pa.

(In continuing actions against combination drugs considered ineffective by the FDA, the agency announced a ban Sept. 14 of 15 prescription cold remedies. The ban was on products made by Lederle Laboratories in Pearl River, N.Y. and by divisions of Charles Pfizer & Co. and Bristol-Myers Co)

Ineffective drugs—The FDA Nov. 27, 1970 had listed 369 drugs that were ineffective or hazardous according to tests performed for the agency by the National Academy of Sciences—National Research Council.

The FDA, since mid-1968, had sought to remove the listed drugs from the market, but many were still in use. In some cases the manufacturers discontinued their products following challenges by the FDA, but others contested the agency's actions.

The list had been distributed to agencies of the federal government following charges from Congressmen that units—such as the Defense Department, Veterans Administration, Public Health Service and Agency for International Development—continued to buy drugs that had been found ineffective or dangerous.

The National Research Council tests were commissioned following passage in 1962 of the Kefauver-Harris amendment, which required proof of a drug's effectiveness and safety before it could be marketed.

The tests were made on drugs already approved for marketing before the law took effect. FDA spokesmen said the drugs on the list and others that would ultimately be declared ineffective comprised more than 12% of the roughly 3,000 products that came on the market between 1938 and 1962.

Most of the drugs on the list were prescription medicine and several were among the 200 most-prescribed drugs in recent years. The list also included non-prescription products such as mouthwash, medicated bandages, throat lozenges and toothpaste. Many of the prescription products were combination drugs that were included in the list although their ingredients taken separately were considered effective. The FDA held that the drugs taken together were no more effective than the components taken separately, and it would be unnecessarily hazardous to take them in a fixed combination.

Inclusion on the list indicated that the FDA had found the product lacked "substantial evidence of effectiveness" or that potential hazards outweighed benefits resulting in "an unfavorable benefit-to-risk ratio."

Combination-drug rules—The FDA Feb. 17, 1971 issued new rules to insure the safety and effectiveness of fixed combination drugs, those containing two or more active ingredients in a fixed dosage form.

The FDA standards would require that each active ingredient in a combination drug contribute to the medicine's effectiveness. The agency statement said the action would insure that combination drugs were used only when the product offered advantages over any one or more of its ingredients taken separately. FDA Commissioner Dr. Charles C. Edwards said the agency recognized that some combinations had a legitimate role in medical treatment.

The agency announcement said, "The new policy affects up to 40% of the most widely sold prescription drugs and most [about 50%, an FDA officer said later] over-the-counter drugs—those sold without prescription."

The new rules were made final by the FDA Oct. 15. The FDA also announced a two-year study of the safety and effectiveness of all non-prescription drugs.

Manufacturers would have to prove that the drugs were safer or more effective in combination, or that a "significant number" of patients would require all the ingredients combined even if taken separately.

Cold remedies questioned. The FDA July 7, 1972 released a report submitted three years earlier by the National Academy of Sciences-National Research Council (NAS-NRC) that found most claims on cold remedy labels to be unsubstantiated.

Twenty-seven representative cold remedies were reviewed in the study. Of 45 claims, the NAS-NRC said manufacturers had provided substantial evidence for only four, while 14 were found "probably effective," five "effective, but," when some doubts were expressed, 14 "possibly effective" and eight "ineffective as a fixed combination," in which cases the combination of singly effective ingredients was considered unsafe or unnecessary for must users.

The remedies included pills, capsules, inhalers, jellies and nose drops, all marketed before 1963. After that date new non-prescription drugs could not be sold without proof of efficacy.

The FDA said that the three-year delay in publishing the report had resulted from the agency's concentration on prescription drugs during that period.

Smith, Kline and French, manufacturer of Contac, which the study found only possibly effective for two of three claims, replied in a July 7 statement that the NAS-NRC had based its study on data submitted prior to September 1966. Since then, the company claimed, it had submitted further, more conclusive verification for the efficacy of Contac.

FDA on drug overuse. The FDA Oct. 8, 1972 released a survey on the use of patent medicines and nonprescription drugs, and said "it is probable that there is an enormous waste of money, not to mention adverse health effects, from misguided consumer experimentation with health products."

FDA Commissioner Dr. Charles C. Edwards charged that manufacturers and distributors "often greatly exaggerate their advertising claims," resulting in overuse of such products as vitamins, mineral supplements and laxatives. He said the survey illustrated the need for "stiffer regulation of the labeling and promotion of nonprescription drugs and more meaningful education of the public."

Edwards said the FDA should be granted power to regulate advertising of the products, which was currently a function of the Federal Trade Commission. The report had found that three of every eight individuals in the 2,914 cross-section sample believed the ads were valid, since, if they were untrue, "advertisers wouldn't be allowed to say them" by federal agencies. Edwards noted that, unlike prescription drug makers, "the promoters of over-the-counter drugs are not restricted as to what their ads may claim."

The study found that 35 million adults had used vitamins and mineral supplements without doctor's advice, and that 75% of the entire sample thought vitamins provided more energy, which the report called "the most common of the misconceptions investigated."

Vitamin doses curbed. The FDA Dec. 13, 1972 issued an order that restricted sharply the amounts of vitamins A and D that could be sold in over-the-counter products.

The agency said the substances were "known to be toxic," and were "heavily promoted in high doses to the consumer." Overdoses of either vitamin could retard physical growth in children. Too much vitamin A could also cause bone lesions, irritability, or enlargement of the liver or spleen, while an excess of vitamin D could cause nausea, listlessness, or a rise in calcium deposits leading to hypertension and kidney failure.

Currently marketed multivitamin products contained as much as 10 times the new permissible limit of vitamin A and 60 times the limit of vitamin D.

Children's-vitamin TV ads withdrawn— Three major drug manufacturers separately informed Action for Children's Television (ACT), a Boston public interest group, that they would cease advertising vitamins on children's television program (reported July 21, 1972).

Miles Laboratories, Bristol-Myers and Hoffmann-LaRoche reported that they had either removed their ads or would do so by Oct. 1. Peggy Charren, ACT president, said the group would continue to petition the Federal Trade Commission to ban all advertising aimed at children.

FDA curbs vitamins & minerals. Acting over protests of the health-food industry, the FDA Aug. 1, 1973 announced final regulations governing the labeling, promotion and sales of vitamins and minerals.

A major rule curtailed the availability of vitamins A and D, which had been found to have adverse physical and mental effects when taken in large amounts. Prescriptions would be required for dosages of vitamin A above 10,000 international units—twice the recommended daily allowance (RDA)—and for dosages of vitamin D above 400 international units—the same as the RDA.

Other vitamin-containing products would be classified in three groups and regulated with varying degrees of strictness: items containing less than 50% of the RDA of a vitamin would be classified as food. Products with 50%-150% of the RDA would be classed as dietary supplements and would have to be labeled as such. Dietary supplements could not be promoted for treatment or prevention of disease. Products with more than 150% of the RDA of one or more vitamins would be classed as drugs and regulated accordingly. All products (except for the high-potency forms of Vitamins A and D) would remain available on a non-prescription basis.

FDA Commissioner Alexander M. Schmidt noted that no vitamin or mineral products were being banned from the market. One of the chief aims of the rules, he said, was to curb deceptive promotional claims.

The rules restricting vitamins A and D were to become effective in 60 days. For the other products, manufacturers were given until the end of 1973 to begin producing labels meeting the new standards and until the end of 1974 to dispose of existing stocks.

Nearly two years later, after litigation, the FDA May 27, 1975 modified its regulations on marketing vitamins and minerals.

Under the 1975 plan, the FDA would permit any vitamin and mineral to be sold in any strength if it were generally recognized as safe. High-strength Vitamin A and D formulations would be restricted as before to prescription sales because of proven harmful effects if consumed in large quantities.

The FDA retained its intention to establish specific composition of products that could be sold as multiple vitamin and mineral products, but producers would be allowed to apply for other combinations and these would be approved, the agency stressed, only if confusion to the consumer could be avoided.

The agency also retained its basic authority to regulate as a drug any vitamin or mineral for which a health claim were made.

Antibiotic misuse—Dr. Henry E. Simmons, director of the FDA's Bureau of Medicine, told the Senate Monopoly Subcommittee that antibiotics overuse resulted in tens of thousands of unnecessary deaths in the U.S. each year (reported Dec. 8, 1972).

Simmons said the drugs were properly used only to treat serious illnesses like typhoid and meningitis, but had been used for such routine discomforts as the common cold. The overuse of antibiotics, Simmons said, had led to development of immune strains of bacteria, and had caused a major wave of hospital blood poisoning from superinfections, which occurred when the antibiotic "kills off one set of microorganisms, thereby allowing another group to flourish."

Witnesses testifying before the subcommittee said at least 60% of antibiotic patients in hospitals could do without the drugs, and that U.S. antibiotic production had more than tripled in 10 years, reaching an annual average of 50 doses for every person in the country.

The FDA said it was consulting medical groups on measures to study and control distribution and use.

Useless & Unsafe Drugs Under Continuing Attack

Caution on use of diabetes pill. The American Medical Association (AMA), concurring with the FDA, urged physicians Oct. 23, 1970 to be cautious in prescribing the diabetes pill tolbutamide, which was marketed by Upjohn Co. under the trade name Orinase and was used by about 800,000 Americans.

The AMA said its Council on Drugs had issued a statement to doctors in which it suggested that they try to control mild diabetes cases in adults by reliance on a regulated diet. If this was unsuccessful, the statement said, the council recommended diet and insulin injections. The AMA's statement said that "the consideration of treatment with oral hypoglycemic agents should be secondary to the use of insulin."

The AMA's action represented an evaluation of an 8½ year study conducted at 12 hospitals by the University Group Diabetes Program. In the study, more than 800 adult patients with mild cases of diabetes were treated with various combinations of insulin, tolbutamide and a strict diet. One conclusion made by the study group was that the combination of diet and tolbutamide was no more effective in prolonging a patient's life than control of the diet alone. The FDA had endorsed the report early in 1970.

Further warnings were issued about oral diabetes drugs. The FDA announced in a letter to physicians, reported May 26, 1972, that it had approved new labeling for all oral diabetes drugs to warn against "apparent increased cardiovascular hazard," and recommending use only when the condition could not be controlled by diet and weight reduction or by insulin injections.

The ruling was the result of a 1961-1970 study by the National Institute of Arthritis and Metabolic Diseases of 823 diabetes patients, which found that those using oral drugs had a cardiovascular death rate 2½ times greater than those using diet or insulin alone. Furthermore, after two or three years of use the oral drugs tended to lose their effectiveness in reducing blood sugar.

About 1.5 million U.S. patients used the oral drugs daily, under the trade names Orinase, Tolinase, Diabinese, Dymelor, Meltrol-50 and DBI.

Another serious warning was issued in 1975. The second major type of oral drug used to fight diabetes was found to have been linked to excessive deaths from heart disease, it was reported Feb. 27. The report was part of a study of oral diabetic drugs by the University Group Diabetes Program (UGDP), which evaluated 1200 diabetic patients over 8½ years. The latest report focused on the drug phenformin, showing a death rate from heart attacks that was three times greater than for those patients treated with insulin injections alone. It also linked the drug with high blood pressure and rapid heart rate.

The UGDP studies cast serious doubt on the use of oral drugs for lowering blood sugar in diabetics. Aside from the dangerous side effects, it was found that a change of diet, or the use of diet and insulin, appeared more efficacious than the oral drugs alone in prolonging the lives of diabetics whose troubles began when they were adults. This was backed up in the report on phenformin.

A study by a special panel of the internationally prestigious Biometrics Society, reported Jan. 28, confirmed the validity of the 1970 UGDP study. The group declared, in the Journal of the American Medical Association, that in the light of the findings it was "the responsibility of the proponents of oral agents to conduct scientifically adequate studies to justify the continued use of such agents."

In a related development, licensing procedures for a new diabetes drug, developed by the Salk Institute, came under strong criticism from the Justice Department. According to a March 19 report in the Wall Street Journal, Salk had proposed to grant patent licenses for the drug, somatostatin, to four companies for clinical testing necessary before the FDA could approve its sale. Additional licenses would not be granted for three years to provide incentive for investing in the testing procedures, according to the institute. But the Justice Department contended that the three-year head start would discourage other companies from buying the patent rights.

Tests reportedly had shown that human diabetics given somatostatin, together with insulin, had their blood sugar lowered below levels achieved with insulin alone. The drug, a brain hormone, was said to work by inhibiting the release of glucagon, another natural hormone thought to be responsible for maintaining high levels of sugar in the blood of diabetics.

FDA bars uncertified drugs. The FDA told two drug companies Feb. 1, 1971 to stop selling a pair of medicines that had been marketed in violation of a law governing "new" drugs. At issue was a law that no drug legally classified as "new" could be sold without FDA approval of a new-drug application.

The two companies—Smith Kline & French Laboratories, maker of a non-prescription decongestant and painkiller called Ornex, and Ayerst Laboratories, producer of a glaucoma treatment called Epitrate—had claimed their products were legally "old drugs" whose active ingredients had been medically accepted for years. The FDA acted on the basis of a letter Jan. 28 from Rep. L.H. Fountain (D, N.C.), who complained that the agency had taken no action although he had brought the matter to its attention two months before.

(The FDA also told Cord Laboratories and Linden Laboratories to recall their versions of chlorpromazine, a tranquilizer, because the products lacked approved new-drug applications.)

In another case involving the "new drug" provisions of the federal Food, Drug and Cosmetic Act, the Justice Department announced Jan. 19 that Dow Corning Corp. (Midland, Mich.) had entered pleas of nolo contendere in a 1967 indictment charging violations involving a silicone fluid, best known for its use to augment women's figures. The government charged that the drug was shipped illegally and misbranded for its use as an injection into human beings. A federal court in Bay City, Mich. July 14 fined Dow Corning $5,000 in the case.

L-dopa approved. The FDA June 4, 1970 cautiously approved the marketing of L-dopa as a prescription drug for treating persons afflicted with Parkinson's disease. The FDA approved L-dopa, clinically known as levo-dihydroxyphenylanine, in an unusually short time as a result of heavy public pressure.

In announcing approval of the drug, FDA Commissioner Dr. Charles C. Edwards stressed that L-dopa was to be used with caution because it was known to have dangerous side effects. He said that the FDA, for the first time, was requiring the two companies that would market the drug to continue their studies of patients who use it.

Edwards said that L-dopa "shows promise of being one of the major drug discoveries of recent years" despite its dangers. He added that "possibly as many as a million Americans" suffered from Parkinson's disease.

The commissioner said that the compound would be reviewed yearly by the FDA.

DES linked to cancer in women. The FDA was accused Oct. 26, 1971 of sidestepping for 4½ months a decision on banning the use of synthetic estrogens by pregnant women.

A drug in the synthetic estrogen family—diethylstilbesterol—had been linked to a number of cases in which young women whose mothers had taken the drug during pregnancy had been afflicted with vaginal cancer.

According to an article in the Washington Post, the number of known cases tying vaginal cancer in young women to their mothers use of DES was 60.

The Post article said that the FDA was asked by the New York State Department of Health in June to "initiate immediate measures to ban the use of synthetic estrogens during pregnancy." The appeal was made after cancer researchers linked 13 cases of vaginal cancer to the drug. Dr. Hollis S. Ingraham, commissioner of health in New York, in a letter to the FDA commissioner, Dr. Charles Edwards, said his department had begun a program of "continuous surveillance and monitoring" to try to detect the disease as early as possible. Ingraham urged Edwards to initiate a similar program on a national basis.

The FDA replied Aug. 10 by asking for the records of five of the cases. At the same time, the FDA said it was "actively evaluating" eight other cases linking DES to vaginal cancer reported by physicians at the Massachusetts General Hospital in Boston.

Intravenous fluids recalled. The Food and Drug Administration (FDA) March 22, 1971 ordered the recall of Abbott Laboratories' intravenous fluids because of 350 cases of blood poisoning in hospitals. Hospitals were advised not to use the Abbott products unless absolutely necessary.

The FDA had issued its first alert March 13, urging the users to handle the products with special precautions and ordering Abbott to cease further shipments until manufacturing problems were solved. The agency stiffened its warning after learning that precautions were not being taken and new evidence was uncovered about potential risks. Twenty-one hospitals attributed nine deaths to the contaminated products.

Vertigo drug recalled. The FDA withdrew marketing approval in December 1972 for a controversial drug against vertigo, Serc, after hearing evidence that the drug increased episodes of the ailment.

Drugstore stocks of Serc would be recalled, although drug bureau director Dr. Henry E. Simmons said the drug was safe.

FDA reviews nonprescriptive drugs. The FDA Jan. 4, 1972 announced plans for its first full review of all nonprescriptive drugs on the market.

According to the FDA, the principal aim of the program, which would cover a three-year span, was to assure the consumer that medications sold over the counter did what the label promised. Presently, consumers depended on previous experience and the manufacturer's word in selecting the more than half a million drugs available without a prescription.

In announcing the program, FDA Commissioner Dr. Charles C. Edwards said that because everyone could not and should not go to a doctor for minor illnesses, self-treatment was "essential to the nation's health care system." Edwards called the FDA program unprecedented in scope and intensity.

The FDA had tested most of the drugs to be reviewed for their safety but not, in most cases, for their effectiveness. Many of the over-the-counter medications went on the market before 1962, the year in which Congress gave the FDA authority to tests drugs for effectiveness.

Edwards said the review would be conducted by panels of non-government scientists on a class-by-class rather than a drug-by-drug basis.

Review speedup ordered—U.S. District Court Judge William Bryant in Washington ordered the FDA to complete work on its review of 3,600 prescription drugs, and set a one-year limit for a ban on over 100 drugs so far found to be ineffective, it was reported Oct. 12.

The agency had been sued by the American Public Health Association, which charged it with failing to enforce the 1962 drug law amendments. The 1962 provisions required the FDA to review all prescription drugs marketed between 1938 and 1962, ban those found ineffective, and ban excessive advertising claims for the rest. The agency had completed preliminary reviews on the drugs, but final actions on hundreds of cases had been delayed by legal challenges from drug companies, and by prolonged additional testing by the companies.

Besides the one-year limit on ineffective drugs, Judge Bryant set a two-and-a-half year limit for action on "possibly effective" drugs, three-and-a-half years for "probably effective" drugs and four years for the rest. FDA Bureau of Drugs Director Dr. Henry E. Simmons said the ruling would prevent the agency from allowing most delays for testing, although tests could take as long as two years for drugs used in chronic conditions.

By the time of the court order, 341 of 493 drugs found ineffective had already been removed from the market, as had 113 of 723 products found possibly ineffective.

Antacid rules. The FDA June 4, 1974 issued final rules requiring makers of non-prescription antacid products to meet new standards for safe and effective ingredients and to limit labeling claims.

The regulations limited antacid products to 13 ingredients recognized as safe and effective and required that active ingredients be listed on labels. Labels would have to include a section warning of possibly harmful effects of using the product in conjunction with other drugs.

The order also limited labeling claims for antacids to the treatment of heartburn, "sour stomach" and acid indigestion, barring previous claims that the products were effective against "nervous or emotional disturbances," "cold symptoms" and "morning sickness."

Rejecting protests by some consumer groups, the FDA ruled that products containing a combination of antacids and a pain killer could still be produced. Labels, however, would have to state that the product was to be used for a combination of symptoms—headache and upset stomach—and not for upset stomach alone. The protesting groups had requested a ban on Alka-Seltzer, made by Miles Laboratories Inc., because of possible stomach hazards from the aspirin ingredient. The FDA said manufacturers would have one year to conform with the rules.

The FDA's preliminary proposals on the advertising and labeling of antacid products had been issued April 4, 1973. It was the first of a series of recommendations on regulating the vast over-the-counter drug market.

On the advice of an independent panel of medical experts who reviewed about 150 products submitted by drug companies, the FDA said most of the products in the $100 million-a-year antacid market were effective for control of acid indigestion, "sour stomach" and heartburn. But at least nine products containing bile salt would be banned. These products, not among the major sellers, were thought to promote hydrochloric acid secretion, which antacids were designed to counteract.

Another group of products, including Di-Gel, manufactured by Plough Inc., and Mylanta, made by ICI America Inc., could remain on the market for two years to allow manufacturers to gather information on the effectiveness of various ingredients.

Antacid labels would not be permitted to claim usefulness in treating colds, nervous tension headaches, nervous emotional disturbances, food intolerance or alcohol consumption. Labels would have to list all active ingredients and include a warning against use for over two weeks without a physician's advice.

In another provision, FDA recommended that no laxatives be added to antacids except to counteract the effect of the antacid, and not to make dual claims.

In a statement, Miles said the "strongly buffered aspirin solution" in Alka-Seltzer did not contribute to stomach damage, but the Health Research Group, associated with consumer activist Ralph Nader, issued a statement calling for a total ban on antacid-aspirin combinations.

Panel cites equivalent drug differences. A report to Congress by the Office of Technology Assessment (OTA) July 12, 1974 indicated that prescription drugs containing the same active ingredients did not necessarily produce identical therapeutic results. The OTA found "roughly a score" of chemically equivalent drugs produced by the same or different manufacturers that could be absorbed into the blood at different levels and speeds. This was potentially dangerous, the panel said, for drugs that were toxic at high levels.

Robert W. Berliner of Yale Medical School, chairman of the OTA panel, said that 85%-90% of ethical drugs would not require screening for equivalency, but he urged greater FDA control over the manufacturing of medicines that did. He also proposed creation of FDA advisory groups to make lists of interchangeable drugs.

C. Joseph Stetler of the Pharmaceutical Manufacturers Association (PMA) called the OTA's report "superb," and claimed that it undercut the new Health, Education and Welfare (HEW) Department policy of limiting Medicare and Medicaid drug reimbursement to the lowest-cost drug generally available.

However, Berliner disputed Stetler's assessment, arguing that HEW could act promptly to insure equivalency among the 10%-15% of drugs requiring screening.

Sen. Edward M. Kennedy (D, Mass.), chairman of the Technology Assessment Board overseeing the OTA and the Health Subcommittee of the Senate Labor and Public Welfare Committee, had requested the study.

Kennedy had released statistics May 2 showing that in 1973, 20 leading drug concerns had given doctors, nurses and other health professionals promotional gifts valued at $14 million. These firms had also distributed more than two billion free drug samples. Kennedy said such marketing practices were indefensible.

Testing rules proposed—The FDA June 19, 1975 announced plans for new testing standards to ensure that different brands of the same drug would be equally effective.

The standards would cover 137 different drugs. Manufacturers would be required to demonstrate on these that their product was equivalent to a standard, or "reference" drug, designated by the agency.

Heart drug testing tightened. The FDA Jan. 2, 1974 set plans for batch-by-batch testing of the heart stimulant digoxin, a drug prescribed for 3.5 million Americans to increase forcefulness of their heartbeats. The move was designed to insure uniform standards for the rate at which digoxin dissolved in the upper respiratory tract, a fact important to doctors needing to know proper amounts to prescribe. The FDA indicated the action was directed at less than 10% of the digoxin manufactured.

Curbing 'pep pills.' The FDA Aug. 5, 1970 announced legal actions to sharply limit the use of amphetamines—drugs known as "pep pills." Food and Drug Commissioner Charles C. Edwards said the drug industry produced enormous amounts of the drug, which he said had only limited medical usefulness. He said the industry "has not faced its responsibilities with these drugs.... It is time for the manufacturers to accept the challenge of working closely with the FDA and the Department of Justice to stop unnecessary production of amphetamines."

The agency ordered changes in amphetamine labeling to restrict claims of effectiveness and strengthen warnings of hazards. Labels could claim effectiveness for three medical uses: narcolepsy, an uncontrollable urge to sleep; hyperactivity in children with minor brain damage; and obesity, when short-term use of the drug would be allowed as an appetite suppressant in a weight reduction treatment based on restriction of calories.

The FDA ordered the drug industry to produce data within a year to validate claims made for amphetamine products. Although the FDA action would not limit a doctor's right to prescribe the drug, it would increase his exposure to malpractice suits if he deviated from the recommended uses.

The FDA estimated that drug companies manufactured 3.5 billion doses of amphetamines annually, with almost 40% sold illegally. In earlier testimony before a Congressional subcommittee, Dr. Sidney Cohen, a National Institute of Mental Health officer, cited three types of amphetamine abuse: occasional use by students, businessmen, truck drivers or athletes to stay awake or produce extra bursts of energy; daily use of large amounts of the drug to produce an emotional lift; and a comparatively new use by injection into a vein to produce an effect much like that of cocaine.

The FDA said the drug could induce "extreme fatigue and mental depression" after the initial effect wore off and continued use could produce "psychosis, often clinically indistiguishable from schizophrenia."

Thomas N. Rauch, president of Smith, Kline & French Laboratories, the leading manufacturer involved, said Aug. 5 that the company had been urging passage of more restrictive drug-abuse legislation. "As we have said before Congressional committees," Rauch added, "the company's amphetamine products are not supplying the illicit traffic."

The FDA announced Dec. 2 that it had succeeded in a two-year effort to remove a class of diet pills from the market. The agency said Lemmon Pharmacal Co. (Sellersville, Pa.), the last of 112 companies that formerly made appetite-depressant pills composed of synthetic thyroid hormone combined with amphetamines, had agreed under federal court order to recall the pills from the market. The National Research Council had found that the thyroid-amphetamine combination could cause heart damage and did not work for people with normal thyroid glands. Of the 112 manufacturers that made the pills, the FDA had filed separate suits against six companies. The rest withdrew their products voluntarily or after the agency threatened court action.

Dr. Henry E. Simmons, FDA Bureau of Medicine director, told the Senate Monopoly Subcommittee Dec. 14, 1972 that the FDA would distribute the results of a test of amphetamine-related diet pills to 600,000 medical professionals. He said the FDA would require that manufacturers stress the drug's limitations and hazards on labels, and might move to place most of the appetite-suppressants under the Controlled Substances Act, as had already been done with pure amphetamines.

Simmons reported that a study by an advisory panel found that the drugs had an "extremely limited" effectiveness, and had caused side effects such as nervousness, insomnia and habituation in susceptible patients. He said, however, the agency would not ban the products, "because the treatment of obesity is particularly difficult," and "the physician should have the use of all adequately tested therapeutic aids."

Some 26 million prescriptions for weight-reducing drugs had been filled in 1971, earning drug companies about $65 million.

The FDA and Bureau of Narcotics & Dangerous Drugs (BNDD) April 1, 1973 ordered the recall of all diet drugs containing amphetamines, with the objective of eliminating them from the market by June 30. The order applied to injectable amphetamines and all combination diet pills composed of amphetamines and other substances such as vitamins or tranquilizers.

In an attempt to further curb amphetamine abuse, the BNDD announced April 1 a 39% cut in the legitimate production quotas of amphetamines and methamphetamines. This cut from 1972 levels followed an 80% quota reduction from 1971. Since 1971, legitimate production quotas had been reduced from 9,356 to 992 kilograms for amphetamines and from 4,926 to 561 kilograms for methamphetamines.

FDA probes 'mood drugs.' The FDA, in a move announced Aug. 1, 1971 in the Federal Register, began a study of the efficacy and safety of nonprescription tranquilizers and sleeping pills. The action gave drug manufacturers 180 days to submit "the best available evidence" of safety and effectiveness of the numerous over-the-counter (OTC) products that contained an antihistamine called methapyrilene, including such preparations as Compoz, Nytol, Sominex, Excedrin P.M. and Dormin.

In Senate testimony July 21, Dr. Charles C. Edwards, FDA commissioner, had said the study of mood drugs would be the first part of an assessment of all over-the-counter medicines. Edwards told the Monopoly Subcommittee of the Senate Select Committee on Small Business that past emphasis had been on the safety of OTCs rather than whether they met advertised claims of effectiveness.

Edwards said there were more than 90 nonprescription sleep aids on the market and at least 100 preparations advertised as sedatives or relaxants. He said the products often contained the same basic ingredients: "It is difficult to determine how the manufacturer has decided to market the product as a sleep aid, a daytime calmative or sedative." He said another category of OTC mood drug advertised as stimulants was represented by about 60 products, all containing 100 to 200 milligrams of caffeine, roughly equivalent to the caffeine in one cup of coffee.

Dr. Karl Rickels, a University of Pennsylvania psychiatrist, testified July 22 on clinical tests that Edwards had called "one of the few, or perhaps the only well-controlled evaluation of OTC sedatives." Rickels said a test of Compoz, as "the prototype of a group of OTC tranquilizers," showed that neither that drug nor aspirin was more effective in patients than a placebo and that neither Compoz nor aspirin was as effective as Librium, a prescription drug, in relieving nervous tension.

Methaqualone use restricted—Methaqualone, a tranquilizer described by the Drug Enforcement Administration (DEA) of the Justice Department as "the heavily abused fad drug among young people," was ordered placed under schedule II of the Controlled Substances Act, the DEA announced Sept. 27, 1973.

The action followed a ruling by an administrative law judge that "methaqualone and its salts may lead to severe psychological and physical dependence."

Under schedule II requirements, the DEA would set production quotas, prohibit refillable prescriptions, prohibit export or import without DEA authorization, and prohibit the sale and manufacture except through use of DEA order forms.

Among other drugs under schedule II were cocaine, morphine, methadone, and methamphetamine. Methaqualone was produced under the trade names of Quaalude, Sopor, Parest, Somnafac and Optimil.

Valium, Librium to be controlled—The DEA announced Aug. 15 that Hoffman-LaRoche, manufacturer of the tranquilizers Valium and Librium, had agreed not to contest the placing of the drugs under schedule IV of the Controlled Substances Act.

Under schedule IV, the DEA would require records and reports on manufacture, distribution and sale of the drugs. Valium and Librium, the two most widely prescribed drugs in the U.S., would join phenobarbital and other long-acting barbiturates in schedule IV.

In another action announced Nov. 13, the DEA said it had placed the barbiturates amobarbital, secobarbital and pentobarbital under schedule II of the Controlled Substances Act. These drugs, often prescribed as sleeping pills, were marketed under the trade names of Seconal, Tuinal, Amytal and Nembutal.

Panel scores sedatives, sleep aids. None of the ingredients in currently marketed over-the-counter sedatives and sleep aids was recognized as safe and effective by a **panel of experts headed by Karl Rickels, the FDA disclosed Dec. 4, 1975.**

In another category of over-the-counter drugs, stimulants, only one major ingredient was found fully safe and effective—caffeine, commonly found also in coffee, tea and cola drinks.

Tests show aspirin may increase spread of colds. A recent study by a team of researchers on the effects of aspirin on cold sufferers showed an increased ability for spreading the virus over a longer period of time. The researchers, from the University of Illinois, reported on this in the March 24, 1975 issue of the Journal of the American Medical Association. They said that aspirin may suppress white blood cells, the body's normal defense mechanism against colds (suggested in earlier studies), allowing viruses to multiply at a high rate. The report further noted that because those with colds felt better after taking aspirin they might be encouraged to stay on the job or go out in public, increasing contagion danger.

During the research project, students who came down with colds after injections with a virus were given either aspirin or a placebo—a pill which looked like aspirin but contained no drug at all. Researchers said those given aspirin showed "measurable, but not great" relief from cold symptoms. However, the test subjects also showed up to a third more viruses in nasal samplings after taking aspirin. Three days after being infected nearly 80% of the aspirin-users excreted some virus as opposed to only 50% of the placebo-takers. Aspirin was probably the most widely used nonspecific remedy for symptoms caused by viral infections of the respiratory system.

(The FTC was reported July 22, 1974 to have tentatively accepted a consent agreement prohibiting Sterling Drug Inc. from claiming that its Lysol brand and other household disinfectants prevented colds and other respiratory diseases.)

Aerosol chemical curbed. The FDA Aug. 13, 1973 ordered drug firms to submit lists of products containing trichloroethane, a chemical used as a solvent for active ingredients in aerosol cold remedies. The FDA also proposed to have the chemical declared "not generally recognized as safe," requiring manufacturers to demonstrate the safety of new products containing it before they could be marketed.

The FDA had ordered six brands of aerosol cold sprays recalled July 2 and July 9 after learning of 18 deaths associated with the product since 1968. The FDA had said most of the deaths involved "abuse or gross misuse" of the sprays (including "aerosol sniffing" to obtain a drug high). But the death of a five-year-old girl occurred under apparently proper use.

According to the FDA, trichloroethane acted as an anesthetic when inhaled and caused significant disruptions in heartbeat.

Medical Practices Criticized, Industry-Physician Tie Seen

Nader group scores U.S. doctors. A team of Ralph Nader's consumer investigators charged Nov. 8, 1970 that the U.S. medical profession was doing a poor job of supervising the quality of health care delivered by doctors to their patients.

In a 250-page report the team noted that while some of the best medical care in the world was practiced in the U.S., the American medical profession had an almost complete lack of internal quality control. The report said this lack had "allowed a very large measure of very poor medicine to be practiced."

Dr. Walter C. Bornemeier, president of the American Medical Association (AMA), said the doctors' group had received a copy of the document, but that there had not been time to study it thoroughly. He called the report comprehensive and deserving of objective consideration.

The team proposed a National Board of Medicine that would have jurisdiction over all health care programs that used federal funds. The board, the report said, would be expected to use its jurisdictional power to require a uniformly high standard of professional performance by doctors. The report said that at the present time, "every citizen is at the mercy of a system devoid of uniform, enforced standards of quality."

The study, entitled "One Physician—One Life," was directed by Dr. Robert S. McCleery, a consultant to Nader's Center for Study of Responsive Law and a former Food and Drug Administration (FDA) officer. It was prepared by Louise T. Keely, Mimi Lam, Russell E. Phillips and Terrence M. Ouirin.

AMA drug policy criticized. Three former top advisers to the American Medical Association (AMA) accused the organization of being "a captive of and beholden to the pharmaceutical industry." Their criticism was delivered Feb. 6, 1973 in testimony before the Senate Monopoly Subcommittee of the Small Business Committee. The advisers were the last two chairmen and a former vice chairman of the AMA's Council on Drugs, an independent group of scientists and doctors established by the AMA in 1905 to advise the medical profession on drugs. The council was abolished October 1972 in what the AMA called an economy move.

Dr. John Adriani, council chairman from 1968 to 1970, and Dr. Harry C. Shirkey, Adriani's successor, both of Tulane University, and former vice chairman Dr. Daniel L. Azarnoff, of the University of Kansas testified before the subcommittee. The following summary of their combined testimony was reported by the Feb. 7 Washington Post and New York Times:

The AMA had committed itself to publish a complete, unbiased guide to prescription drugs. Drawing on over 300 experts, the Council on Drugs completed the report in 1971 at a cost of over $3 million and readied the report for distribution to members. In January 1971, Max H. Parrott, chairman of the board of directors of the AMA, told the council that publication of the study would have to be delayed for a few months so the book could be reviewed by people he called "our friends,"—the Pharmaceutical Manufacturers Association (PMA). Actually the PMA had already been given draft copies. Although the council initially demurred, it later accepted. Soon after, the PMA submitted "three or four crates" of proposed revisions, which the council dealt with by making about 35 token revisions in areas such as dosage sizes and revised formulations. The council stood fast against any substantive revisions, especially against condemnations of heavily advertised drug combinations.

When the book appeared, Dr. Parrott attempted to tone down the report by adding a cover letter that said that some of the condemned combination drugs "may be justifiable."

A second clash came in September 1972, when the AMA board was given an advance look at the second edition of "AMA Drug Evaluations." Many medicines had been evaluated as "not recommended," a rating that board representative Dr. Richard Palmer asked be deleted. The council instead proposed that an explanation accompany each appearance of "not recommended," a compromise that was unacceptable to the board.

One month later the council was abolished and the task of completing the second drug manual was turned over to paid employes of the AMA.

Dr. Adriani testified that the "not recommended" designation left the AMA board with "no choice but to appease the pharmaceutical industry." The alternative he said, was to sacrifice ad revenues in the AMA Journal of Medicine.

Court supports review of doctors' Medicare billing. A 1972 federal law that gave the government the right to review billing for Medicare and Medicaid was ruled constitutional by a three-judge federal panel May 8, 1975. The law had been contested in a 1973 suit brought by the Association of American Physicians & Surgeons against the Department of Health Education and Welfare.

The suit challenged the legality of legislation known as the Professional Standards Review Act, which was an amendment to the 1972 Social Security Act. Under the act, doctor "peer review" groups called Professional Standards Review Organizations (PSROs) had already begun to be set up in several areas of the country.

In the ruling, which was unanimous, the judges said that the law didn't "bar physicians from practicing their profession," but only provided "standards for the dispensation of federal funds." The panel ruled that Congress had a constitutional right to see to it that physicians were kept from abusing Medicare and Medicaid funds.

Kennedy criticizes drug promotion. Sen. Edward M. Kennedy (D, Mass.) accused the pharmaceutical industry of using techniques to promote sales of their drugs that smacked of "payola." Kennedy's charge was made amid Senate subcommittee testimony by former drug salesmen that the drug industry offered doctors color television sets, freezers and expense-paid Bermuda "seminars" in hopes of inducing them to prescribe certain drugs.

The former salesmen appeared before the Health Subcommittee March 8, 1975. They told of promotional schemes offering "gifts" to pharmacists, officials of hospitals or clinics and doctors who ordered or prescribed large amounts of a company's products. While they expressed high regard for their former employers, the witnesses also testified that they were under great pressure to sell but under relatively less pressure to educate physicians and pharmacists on the hazards and limitations of their drugs.

The subcommittee March 12 took testimony from executives of four leading drug manufacturing firms, who defended industry marketing practices, contending they were intended to provide doctors with a careful balance on the good and bad points of their products.

Jan Dlouhy of the Lederle Labs division of American Cyanamid Co. said: "I do not accept the proposition that a physician, after all his years of training, with all his interest in his patient's well-being, and with his professional reputation at stake, will have his judgment swayed and will use inappropriately a product simply because of a salesman presentation—even if overzealous on occasion."

Openly skeptical, Kennedy responded that doctors were inadequately educated about drugs in medical school and, forced to choose among 20,000 brand names for 700 drug entities, tended to rely excessively on information from the drug manufacturers.

Kennedy also charged that huge outlays to promote medicines had led to irrational prescribing. Kennedy said adverse drug reactions killed 30,000 persons annually and that 50,000–100,000 deaths a year could be attributed to treatment-resistant bacteria, which had emerged, in part, because of misuse and overuse of antibiotics.

Previously, the subcommittee heard testimony Feb. 25 that more than half the antibiotics given hospital patients were not needed or had been incorrectly prescribed.

Dr. Sidney Wolfe, director of Ralph Nader's Health Research Group, blamed the drug industry for the unnecessary use of medicines. "A well trained actor could probably prescribe drugs as well as the thousands of American doctors whose prescribing practices reflect drug company indoctrination in lieu of scientific evaluation." Wolfe cited unpublished drug industry statistics that two of every three Americans who saw doctors about common colds were given antibiotics that were ineffective.

Dr. James A. Visconti of Ohio State University's College of Pharmacy told the subcommittee of a study he participated in, which showed that only 13% of the prescriptions for antibiotics given 340 hospital patients were judged "rational" by an evaluating team of doctors and pharmacists. Of the remaining prescriptions, 65% were called "irrational" and 22% "questionable," he said.

Health Devices

Warning on Relaxacizor. Government investigators have charged that many devices designed to help consumers exercise, lose weight and improve health in general actually endangered the health of the users. The government took action against one such device in the spring of 1970.

The FDA warned consumers April 25 not to use an electrical exercise and weight reducing device called the Relaxacizor. The agency said the device, currently in the hands of more than 400,000 consumers, "has a serious potential for damage to the heart and other vital body organs." The warning cited an April 14 federal court order in Los Angeles in which Judge William P. Gray found "a wide spectrum of conditions in which the Relaxacizor is hazardous and contraindicated, such as intra-abdominal, gastrointestinal, orthopedic, muscular, neurological, vascular, dermatological, kidney, gynecological, and pelvic disorders."

Gray, ruling in an action brought by the Justice Department at the urging of the FDA, had issued a permanent injunction against interstate distribution of the device, manufactured by Eastwood General Corp. of Los Angeles (formerly Relaxacizor Inc.) and distributed by Relaxacizor Sales Inc. The machines, which caused muscle contraction by providing electrical shocks to the body, had been sold since 1949 at prices ranging from about $100 to $400. The FDA said its warning applied to similar devices sold by other companies.

Shatterproof eyeglasses required. The FDA Sept. 30, 1970 issued a rule requiring shatterproof glass in all eyeglasses and sunglass lenses. FDA Commissioner Charles C. Edwards said the action was "a very significant step to protect the American public from eye injuries."

Edwards said that an estimated 100,000 adults and 20,000 children were injured every year by accidents involving shattered glass lenses. He said that only 25% of the prescription glasses worn by an estimated 100 million Americans were impact-resistant. Jerome Miller, executive secretary of the Guild of Prescription Opticians of America, said Sept. 30 that about half the glasses currently sold had shatterproof lenses.

Dr. West toothbrush criticized. The FTC charged Dec. 4, 1970 that Dr. West's "Germ fighter" toothbrushes, manufactured by the Chemway Corp., did not contain chemicals that fought mouth bacteria as advertised and that mercury chemicals on the toothbrush "may constitute a danger to the consumer by adding to the body's burden of mercury." The agency's tentative order would require the company to discontinue its old advertising and repeat FTC charges in any new advertising. The company denied the charges and said it had stopped selling the product "earlier this year."

Diagnostic kit rules asked. The FDA Aug. 16, 1972 made public rules to begin regulating the diagnostic product, or test kit industry.

Some 4,000 diagnostic products would be subject to new labeling requirements, including performance characteristics, directions and warnings. Included were products used to test blood sugar and hemoglobin, to detect vaginal cancer or take throat cultures, for blood tests, and to determine pregnancy or drunkenness. The FDA said an increase in the number of such products had forced a stricter regulation policy.

FDA criticized on pacemakers. Sen. Abraham A. Ribicoff March 12, 1975 called for tighter industry and federal regulation over heart pacemakers, electronic devices surgically implanted to regulate the heartbeat of cardiac patients.

Ribicoff, chairman of the Senate Government Operations Committee, cited a General Accounting Office report criticizing FDA response to recalls of defective pacemakers by four manufacturers. The report found the agency lax in identifying industry problems, testing products and enforcing and formulating standards.

In tracing 68 of the recalls, the GAO found seven deaths and two injuries attributable to defective pacemakers. The total number of pacemakers in use in the United States was estimated at 125,000.

FDA Commissioner Alexander M. Schmidt said March 13 he considered the criticism "excessive" even though the GAO report "correctly identifies the scope and the seriousness of the need for improved medical device regulations." He said the agency had no authority under law to issue regulations in this area and urged passage of legislation to put medical devices such as pacemakers into a regulated category similar to drugs.

Two weeks earlier the FDA Feb. 27 had announced the recall of 1,241 already implanted pacemakers made by the General Electric Co., because of potential malfunction. A second recall, of about 4,288 pacemakers made by Cordi Corp. of Miami, Fla., also was announced. The FDA advised doctors to monitor the Cordi pacemakers.

30-day trial for hearing-aid sales. The FTC June 17, 1975 announced a new trade rule designed to protect hearing-aid customers by allowing them to cancel a purchase within 30 days and get most of their money back. The rule would proscribe deceptive sales techniques and advertisements. The agency said many consumers bought hearing aids "from which they do not receive any significant benefit." The 30-day trial period was the longest such period ever ordered by the agency.

Birth Control Aids

Pill safety probed. Following reports that some users of birth-control pills had died of blood clots, the FDA early in 1963 ordered a study of the problem. The five-month scientific investigation was conducted by an FDA-appointed panel of experts headed by Dr. Irving S. Wright of Cornell University. On the completion of the study, the FDA announced Aug. 3 that Enovid, a progesterone hormone used to suppress ovulation and to correct some gynecological disorders, had been proven safe enough to remain on the market, available to woman by doctor's prescription. But it warned against its use by women over 34 years of age.

According to the announcement, Enovid had been used by 1,300,000 women in 1962. Currently, more than two million women were using Enovid or Ortho-Novum, a newer birth-control pill marketed by Ortho Pharmaceutical Corp. Since 1961, blood clots in 350 Enovid users were reported, and 35 died. The panel found no evidence that Enovid caused blood clotting. It also found that: (1) of the 35 deaths, only 12 or 14 were caused primarily by blood clots; (2) there was no significant difference in deaths from blood clots between Enovid users and non-users through age 34; (3) the death rate for women aged 35 to 39 was 2.4 times greater among Enovid users, and among those aged 40 to 44 it was 3.8 times greater.

The FDA announcement directed G. D. Searle & Co., manufacturer of Enovid, to list on its labels the pill's "apparent hazard" to older women, to women with certain cancers and liver diseases and to those predisposed to blood clots in the veins and lungs.

Dr. Joseph F. Sadusk, chief of the FDA's Bureau of Medicine, reported to a House Appropriations subcommittee April 15, 1965 that the five birth-control pills the FDA had already approved had proved so effective and safe so far (since 1961) that it had been unnecessary to withdraw any from the market. But he added: "We still must answer for the lady who is taking them and how safe it is for her to take these pills over a prolonged period of time." (The approved pills contained two hormones administered simultaneously to achieve the desired effect of blocking ovulation and thereby preventing conception. The five companies marketing these pills: G. D. Searle & Co.; the Ortho division of Johnson & Johnson; Upjohn Co.; Parke, Davis & Co.; the Syntex Corp.)

Mead Johnson & Co. reported April, 18, 1965 that it had received FDA approval to market the first "sequential" oral contraceptive in the U.S. When this contraceptive was used, first one and then two hormones were administered to women over a 21-day period. Eli Lilly & Co. announced May 4 that it had become the second company to win FDA approval to market a sequential oral contraceptive.

In its Second Report on Oral Contraception, the FDA said Sept. 4, 1969 that it found "the ratio of benefit to risk sufficiently high to justify the designation safe" for use of birth control pills. But Dr. Louis M. Hellman, chairman of the committee that authored the report, said there was "a clear-cut cause and effect" relationship between the pill's use and deaths caused by blood clotting disorders. The report said the risk of death from blood clotting to pill users was 4.4 times greater than for non-users, at the rate of three deaths per 100,000 users a year. Hellman warned women having histories of blood clotting ailments, persistent headaches, breast cancer or lumps in their breasts not to use contraceptive pills.

The report said that users of the sequential pills suffered a higher incidence of blood clotting than did users of the ordinary birth-control pills.

The report added that only one woman in 1,000 would become pregnant in a year through use of regular birth control pills. The "failure rate" for sequential pills was reported to be five times as high.

The report concluded that no connection could be found between cancer and birth control pills. But it called for a major study to determine if such a relationship existed. The report was based on information collected at 48 hospitals from findings on 350 women.

A study sponsored by Planned Parenthood of New York and the Sloan-Kettering Institute-Memorial Hospital had indicated that there was a higher incidence of early cervical cancer among women who used birth-control pills than among women who used diaphragms.

The study, headed by Dr. Myron R. Melamed, did not suggest a causal relationship between cervical cancer and the pill, only that there was a "small but significant difference" between women who used a diaphragm and those who took birth control pills. "The reason for the difference," the report said, "is not apparent from the data." The report, published in the British Medical Journal July 26, was based on 27,508 women who took the pill and 6,809 who used the diaphragm.

The study had been submitted for publication in February to the Journal of the American Medical Association. The association decided not to publish it after three independent pathologists called upon to review the report reportedly criticized the study, mainly because it did not deny or confirm a causal relationship between oral contraceptives and cervical cancer.

Devices termed inadequate. The Rockefeller Foundation, in its five-year review and annual report, issued May 9, 1969, warned that within a few years the intrauterine device (IUD) and oral contraceptive pills would prove inadequate to control increases in population. The report said that the pill had caused a small but increasing number of blood clotting disorders and pulmonary embolisms. In a number of countries the IUD had been discarded by half its users after two to three years, while for the remaining half, the report said, the device had not proved satisfactory for various reasons.

The foundation had spent $150 million in the last five years for birth control research, but it said little first-rate research was being done on improving methods of contraception.

Warning on pill. The FDA Jan. 19, 1970 asked the nation's doctors to familiarize themselves with the risks involved in the use of birth control pills and to explain to their patients the potential long-range side effects of the pills. The FDA sent letters to 381,000 hospital administrators and physicians, asking them to keep informed about the latest information linking birth control pills to blood clotting problems.

The letters, signed by Commissioner of Food and Drugs Charles C. Edwards, also urged the doctors to study the FDA's newly revised pill labeling system which cited the risks of thromboembolic (blood clot) problems in the use of the pills. The revised system was inaugurated in September 1969 after the FDA's Advisory Committee on Obstetrics and Gynecology had conducted a full review of the pills' potential hazards.

"In most cases a full disclosure of the potential adverse effects of these products would seem advisable, thus permitting the participation of the patient in the assessment of the risk associated with the method," the letter said.

The government announced April 7 that it had accepted a compromise warning statement to accompany all birth-control pills sold.

Three earlier versions of the statement cautioning women about the potential hazards of the pill had evoked strong opposition from some physicians and firms that manufactured oral contraceptives.

The new statement accepted by the government was shorter and less emphatic about the potential dangers of the pills than the others.

The new draft said: "The oral contraceptives are powerful, effective drugs. Do not take these drugs without your doctor's continued supervision. As with all effective drugs they may cause side effects in some cases and should not be taken at all by some...." The statement also warned women to consult their doctors if they noticed any of the following while taking the pills: "1. Severe headache. 2. Blurred vision. 3. Pain in the legs. 4. Pain in the chest or unexplained cough. 5. Irregular or missed periods."

Congressional hearings on pill—At Senate subcommittee hearings, which opened Jan. 14, prominent physicians disagreed on the potentially dangerous side effects of birth control pills. Sen. Gaylord Nelson (D, Wis.), chairman of the Monopoly Subcommittee of the Senate Select Committee on Small Business, said he had called the hearings to question whether the pills' manufacturers had deliberately under-emphasized the risks involved in using birth control pills.

Dr. Hugh J. Davis, a Johns Hopkins specialist in birth control devices, told the senators Jan. 14 that he feared that birth control pills may cause breast cancer that would remain undetected for years. Dr. Davis questioned whether it was wise to have "millions of Americans on the pill for 20 years and then [we] discover it was all a great mistake?" About 8½ million American women were reported using birth control pills.

Dr. Roy Hertz, of the Population Council and Rockefeller University, agreed with Davis. Hertz testified Jan. 15 that only two facts about birth control pills had been substantiated: the pill's high degree of effectiveness in preventing pregnancy and the pill's ability to cause blood clotting problems. Hertz said all doctors prescribing birth control pills should treat each patient as though she were part of a research program. He advocated such safety measures, he said, because too many important questions about the pill's long-range side effects remained unanswered. Hertz also cited examples of laboratory experiments in which animals treated with synthetic hormones similar to those found in the pills developed certain strains of cancer.

Dr. Robert W. Kistner, a specialist in research and treatment of illnesses related to the female reproductive system at the Harvard Medical School, disagreed with Davis and Hertz. Kistner said animals treated with birth control-hormones in laboratory experiments had produced a protective effect against cancer-producing agents. Among the patients at the Boston Hospital for Women, Kistner said, there had been no appreciable increase in the incidence of pre-cancerous conditions in the female cervix between 1964 and 1969 despite an increase in the number of women using birth control pills.

A third physician to testify Jan. 15 said the manufacturers of birth control pills had failed to inform doctors about the true risks of the pill. Dr. Edmond Kassouf said manufacturers were still distributing information that failed to say anything about current data linking birth control pills to blood clotting problems. He said the risks were often distorted or minimized and in some cases denied by the pills' manufacturers.

'Mini-pill' testing halted—Syntex Laboratories announced Jan. 19 that it was suspending clinical tests of its "mini-pill" oral contraceptive pending further study of experiments that produced signs of breast cancer in dogs treated with the drug. The mini-pill was so dubbed because it contained only half a milligram of a progestin called chlormadinone acetate.

A spokesman for Syntex said that five dogs treated with the contraceptive developed nodules (lumps containing bacteria) in the breast tissue. One of the nodules, the spokesman said, was found to be cancerous.

The mini-pill was being taken experimentally by thousands of women in the U.S. and was marketed in France, Mexico and Great Britain. The Syntex spokesman said there had been no reports from any of the pills' users that

DRUGS, MEDICAL DEVICES & HEALTH

unusual changes in breast tissue had occurred.

2 pill brands discontinued. Two large pharmaceutical houses Oct. 23, 1970 voluntarily discontinued the production of two brands of birth control pills whose chemical ingredients might have contributed to tissue changes in dogs. The action taken by Eli Lilly & Co. and the Upjohn Co. was made public by the FDA.

FDA Commissioner Dr. Charles C. Edwards Oct. 23 called the halt in production of the two brands of oral contraceptives "the only prudent course." At the same time Edwards said that there was no cause for alarm among women taking the pills.

The Eli Lilly product was marketed under the name C-Quens. Upjohn used the trade name Provest.

Edwards said that women using either of the two pills should continue to do so until their physicians told them otherwise.

The FDA had required continuing studies of the active chemicals in birth control pills and it was in one such study that dogs developed noncancerous nodules in their breasts when treated with large doses of two chemicals. One of those chemicals was an active ingredient in Provest. The other chemical was part of the makeup of C-Quens. The chemical in Provest was identified as medroxyprogesterone acetate, while the chemical in C-Quens was chlormadinone acetate.

DES OKd for emergencies. The FDA announced Feb. 21, 1973 its approval of the use of a morning-after contraceptive pill for women in emergency situations such as rape and incest. FDA Commissioner Charles C. Edwards said the agency was in the process of relabeling the drug diethylstilbestrol (DES), a synthetic estrogen, which for over 30 years had only been approved for use in certain gynecological disorders.

The drug had been associated with cancer of the vagina and cervix in the children of some women who were treated with it during pregnancy. (DES had been banned by the FDA in 1972 as a growth hormone in cattle feed as the result of an agency regulation forbidding the use of any substance that might have cancer-causing properties.)

The decision to allow limited use of DES was criticized by Dr. Peter Greenwald, director of the Cancer Control Bureau in the New York State Health Department. Testifying Feb. 22 before a Senate labor and public welfare subcommittee, he said doctors would interpret the action on DES as a go-ahead and prescribe it whenever they wanted, despite the risks.

Dalkon IUD moratorium. The FDA June 28, 1974 ordered a ban on the manufacture and sale of the intrauterine device (IUD) known as the Dalkon Shield. It acted after reports that four women who used this contraceptive device had become pregnant and had died.

The six-month moratorium on the marketing of the Dalkon Shield was ended by the FDA Dec. 20 after A. H. Robbins Co., manufacturer of the device, had agreed to register all new users of the shield, as well as follow their progress. Data to be reported to the FDA by Robbins was to include the number and kind of adverse reactions, the rate at which the device was expelled by women and other details.

In October, an FDA advisory panel of medical experts had concluded that the Dalkon Shield didn't pose greater risk to women than other intrauterine contraceptives. The FDA had said Aug. 21 that it had learned of 11 fatal and 209 nonfatal septic abortions—spontaneous abortions resulting in infection—among the women fitted with the shield.

The October 1974 study had discovered that the shield's multifilament string, or "tail," could draw bacteria up into the uterus. Robbins, therefore, announced Jan. 20, 1975 that it was recalling all domestic stocks of the shield and would not return them until the second half of 1975 when a new mono-filament tail had been developed.

The FDA, in a Senate hearing Jan. 28, pledged to control testing of the revised model in order to obtain reliable data on its safety. The promise was partly in response to complaints by the advisory panel, and the resignation of one of its members, that the agency had not done enough to control the testing of the new model. It was reported Jan. 21 that the Planned Parenthood Foundation of America and the U.S. Agency for International Development were permanently discontinuing distribution of the shield.

Smoking & Health

Long controversy over the apparent health hazards of smoking led finally to legislation banning cigarette commercials from radio and TV and requiring health warnings on labels and advertising.

Filter-tip deceit charged. The House Government Operations Committee Feb. 19, 1958 had approved a report accusing cigarette manufacturers of deceiving the public by advertising that their higher-priced filter-tip cigarettes provided greater health protection than plain cigarettes. "Actually," the report said, "most filter cigarettes produce as much or more nicotine and tar as cigarettes without filters." The report said the FTC had been "weak and tardy" in policing these "deceptive practices and misleading advertising." Cigarette industry spokesmen denied the charges. Lewis Gruber, P. Lorillard Co. president, told the Washington Advertising Club March 12 that the tobacco industry was more concerned over the cigarette-health issue than Congress, doctors and smokers "because we have more at stake."

The Wall St. Journal reported Dec. 28, 1960 that the filter-tip cigarette (popularized as a result of controversy over cigarettes as a contributor to lung cancer) had proved more profitable than the non-filter type because (1) the filter was cheaper than its equivalent in tobacco and permitted use of less costly "reconstituted" tobacco, (2) cigarettes were being made thinner and (3) smokers consumed more filter-tip cigarettes a day because of their mildness.

Lung-cancer connection. Dr. Leroy E. Burney, then surgeon general of the U.S. Public Health Service, had charged in an article in the Journal of the American Medical Association (made public Nov. 26, 1959) that (a) smoking was the "principal" cause of the U.S.' increase in lung cancer, (b) cigarettes apparently were three times worse than pipes and seven times worse that cigars as a lung-cancer cause and (c) no filter or tobacco treatment materially reduced or eliminated the hazard of lung cancer. Burney added that air pollution also apparently was a cause of the lung-cancer increase.

Dr. Oscar Auerbach, N.Y. Medical College associate professor and East Orange (N.J.) Veterans Administration Hospital scientist, reported at the AMA meeting in Dallas Dec. 4 that (a) lung tissue studies of 238 men smokers showed cell changes that "probably represent a change toward cancer" and (b) the extent of these changes "depend almost completely on the number of cigarettes smoked."

Both reports were challenged by the Tobacco Institute and the Tobacco Industry Research Committee as statistically unsound and ignoring contradictory evidence.

Dr. John H. Talbott, editor of the Journal of the American Medical Association, said editorially Dec. 11 that there was insufficient evidence to prove the case for either side.

Surgeon General's report. U.S. Surgeon General Luther L. Terry Jan. 11, 1964 released a federal report that described cigarette smoking as a definite "health hazard" that "far outweighs all other factors" as a cause of lung disease. The report, "Smoking and Health," noted that 70 million Americans were cigarette smokers during 1963.

The report was prepared by a federal advisory committee appointed by Terry Oct. 27, 1962 to evaluate and reprocess existing studies and statistics on the relationship between smoking and health. Terry served as the committee's chairman.

Chief concern of the committee was the rising death rate in the U.S. from lung cancer, arteriosclerotic (mainly coronary) heart disease and chronic bronchitis and emphysema.

The committee evaluated three kinds of evidence—animal experiments, clinical and autopsy studies and population data. Its conclusions were based primarily on the combined results of seven population studies involving men selected at random and observed until death. On the basis of an analysis of the deaths of 37,391 of the 1,123,000 men involved in the seven studies, the committee concluded that:

(1) The death rate, from all causes, was 68% higher for smokers than for nonsmokers. For coronary artery disease, the leading cause of death in the U.S., the death rate was 70% higher; for chronic bronchitis and emphysema, leading causes of severe disability, the rate was 500% higher; for cancer of the lungs, the most common site of cancer in men, nearly 1,000% higher. The death rate for cancer of the larynx and of the esophagus, for oral cancer, for peptic ulcer and for a group of circulatory diseases was also higher for smokers.

(2) The number of cigarettes smoked daily, the age at which the habit started and the degree of inhalation affected the death rate. Men who smoked fewer than 10 cigarettes daily had a death rate, from all causes, about 40% higher than nonsmokers. The death rate of those who smoked 10-19 cigarettes was about 79% higher; the rate for those who smoked 20-30, about 90% higher; the rate for those who smoked 40 or more, 120% higher. The death rate of those who started smoking before 20 years of age was higher than those who began after 25.

(3) Cigarette smoking was a much greater causative factor in lung cancer than air pollution or occupational exposure.

(4) There was no evidence that nicotine substantially caused disease. Certain components of tobacco smoke—polycyclic aromatic hydrocarbons—had been found to cause cancer in animals.

(5) There was no link between tobacco and cancer of the stomach.

Advertising curbs. The FTC Jan. 13, 1964 announced plans not only to require that every cigarette pack contain a warning to the public on the hazards of smoking but to force advertisers to eliminate statements enhancing the pleasures and advantages to be derived from smoking.

FTC Chairman Paul Rand Dixon announced June 24 that cigarette advertisements and labels would be required to carry a warning "clearly and prominently" stating that cigarette smoking "may cause death from cancer and other diseases." The announcement was made by Dixon in testimony before the House Commerce Committee, which had opened hearings June 23 on bills to strengthen federal control of cigarette labels and ads.

The board of TV directions of the National Association of Broadcasters Jan. 29, 1964 had adopted regulations opposing commercials (a) that depicted cigarette smoking "in a manner to impress youth ... as a desirable habit worthy of imitation" or (b) that "convey[ed] the impression that cigarette smoking promotes health or is important to ... personal development." (Tobacco advertisers had spent $134,600,000 on TV and $19 million on radio during 1963.)

American Tobacco Vice President Robert K. Heimann announced Jan. 29 that, following the expiration of current contracts, his firm would no longer sponsor sports events on radio and TV.

Nine of the U.S.' major cigarette manufacturers announced Apr. 27, 1964 that they had adopted an advertising code barring cigarette ads from school publications, from newspaper comic strips and from any other publications "directed at persons under 21." The code provided that models used in cigarette ads must be at least 25 years in age and in appearance. The code went into effect June 22, the day the Justice Department gave the industry immunity from criminal antitrust action in applying the code.

The code also banned: (1) Cigarette ads that depicted "as a smoker any person participating in, or having just participated in, physical activity requiring stamina or athletic conditioning beyond that of normal recreation." (2) Ads claiming that smoking was "essential to social prominence, distinction, success or sexual attraction." (3) "Testimonials from athletes," entertainment celebrities or others with "special appeal" to people under 21. (4) Ads claiming a "representation with respect to health" unless the administrator determined the scientific justification of the claim.

The agreeing companies were American Tobacco Co., Brown & Williamson Tobacco Corp., Larus & Brother Co., Inc., Liggett & Myers Tobacco Co., P. Lorillard Co., Philip Morris, Inc., R. J. Reynolds Tobacco Co., Stephano Brothers, Inc. and the U.S. Tobacco Co.

The Federal Communications Commission (FCC) ruled June 2, 1967 that radio and TV stations broadcasting cigarette commercials would have to provide "a significant amount of time" for "the other side of this controversial issue of public importance—that however enjoyable, such smoking may be a hazard to the smoker's health."

Bill requires warning. Legislation requiring that cigarette packages, cartons and containers be labeled with health warnings was passed by Senate voice vote July 6, 1965 and 285–103 House vote July 13 and was signed by President Lyndon B. Johnson July 27.

The warning statement—"Caution: Cigarette Smoking May Be Hazardous to Your Health"—was required as of Jan. 1, 1966. It was to be put in a "conspicuous place" and be in "conspicuous and legible type." The bill barred, until July 1, 1969, any requirement of a health statement in cigarette advertising. It also barred the requirement of any other statement on cigarette packages.

An FTC regulation requiring that a health warning be carried on cigarette packages and advertising had gone into effect July 1, but it had not been enforced because of the pending legislation, which subsequently superceded the order.

The FTC June 30, 1967 filed with Congress a report on the impact of the first 18 months of the 1965 labelling act on the smoking habits of Americans and the advertising practices of the tobacco industry. An FTC survey showed that 82% of those interviewed felt that the warning label on cigarette packages was not impressing smokers with the hazards of smoking. There was "virtually no evidence" that the label "had any significant effect," the FTC report stated. In spite of its voluntary advertising code, the tobacco industry had continued to represent smoking as enjoyable and even healthful, the report charged.

Health, Education & Welfare Secretary John W. Gardner July 12 supported the FTC appeal for more significant labelling. He urged Congress (1) to strengthen the warning label to state that smoking was "clearly hazardous to health," (2) to require that the warning appear in advertising as well as on labels and that (3) both labels and advertising identify the tar and nicotine content in cigarettes. Gardner stressed that the action was imperative to inform the public, especially young people, on the dangers of the smoking habit in the light of new evidence disclosed by the Public Health Service (PHS) in a report also submitted to Congress July 12.

The first government report ranking cigarettes by brand names according to their tar and nicotine content was made public Nov. 27, 1967 by the Consumer Subcommittee of the Senate Commerce Committee. The tests, made by the FTC on its smoking machine in Washington, showed that Marvel filter cigarettes ranked lowest in tar content among 59 varieties of cigarettes tested. Long-length nonfilter Chesterfields ranked highest. Raleigh nonfilter cigarettes ranked highest in nicotine content and 4th in tars. Sen. Warren G. Magnuson (D, Wash.), subcommittee chairman, said the results "will enable a smoker who is unable or unwilling to give up smoking to select the least hazardous cigarettes on the market." This view was challenged by the Tobacco Institute, which said that there was no proven relationship between tar and nicotine levels and human health and that the FTC study was faulty in many ways.

Networks reject ad ban. The National Broadcasting Co. (NBC) Aug. 11, 1969 rejected a July 8 request by the Television Code Review Board that cigarette advertising be phased out by Jan. 1, 1970. In a letter to Sen. Frank E. Moss (D, Utah), chairman of the Commerce Committee's consumer subcommittee, NBC President Julian Goodman said that ending cigarette advertising would cause "considerable economic disruption in

DRUGS, MEDICAL DEVICES & HEALTH

broadcasting." Current cigarette contracts were scheduled to expire in September 1970, and Goodman said he could not understand why it was necessary to move up the termination date by eight months.

In early August the American Broadcasting Co. had rejected the proposed advertising ban. The network recommended that Congress enact legislation to ban the manufacture of cigarettes if it thought smoking was "a clear and present danger" to health. The Columbia Broadcasting System, Inc. was reported Aug. 11 to have agreed to allow cigarette manufacturers to withdraw their ads if Congress would allow the withdrawal without threat of an antitrust suit.

Bill bars cigarette ads. After considerable controversy, Congress in March 1970 passed a compromise bill outlawing cigarette commercials on radio and TV starting Jan. 2, 1971. President Richard M. Nixon signed the measure April 1, 1970. The cut-off date was chosen to permit cigarette companies to broadcast commercials during the widely viewed telecasts of football bowl games.

The bill signed by Nixon would also strengthen the warning on cigarette packages to read: "Warning: The Surgeon General has determined that cigarette smoking is dangerous to your health." The bill also authorized the Federal Trade Commission to require warnings in other cigarette advertising after July 1, 1971, if it voted to do so.

Cigarette ad spending tripled. The Tobacco Institute said Jan. 18, 1972 that six major cigarette advertisers in 1971 shifted more than $132 million to newspaper, magazine and outdoor advertising after the ban on cigarette advertising on television and radio went into effect Jan. 2, 1971.

Although advertising was tripled in publications and outdoor advertising, total outlays of $200 million represented a 28% decline from 1970 expenditures.

Ads to have warnings. The FTC said Jan. 31, 1972 that the six largest cigarette manufacturers had agreed to include a "clear and conspicuous" health warning in their cigarette advertisements.

The FTC had warned the companies in July 1971 that it would start court action unless they agreed to display the health warnings.

The six companies signing the consent agreement accounted for 99% of all cigarette production in the U.S. and virtually all the cigarette advertising. They were American Brands, Inc.; the Brown & Williamson Tobacco Corp.; Liggett & Myers, Inc.; the Lorillard Division of Loews Corp.; Philip Morris, Inc.; and the R. J. Reynolds Tobacco Co.

During the past year, advertisements by all of the companies except American Brands had included pictures of cigarette packages which carried the statement: "Warning: the Surgeon General has determined that cigarette smoking is dangerous to your health." Federal law required that all cigarette packages carry that warning.

FTC spokesmen had said that the warnings displayed voluntarily in the cigarette advertisements were not sufficiently conspicuous.

Under the consent order, the same warning had to be displayed in a black-bordered space at the bottom of each advertisement.

Little cigar ads banned. President Nixon Sept. 21, 1973 signed legislation banning advertisement of little cigars on radio and television.

The law defined a little cigar as any roll of tobacco other than a cigarette, 1,000 of which weighed less than three pounds.

In reporting the bill to the House floor, the House Commerce Committee had stated that to allow advertising of little cigars to continue "would promote the impression that it is safer to smoke little cigars than cigarettes."

Food

Standards & Inspection; Filth & Laxity Charged

Under federal law, the Food & Drug Administration and the Department of Agriculture are the principal agencies responsible for requiring that food sold to consumers is pure, wholesome and safe and that it conforms with standards designed to assure that the consumer gets essentially the product he pays for.

Federal standards. Under the Federal Food, Drug & Cosmetic Act, the Food & Drug Administration (FDA) enforces three kinds of mandatory standards for food shipped across state borders. These are standards of:

(a) Identity, which define a specific food product and its mandatory ingredients, although the standards permit the use of optional ingredients in addition to the required ones;

(b) Minimum quality, which provide minimum standards for such factors as tenderness, color and freedom from defects for a number of canned fruits and vegetables; and

(c) Fill of container, which specify how full a container must be to avoid deception.

The U.S. Department of Agriculture (USDA) has established mandatory minimum content requirements for federally inspected meat and poultry products under the Federal Meat Inspection Act and the Poultry Products Inspection Act. These rules specify that a federally inspected meat or poultry product must meet specified content requirements (for example, at least 25% beef in "beef stew"), although different companies can use distinctive recipes once the minimum content requirement has been met.

The USDA has also established mandatory complete standards of identity (setting specific and optional ingredients) for these products: chopped ham, corned beef hash and oleomargarine.

Voluntary grade standards have been set by the USDA for some 300 food and farm products under the Agricultural Marketing Act of 1946 and related statutes. The department, for a fee, provides official grading services, often in cooperation with state agencies, to packers, processors, distributors or others who seek official certification of the grade of their products.

Similar voluntary grade standards and grading services for fishery products are provided by the Department of Commerce's National Marine Fisheries Service. This program provides also for official inspection for edibility and wholesomeness, and many of its standards specify the amount of fish component required in a product.

Wholesome Poultry Act passed. A bill extending federal poultry inspection standards to poultry sold within a state was passed by voice votes of the House and Senate Aug. 2, 1968 and was signed by the President Aug. 18. Called the Wholesome Poultry Products Act, the bill had been requested by the President in his Feb. 6 message to Congress on consumer matters. It provided for financial and technical aid to the states for establishing inspection systems at least equal to federal standards on poultry shipped interstate. The states would have 2 years to establish such programs. After that time federal inspection programs would be extended to states not acting to establish their own.

The legislation covered an estimated 1.6 billion pounds of poultry (about 13% of the U.S. output).

Poultry plant takeovers—The Agriculture Department announced Sept. 1, 1970 that intrastate poultry plants in 14 states would be brought under federal inspection because of state consumer protection laws that failed to meet federal standards. The action was taken under provisions of the Wholesome Poultry Products Act. Plants or planned plants in the following states were affected by the action: Arkansas, Colorado, Georgia, Idaho, Maine, Michigan, Minnesota, Montana, New Jersey, North Dakota, Oregon, South Dakota, Utah and West Virginia.

The General Accounting Office reported Nov. 16, 1971 that "unacceptable" sanitary conditions existed in most of 68 poultry plants inspected randomly, including 17 that had been found negligent in 1969 and 1970.

As in two earlier reports to Congress, GAO found the Agriculture Department's Consumer and Marketing Service largely responsible for lax enforcement, and it recommended creation of a separate inspection agency.

State meat law upheld. U.S. Court Judge Noel P. Fox ruled Nov. 12, 1971 that meat processors selling in Michigan must comply with a state packaging law tougher than federal regulations.

Armour & Co. of Chicago, Wilson & Co. of Phoenix, Ariz. and George A. Hormel & Co. of Austin, Minn. had challenged the state law on grounds that the U.S. Wholesome Meat Act of 1967 had been designed to unify standards. The Michigan law mandated 12% protein content and barred organ meats in hot dogs, sausages and similar products.

Filth tolerance disclosed. The FDA released March 28, 1972 a list of maximum limits of "natural" contamination beyond which its inspectors initiated action against food processing plants. The limits, which had been in existence as early as 1911, were publicized in response to consumer and industry pressure.

The contaminants, which were not considered by the FDA to be health hazards in small quantities, included insect parts and eggs, rodent excreta, worms, hairs, mold, bacteria, rot and cysts. The products covered ranged from fresh fruits and vegetables, grains, spices, coffee beans and fish to juices, flour, jams and canned fruits.

Dr. Virgil O. Wodicka, head of the FDA Bureau of Foods, said the limits had been chosen "essentially on esthetic grounds," and that if all such impurities were banned "there would be no food sold in the United States."

Filthy plants scored. A General Accounting Office (GAO) report in April 1972 assailed "deteriorating" conditions in the food processing industry. It noted that, according to the FDA, the U.S. food industry comprised "some 60,000 establishments whose output results in about $110 *billion* in purchases by consumers each year."

The GAO report, presented to Congress April 18, found that 40% of a sample of 97 food plants operated under unsanitary conditions, 24% with "serious" sanitation problems. Among the violations found were rodent excreta and insects in raw or finished products, use of pesticides near processing areas, use of unsanitary equipment and "dirty and poorly maintained areas over and around food processing locations."

GAO claimed that the FDA had been unable to "provide the assurance of consumer protection" required by the law," partly because of staff shortages and obsolete record-keeping. Congress was advised to give the FDA fine levying power as a middle course between warning letters and time-consuming court action.

FDA Commissioner Charles C. Edwards, replying May 17, asserted that recent "priority attention to microbiological problems such as salmonella and botulism" had led to a decline in "general sanitary practices." Edwards announced a new inspection program that would require appointment of 300 more inspectors added to the 210 currently responsible for the inspection of 60,000 plants.

Food bacteria curbed. The FDA proposed a maximum level on nonharmful bacteria in certain foods, above which the product label would be required to read "Below Standard in Quality— Contains Excessive Bacteria," it was reported Oct. 27, 1972.

The products in the initial order were certain frozen, ready-to-eat cream pies and unflavored gelatin. Fewer than 2% of the pies and no sample of gelatin exceeded the new maximum.

U.S. assumes state meat control. The Department of Agriculture assumed all meat inspection power in Pennsylvania July 17, 1972 because state authorities had failed to raise inspection standards on intrastate plants to levels required by the 1967 Wholesale Meat Act.

Although Pennsylvania officials claimed the transfer of inspection powers would drive small plants out of business and raise costs and consumer prices, Richard E. Lyng, U.S. assistant secretary of agriculture, said in Washington that infrequent and lax inspection in Pennsylvania had led to inadequate hygenic, waste and pest control conditions.

The federal government had taken similar action in six other states— North Dakota, Kentucky, Nebraska, Minnesota, Montana and Oregon, and had notified Missouri that it would be added to the list in August.

Meat inspection found lagging. An internal investigation by the Department of Agriculture of its meat and poultry inspection service, conducted in 1972 by the department's Office of the Inspector General, found dangerous and unsanitary conditions in 38 of 88 processing plants checked in a random survey. A secret report on the investigation was made public June 17, 1973 by Rep. John Melcher (D, Mont.).

Conditions ranging from poor sanitation practices to "filth" were found in the plants, 11 of which were deemed "unacceptable."

The department, in an October 1972 response to the report, said improper conditions had been corrected in 30 of the 38 plants.

The report also cited low morale, confusion and misconduct among inspectors and inadequate supervision of the inspection of meat imports, partly because of a lack of coordination between customs and agriculture officials. Illegal meat products from China, unfit horsemeat from Mexico and canned meat products from various countries were allowed entry without inspection, the report noted.

Clayton Yeutter, assistant secretary for consumer and marketing affairs, said after the release of the report that the department was acting on the charges of misconduct and implementing other recommendations of the report. Yeutter said he agreed with the finding that department laboratories spent too much time analyzing the fat and water content of meat products and not enough time checking for harmful residues and additives.

Shellfish danger. The General Accounting Office said March 30, 1973 that a review of shellfish harvesting in four sample states showed that the states and the FDA maintained "inadequate" inspection procedures.

GAO said the states had "allowed growing areas to remain open for harvesting despite indications that the quality of the waters was questionable, if not polluted."

The FDA June 19, 1975 published preliminary rules to strengthen sanitation rules in the shellfish industry, where it had found that harvesting, processing, packaging and storage practices were in many instances "not adequate to assure that consumers receive only safe and wholesome products."

Action Vs. 'Dangerous' Foods

Mercury-tainted fish recalled. The Food and Drug Administration (FDA) announced Dec. 15, 1970 that at least nearly one million cans of tuna fish was being removed from the market because of tests indicating mercury contamination. The agency said, however, that the action was a precautionary measure and that the fish was still safe to eat.

The investigation of mercury in tuna fish followed a Dec. 3 report by Dr. Bruce McDuffie, a chemistry professor at New York State University's Binghamton campus, that he had found a can of tainted tuna. It was believed to be the first time that high levels of mercury had been found in ocean fish, although there had been many reports of mercury-tainted fresh water fish in the U.S. and Canada.

FDA Commissioner Dr. Charles C. Edwards Jr. estimated that from the samples tested, 23% of the 900 million cans of tuna packed in the U.S. in 1970 contained mercury levels above the .5 parts per million (ppm) considered acceptable by the FDA. The highest level found in the cans tested was 1.2 ppm and the average of all samples was .37 ppm.

Dr. Virgil O. Wodicka, director of the FDA Bureau of Foods, said it was unlikely that the mercury came from a single source since many brands of tuna, several species of fish, and fish taken from wide geographical areas had been found contaminated. Wodicka said the "best guess is that the mercury somehow got into the food chain, although we're not even sure of that."

Edwards emphasized that "given the present levels of tuna consumption in this country, the relatively low levels of excess mercury found to date and the fact that even this excess is being removed, we are confident that the American consumer is now and will remain safe from risks of mercury poisoning."

Lots of the following brands of tuna were affected by the action, with the manufacturers agreeing to withdraw the contaminated stock voluntarily: Bumble Bee; Chicken of the Sea; Empress; Grand Union; Orchard Park; Star Kist; and Van Camp.

(Statistics released by the FDA April 28 indicated that food manufacturers recalled products for safety reasons at the rate of about twice a week. The figures showed that during the first 3½ months of 1970, at least 37 recalls took place. FDA officials said that the actual number may have been higher, because some companies may not have reported recalls to the agency. The recalls included 250,000 cases of soup manufactured by Thomas J. Lipton Inc.'s Albion, N.Y. plant because some noodles had been found to be contaminated with a bacteria that caused intestinal inflammation; 460,000 cases of sliced pimentos processed by a National Biscuit Co. factory in Woodbury, Ga. because glass particles had been found in some jars; and 2,000 cases of candy recalled by the Lincoln, Neb. plant of Russell Stover Candies Inc. because of infestation by rodents and insects.)

■ The FDA announced Dec. 23 that excessive amounts of mercury had been found in 89% of samples of frozen swordfish tested and that nearly every brand sold in the U.S. was being removed from the market. Mercury levels found in the swordfish ranged from .18 ppm to a high of .24 ppm, with an average of .93 ppm. The agency said that although the levels were much higher than those found in the tuna samples, only 25 million pounds of swordfish were consumed annually by the American public compared with 469 million pounds of tuna.

The FDA statement said: "There is no cause for alarm as to an immediate health hazard as a result of the swordfish findings." The agency said the government was instituting a strict program to test swordfish before it was imported into the country. About 98% of the swordfish consumed in the U.S. was imported, mostly from Japan.

■ Dr. Barry Commoner, a pioneer in the fight against environmental pollution, charged Dec. 29 that the FDA "appears to be minimizing the hazard" of mercury pollution. Commoner, a George Washington University (St. Louis) ecologist, called for a "total survey" of all foods in the American diet to test for mercury contamination. Pointing out that World Health Organization guidelines for safe mercury levels were 10 times lower that FDA limits, Commoner said: "As in the case of radiation, in which 'acceptable' limits were significantly reduced in the postwar years, the 'acceptable' limits for mercury in food may have to be reduced."

Commoner, who spoke to newsmen before presenting a formal report to the convention of the American Association for the Advancement of Science in Chicago, said: "What we know about mercury pollution suggests to me that it may well emerge as the most serious acute problem among the dismal array of environmental problems which constitute the environmental crisis."

■ The FDA announced Feb. 4, 1971 that all stocks of mercury-tainted tuna had been removed from the U.S. market.

Edwards said the seven-week tuna testing program "showed the problem of mercury in tuna to be less serious than had been feared." He said about 3.6% of the canned tuna supply had been found to be contaminated and that a December 1970 estimate of 23% contamination was based on the initial testing of "the most suspicious lots of tuna."

The agency said that "stocks of [tuna] presently marketed in the United States are within the guideline." About six million pounds of tuna had been removed from stores.

The FDA said swordfish was disappearing from the U.S. market because of disclosures of mercury contamination. The agency said that the "swordfish industry is being called upon to withhold all uncleared shipments voluntarily." The statement said federal officials had seized the fish when voluntary compliance was unsuccessful and that 12,000 pounds of swordfish had been confiscated in Los Angeles in January.

The FDA said Feb. 4 it was also testing 40-year-old frozen fish to determine whether mercury contamination had increased. New York State researchers had said Jan. 5 that levels of mercury found in preserved fish, some caught as much as 43 years ago, were twice as high as the levels that currently barred fish from the market.

■ The FDA warned consumers May 6, 1971 to give up swordfish because of mercury contamination. The agency said more than 90% of the swordfish samples tested during a three-month study contained levels of mercury "substantially" above .5 parts per million (ppm), the upper limit of the FDA safety guideline.

Edwards said the warning was particularly important for children, more susceptible to mercury poisoning, and for women of child-bearing age, because of tests indicating that mercury can cause birth defects. The FDA said the average concentration of mercury in the swordfish specimens studied was more than twice the guideline level and that more than 8% of the samples had concentrations higher than 1.5 ppm.

The FDA said that despite industry cooperation and the seizure of 832,000 pounds of contaminated swordfish, it was unable to keep swordfish with excessive mercury levels off the market as in the case of tuna because the industry was composed of small, scattered operators. The agency had decided on the unprecedented, across-the-board warning because it had been unable to develop a program for certifying the 5%–8% of each swordfish catch likely to meet FDA standards.

Before the first warnings of contaminated swordfish, Americans had consumed about 26 million pounds annually. About 22 million pounds were imported from Japan and Canada, and the rest was caught domestically in Northeastern coastal waters and off California.

■ The President's Council on Environmental Quality issued a report May 6 on toxic substances, declaring that a new health hazard was posed by poisonous metals and other toxic compounds that were becoming a pervasive element of the environment. The report said large accumulations of mercury could "destroy cells of the brain, cause tremors and mouth ulcers, and produce birth defects because of chromosome breakage."

■ In testimony before a Senate Commerce subcommittee on the environment May 20, scientists reported a pervasive and long-lasting danger due to mercury pollution in streams and oceans. Dr. Roger C. Herdman, New York state deputy health commissioner, reported the first documented case of mercury poisoning in the U.S. Herdman said a New York woman, who had consumed 10 ounces of swordfish a day for 10 months "without interruption" as part of a weight-reducing diet, had suffered symptoms of brain damage. In other testimony, scientists reported that hazardous levels of mercury had been discovered in striped bass and that arsenic contamination may also threaten the fish supply.

■ The Environment Protection Agency March 24, 1972 suspended registration of 12 mercury pesticides and fungicides and initiated such procedures on 750 others. Taken together, the poisons accounted for 18% of all commercially used mercury.

Action against DDT. Federal and state action was started in 1968–69 to end the use of the pesticide DDT (dichlorodiphenyl-trichloroethane), which had contaminated birds, fish and other wildlife. (Sweden banned the use of DDT in March 1969, and Denmark did so in June.) The Michigan State Agriculture Commission halted the sale of DDT for mosquito control in 1968, and on April 16, 1969 Michigan became the first state to ban the sale of DDT. Other states took similar action later.

In March 1969, the FDA seized 28,150 pounds of Lake Michigan coho salmon, which had been brought from Oregon a few years previously. According to various reports, the salmon contained 12 to 30 parts per million of DDT residues. The FDA had recommended permitting no more than 3.5 ppm in fish in interstate commerce. But the FDA announced April 22 that it had limited the permissible amount to 5 ppm. Dr. Herbert L. Ley Jr., FDA commissioner, said: "This guideline is intended to protect the public from excessive levels of DDT in fish while a full scientific review is completed. It also gives the fishing industry a specific standard." (The governors of the five Great Lakes states—Michigan, Illinois, Wisconsin, Indiana and Minnesota—had asked the federal government April 20 not to set maximum levels on DDT and other pesticides until the states had studied the matter.)

Secretary of Health, Education & Welfare Robert H. Finch had announced April 21 that he had appointed a Commission on Pesticides & Their Relationship to Environmental Health to make a study of pesticides and their effect on humans. Finch said that "each American body" already had 12 ppm of DDT in its fatty tissue. While the average daily U.S. individual consumption of DDT was only .7 of a milligram, or one-tenth of the maximum daily consumption the U.N. Food & Health Organization had called permissible, Finch pointed out that no amount was desirable. (The U.S. government had called animals unfit to eat if they had 7 ppm of DDT in their fat tissue.) Finch said there was no doubt that DDT used against farm pests rapidly spread "throughout the biological chain" and became "cumulative and persistent" in effect. But he added that DDT had economic benefits and that its future use should be studied "in an atmosphere of scientific detachment, removed from emotionalism."

The Nixon Administration Nov. 20, 1969 ordered the use of DDT in residential areas ended within 30 days. The phaseout was ordered by Secretary of Agriculture Clifford M. Hardin following a meeting of the Environmental Quality Council at the White House. Hardin also announced a government plan to ban "all other DDT uses" by 1971. It was pointed out however, that "exceptions would be made where DDT is needed for prevention or control of human disease and other essential uses for which no alternative is available." The target date for the total elimination of DDT was set for Dec. 31, 1971.

Dan Kleber, an FDA official, announced Dec. 30, 1970 that federal authorities had seized about 8,000 pounds of kingfish caught within 20 miles of Los Angeles because of tests showing a high DDT content. Kleber said it was the nation's first seizure of DDT-contaminated salt water fish.

Tests showed the fish, packed by State Fish Co. Inc. of San Pedro, Calif., contained about 19 ppm of DDT. All of the fish were frozen and sold for both human and animal consumption.

The Agriculture Department said July 23, 1971 that a "significant proportion" of chickens raised in 12 states had been given feed contaminated with a DDT-like chemical used as an industrial coolant. The department said it had "no evidence" that chickens contaminated with polychlorinated biphenyls (PCB) had reached consumers and that it was taking steps to make sure none did.

The contaminant had leaked into fish meal processed at the East Coast Terminal Inc. plant at Wilmington, N. C. for nearly three months before Monsanto Corp., sole U.S. producer of PCB, reported it to the FDA. The contamination had been discovered by independent testing by a large chicken producer, Holly Farms Inc., which destroyed 77,000 birds rather than let them reach the market. The meal had been sold to 64 poultry producers and to hog raisers.

The Agriculture Department said July 29 that tests indicated no evidence that chickens given the contaminated feed were unsafe to eat. It said tests of chickens and hogs showed PCB levels "within acceptable" limits. An FDA preliminary guideline set the maximum acceptable level for the compound at 5 parts per million for chickens.

Rep. William F. Ryan (D, N. Y.) said July 28 he was "shocked and outraged" at the government's handling of the case. Ryan, who introduced legislation July 26 to outlaw all production or use of PCB in the U.S., said the FDA guideline level was "purely arbitrary." He said the FDA and Agriculture Department "hushed up earlier PCB contamination cases and delayed announcement in this case until the chickens had been sold."

In December 1970, the Campbell Soup Co. had discovered PCB contamination in chickens raised in New York State. The discovery led to the destruction of 146,000 chickens.

The FDA said Aug. 13 it had seized 75,000 eggs contaminated with PCB. The agency said lots of the eggs, from layers fed with meal from the Wilmington plant, had been found to contain more than the acceptable level of PCB. The Agriculture Department took action Aug. 17 to halt the sale of 30,000 pounds of processed frozen eggs after discovering unacceptable levels of PCB.

PCB curbs—The FDA July 6, 1973 issued final regulations restricting the industrial use of the PCB group of chemicals. The rules banned PCB use in plants processing or making food, animal feed or food-packaging materials.

The FDA said it would be impossible to totally eliminate PCBs from the food supply because of their "ubiquitous presence" in the environment. Maximum tolerance levels were set for various classes of foods and packaging materials. The chemicals had been linked to liver damage, birth defects and skin discoloration.

Turkeys kept from market—The Department of Agriculture reported July 6 that the Ralston Purina Co. of St. Louis had held 120,000 slaughtered turkeys off the market because of possible contamination with high levels of PCB, apparently from feed.

Tainted chickens ordered killed. The Environmental Protection Agency (EPA) March 23, 1974 ordered destruction of chickens found by the Agriculture Department to be contaminated with Dieldrin, an insecticide known to induce cancer in high concentrations.

While the Agriculture Department had first estimated that as many as 20 million birds were contaminated, the EPA lowered the maximum estimate to eight million, and after additional testing, the EPA said March 25 that the destruction might involve no more than two million, all grown by five Mississippi operators. Officials said it was unlikely that contaminated chickens had been marketed.

The Agriculture Department had detected the contamination during testing in late February; some chickens, the department said, showed concentrations of three parts per million, 10 times the maximum set by the EPA. Traces of Dieldrin had been found in vegetable fats used in chicken feed mixtures, it was reported March 28.

Lettuce taint reported. United Farm Workers Union director Cesar Chavez called Feb. 26, 1973 for an investigation into the use of Monitor-4, a potentially fatal pesticide that had contaminated over 1,500 acres of California lettuce.

The pesticide had been sprayed on some 35,000 acres of lettuce until Jan. 8, when state agriculture officials discovered and destroyed some 10,000 contaminated boxes of lettuce in warehouses. Farmers were legally required to wait up to 14 days before harvesting sprayed lettuce.

FDA officials seized several hundred boxes in St. Louis Jan. 19 and Charlotte, N.C. Jan. 23 and 26. An FDA official in Los Angeles said the residues found were not hazardous, although illegal, it was reported Feb. 27.

Monitor-4 banned on lettuce—The Environmental Protection Agency (EPA) announced March 6, 1973 that it was banning the use of Monitor-4 on all lettuce crops, since "it would be impossible to guarantee" that federal limits of one part per million could be maintained.

Poisoning from canned soup. The FDA July 7, 1971 ordered the recall of all soups, sauces and other products of Bon Vivant Soups, Inc. of Newark, N.J. The action came after the June 30 death from botulism poisoning of a Westchester County, N.Y. man after he ate canned vichyssoise made by the company.

Deadly toxin from Clostridium botulinus bacterium caused the death of Samuel Cochran Jr. and the serious illness of his wife. The disease attacks the central nervous sytem and causes paralysis and death, usually from respiratory failure. Although the bacteria was normally harmless, it could grow and produce the poisonous toxin in the airless atmosphere of improperly processed canned foods.

Tests completed July 2 confirmed that botulism of a type fatal in 70% of all cases of the disease was present in the can of vichyssoise eaten by the Cochrans. The total recall was ordered after four additional cans from the same lot were discovered contaminated with botulism.

The FDA said July 7 it had continued to find defective cans of products made in the Newark factory, but botulism had been discovered only in one lot of vichyssoise. The FDA said July 9 that the contamination was the result of "human error" and was probably caused by the improper heating of the cans. The agency acknowledged July 20 that the plant had not been inspected since May 1967.

The FDA announced July 23 that the recall process was being accelerated because more underprocessing of Bon Vivant products had been discovered. The National Canners' Association (NCA)

FOOD

was reported to be cooperating in the recall.

The FDA began seizing Bon Vivant products Aug. 11 because, it charged, Bon Vivant and the NCA had failed to meet the recall agreement.

An FDA report of Aug. 17 said that none of the company's products could "be considered safe for consumption by man or animal" because of multiple processing flaws discovered after a June death by botulism.

The Aug. 17 FDA report charged that the Bon Vivant plant had frequently undercooked food, maintained inadequate records and ignored problems with its canning equipment. The company had been warned, the report disclosed, in a 1962 memorandum from the American Can Co., lessor of the canning equipment, that it might face "problems of inadequate processing as a result of the borderline cooking times used by the firm."

An FDA spokesman said Sept. 15 that some of the violations might have been corrected by more frequent inspections, but claimed that the agency's 210 inspectors were responsible for 60,000 plants nationally.

Campbell recalls products—Campbell Soup Co. announced Aug. 22 that it was recalling chicken vegetable soup from 16 Southern and Western states because it had discovered botulism contamination. The company said "Clostridium botulinum has been found in chicken vegetable soup packed in Paris [Tex.] on July 15, 1971."

The company said the contamination had been discovered through its own inspection facilities and no illness resulting from it had been reported.

The FDA said Aug. 31 that Campbell was recalling more than 1,100 cases of vegetarian vegetable soup because of possible bacterial contamination. The agency said it had requested the recall as a precautionary measure because FDA inspectors discovered "abnormal" cans at a Campbell warehouse during an investigation following the earlier recall.

The suspect cans in both recalls were packed at Campbell's Paris, Tex. plant. Shipments from the plant had been halted pending study by Campbell and the FDA.

FDA tightens rules—The FDA May 14, 1973 ordered canners of low-acid foods (those in which botulism bacteria grew best) to register their canning processes. Plants could be closed if processes did not meet FDA standards. The rules became effective July 13.

Voluntary recalls criticized. In a report Oct. 23, 1971, the House Intergovernmental Relations Subcommittee charged that the Food and Drug Administration (FDA) had relied excessively in recent years on voluntary recalls of hazardous products. This procedure, the committee said, may have contributed to a poisoning death in the Washington area in March.

According to the subcommittee, the FDA had relied "entirely" on a November 1970 letter from the Skinker Specialty Food Co. of Alexandria, Va., stating that no further stocks of a mislabeled meat tenderizer could be found in its own or its customers' possession. The agency then issued a public warning about the product, which had been found to contain 97% sodium nitrate, a fatal poison.

The report, issued by subcommittee chairman Rep. L. H. Fountain (D, N.C.), maintained that the FDA should have directly monitored the recall effort by sending inspectors to all Skinker customers. An improper reliance on voluntary procedures, the committee concluded, "has led to serious enforcement weaknesses and has reduced the public protection."

Tuna recalled. Star-Kist Foods began a recall of 172,000 cans of tuna that contained an agent that had caused temporary flu-like symptoms in some consumers in the Midwest, the FDA reported Feb. 23, 1973.

Mushrooms checked. The FDA Sept. 25, 1973 ordered a nationwide inspection of all canned mushrooms still in warehouses after finding that half the nation's mushroom canning plants had defective equipment or procedures.

FDA Commissioner Alexander M. Schmidt said that canning companies had cooperated with the FDA in making plant improvements and instituting new mandatory safeguards. But mushrooms processed before the safeguards became effective and currently stored in about 5,000 warehouses would have to be checked.

Earlier in 1973 the FDA had said Feb. 25 that the United Canning Corp. of East Palestine, Ohio was recalling 50,000 institutional-sized cans of mushrooms that might have been contaminated with botulism toxin. The firm had recalled 30,000 cans earlier, it had been announced Feb. 17.

The Stouffer's Food Co. had completed a recall of 14,000 cases of frozen foods Feb. 21 that might have contained mushrooms from the contaminated batch.

A month later the FDA said March 11 that all products containing mushrooms manufactured by the Fred Mushroom Products Co. of South Lebanon, Ohio were being recalled because the agency had found botulinum toxin in one lot of cans on retail shelves.

The Fran Mushroom Co., Inc. of Ravena, N.Y. had recalled at least 800 cases of canned mushrooms sold to the Defense Department, FDA reported April 5. The Center for Disease Control reported that 47 Americans had been stricken with botulism over the past two years, 10 of whom died. None of the recent mushroom cases had caused a reported illness.

Because of possible botulism contamination, the FDA July 21 ordered the recall of up to 336,000 jars of mushrooms that had been produced and packed by Wirth Food Products of Lawrence, Mass. and marketed under five brand names: Carriage Trade, Marinated Mushrooms, Pastene, Purveyor and Wirth.

Contaminant tolerance levels. In 1974 the government again authorized tolerance levels for contaminants in some foods.

The FDA Dec. 6 set formal tolerance levels for lead in evaporated milk, mercury in fish and aflatoxin in peanuts and grains. The action, acknowledging that the FDA could not eliminate all "poisonous and deleterious" substances in food or reduce their levels "without disrupting the food supply," was criticized by scientists and consumer groups.

The lead level in evaporated milk was reduced from .5 parts per million (ppm) to .3 ppm, about five times higher than the level found in raw milk. (The method of sealing milk cans caused the lead level to rise.)

The level for aflatoxin was reduced from 20 parts per billion (ppb) to 15 ppb, a level which caused cancer in laboratory rats, according to a spokeswoman for Public Citizens Health Research Group.

The mercury contamination level would remain at .55 ppm, a level set informally in 1970.

Dirty water found in bottles. The EPA found, it was reported March 1, 1973, a large percentage of bottled water samples contained chemical or biological impurities, and that the bottling companies frequently did not follow adequate quality control or sanitary practices.

The agency tested samples taken from 25 companies, of 500 in the industry. Four of the 50 test batches contained coliform organisms, which were often associated with sewage, and one contained lead that could not be traced to the water source.

According to the EPA, "bacteriological surveillance was judged inadequate in more than half of the firms inspected, while chemical surveillance was inadequate in almost all cases," which, the agency said, "compares most unfavorably with community water supplies."

Additives, Sweeteners, Food Colors & Animal Feeds

The use of additives in foods has long been a cause of controversy. The safety and value of many additives are questioned by many nutritionists and people involved in the consumer movement.

FOOD

As Sen. Gaylord Nelson (D, Wis.) told the Senate March 3, 1975, the U.S. *"probably approves the use of more kinds of food additives than any other nation."* About *"1,000 chemicals [are] now approved by the FDA for use directly in food, and some 2,000 for indirect uses, such as in packaging materials,"* Nelson said. *"The use of food chemicals has more than doubled in the past 20 years, from an estimated 419 million pounds in 1955 to more than one billion pounds today. ... The industry estimates that the average American eats five pounds of additives every year."*

Nelson noted that *"many of these substances are safe, economic to use, and make it possible to process foods with a long shelf and shipping life.... [But] while additives cut costs to producers, they do not necessarily reduce costs to the consumer. For example, a seven-ounce package of imitation eggs, advertised as containing approximately the equivalent of two real eggs, costs 21¢, or 10¢ per egg; a single real egg, medium size, costs 6¢ at 79¢ per dozen...."*

Nelson reported that *"some 600 of the 3,000 [FDA] approved additives are 'generally recognized as safe' (GRAS), thus exempted from testing and new approval by the FDA under the food additives law. These GRAS-list items are now subject to review by the FDA. Some GRAS substances have been found to be harmful, or are being questioned, because of new scientific evidence that they may not be as safe as previously thought."*

Scientists back additive curb. An informal conference of about 100 scientists and lawyers in New York agreed overwhelmingly that the 1958 Delaney Clause of the Food and Drug Act, which barred all food additives which could in any quantity induce cancer in men or animals, be retained for the present, it was reported Jan. 21, 1973.

The two-day conference, sponsored by the New York Academy of Sciences, was planned after Food and Drug Administration (FDA) Commissioner Charles C. Edwards joined industry critics of the clause. Edwards and other critics, testifying in September 1972 before the Senate Select Committee on Nutrition and Human Needs, said the clause was unscientific in allowing absolutely no qualifications, since current test methods could reveal traces of carcinogens so minute as not to be a health problem. They also argued that the clause could be interpreted as banning an additive if one cancer developed in one test animal. Edwards said the clause was difficult to enforce because of "conflicting, inconclusive" data.

Most conference participants reportedly said it would be impossible at present to determine safe levels of carcinogens, especially since the resulting cancer could be delayed as much as 20 years.

Review set—The FDA July 25, 1973 announced new procedures for examination of the 533 food additives on the "GRAS" list (generally recognized as safe), under which a committee of scientists from the Federation of American Societies for Experimental Biology would evaluate all safety data already gathered on the substances. The committee would be required to hold public hearings. The new procedures supplemented review steps, including data gathering, already taken under a 1969 Administration order.

The FDA also announced July 25 the results of its evaluation of four additives. The GRAS status of parabens, mannitol and sorbitol—used as preservatives and sweeteners—was confirmed. The fourth additive, carob bean gum, a widely-used stabilizer, was frozen at current use levels pending further studies of possible hazards.

In action July 26, the FDA issued final rules allowing addition of amino acids to increase the protein content of soy products and cereals.

Cyclamates recalled. Health, Education & Welfare Secretary Robert H. Finch Oct. 18, 1969 ordered the widely used artificial sweeteners called cyclamates removed from the consumer market by Feb. 1, 1970.

Finch said the sweeteners had been withdrawn from the government's list of substances recognized as safe in foods because laboratory evidence had linked concentrated doses of cyclamates with bladder cancers in rats. Finch emphasized, however, that there was no present evidence linking the sweeteners with cancers in man.

Companies using the sweeteners in the production of general-purpose foodstuffs and beverages were ordered to discontinue producing them immediately. Soft drinks with cyclamates were ordered off the market by Jan. 1, 1970, and all other foodstuffs using the sweeteners by Feb. 1, 1970. Finch said the beverages were placed on a more accelerated recall schedule because they were so widely used and because they contained relatively large quantities of the sugar substitutes. (About 70% of cyclamates was used in the form of soft drinks such as Tab, Diet Pepsi, Diet Cola and others.)

(A spokesman for the Soft Drink Association said Oct. 18 that the industry would "immediately suspend production" of low calorie soft drinks containing cyclamates.)

Finch said foods containing the artificial sweeteners would not be withdrawn from the market entirely. Finch said some products containing cyclamates "would continue to be available to persons whose health depends on them, such as those under medical care for such conditions as diabetes or obesity."

But the recall would deeply affect the public and the cyclamate-producing industry. The National Academy of Science had estimated that nearly 75 per cent of the U.S. public consumed some form of the sugar substitutes. The industry that produced and marketed goods containing the sweeteners had been estimated as a billion-dollar-a-year enterprise.

The major producer of bulk cyclamate was the Abbott Laboratories in Chicago. Officials of the firm said they would comply immediately with the government's order at a financial loss of $16 million annually.

The largest users of cyclamates, the soft drink companies, said they were moving rapidly to prepare for the market new low-calorie, cyclamate-free products.

Background—Dr. Michael Sveda, 57, Greenwich, Conn., created cyclamate in 1937. He accidentally developed a crude forerunner of cyclamate while attempting to discover a new fever-depressant while working for his Ph.D at the University of Illinois. Sveda joined duPont Company and assigned the patent for cyclamate to the firm. After a decade of laboratory testing, cyclamates went on the consumer market in the early 1950's.

The use of cyclamate in foodstuffs was first questioned in 1966 when two Japanese scientists discovered that a metabolic product of cyclamate could cause severe skin irritation in some persons.

Lag on recall conceded—Dr. Charles C. Edwards, commissioner of the FDA, conceded in testimony before House investigators June 10, 1970 that cyclamates should have been withdrawn sooner.

Edwards told Rep. L. H. Fountain (D, N. C.), chairman of the House Committee on Government Operations, that "there is no question that it should have been done earlier," when asked about the government's ban. Edwards declined to say how much earlier.

Another health official who appeared before the committee, William W. Goodrich, assistant HEW general counsel, said that the government's action had not been taken sooner because of lack of agreement in the scientific study groups that advised the FDA about cyclamates.

Ban expanded—The FDA Aug. 14, 1970 reinstated its total ban on the use of cyclamates in all foods, including those labeled "drugs" for diabetics or people needing to restrict intake of calories. The government had first banned cyclamates in October 1969, but had modified the order in February to exclude use of the sweetener as a drug.

The new order would make it illegal to sell any food, drug or soft drink containing cyclamates as of Sept. 1, 1970. The agency said its Medical Advisory Group on Cyclamates had "reviewed its recommendation" and decided on a total ban of the chemical "in the light of scientific evidence available to date."

The new evidence showed that much smaller amounts of cyclamates than previously tested produced cancer in rats. The agency said use of the chemical at a safe level would result in an "insignificant caloric reduction having no practical value for the obese or the diabetic patient."

Saccharin curbed. The FDA Jan. 28, 1972 removed saccharin from its list of food additives "generally recognized as safe," after studies showed that mice fed large doses of the artificial sweetener developed bladder tumors.

FDA Commissioner Dr. Charles C. Edwards said the action was taken to limit saccharine use to current levels while research continued. If the tumors were then found to be cancerous, and could be attributed to the saccharine, authorities would outlaw the product.

The latest action would require food processors to list saccharine content on package labels. The FDA, following National Research Council advice, recommended a maximum adult daily use of one gram, the equivalent of seven 12-ounce bottles of diet beverage or 60 small tablets.

A special study group of the National Academy of Sciences-Research Council had reported to the FDA July 23, 1970 that saccharin posed no known health hazard to its users. The panel said its findings were made "on the basis of available information."

But the eight-man study group recommended further laboratory tests of the sweetener despite an "80-year history of saccharin use by man without evidence of adverse effects."

The FDA had requested the study in March 1969 after a University of Wisconsin researcher had reported that combinations of saccharin and cholesterol injected in the urinary bladders of mice caused cancers of that organ in some of the mice.

The FDA reported May 21, 1973 that a pathology report on a two-year rat feeding study showed "presumptive evidence" that saccharin caused cancerous bladder tumors on three of 48 rats fed saccharin as 7.5% of their diet.

But the FDA said Jan. 9, 1975 that its researchers had been unable to determine conclusively whether saccharin caused cancer in test animals. The agency said that pending further studies, current curbs on the sweetener would continue.

3 firms ban MSG. The three largest American baby food makers, Gerber, H.J. Heinz and Beechnut, announced Oct. 24, 1969 that they would stop using the food flavor enhancer MSG (monosodium glutamate) in their products pending further study of the chemical's safety.

The agency acted after Winton B. Raskin, deputy FDA commissioner, had announced Oct. 22 that the FDA intended to review at least four food additives, including MSG. Raskin said the chemical's safety had come under scrutiny after a St. Louis scientist linked MSG to brain damage in infant mice.

The scientist, Dr. John W. Olney, reported Oct. 23 that he had fed infant mice MSG in doses greater than those in baby food and had produced brain damage in the portions of the mice's brains regulating appetite. Dr. Olney said the new evidence, added to research he had done previously, had convinced him that MSG should be removed from baby food.

In announcing the recall of the chemical, Daniel F. Gerber, chief executive officer of Gerber Products Company, said he doubted that MSG had any potential harm for human beings. He said the public had been unnecessarily alarmed and confused by the "unconfirmed body of evidence" against the chemical's use.

The Heinz Company said it planned to discontinue the use of MSG in current products "in full confidence that the industry practice will be vindicated by scientific findings of a more valid order than those that have been used to promote the current controversy."

Sen. George S. McGovern (D, S.D.), chairman of the Senate Select Committee on Nutrition and Human Needs, also criticized MSG Oct. 24. He said MSG "does not serve any nutritional purposes in baby food and there is no need to take any risk with a child's health until it has been proven safe."

Most manufacturers agreed that MSG was added to baby foods to make it more palatable to the mother. Gerber, Heinz and Beechnut accounted for about 80 per cent of the MSG on the market.

Background of MSG—Some researchers had claimed the ancient Chinese used MSG in cooking.

In 1908 Dr. Kikunae Ideka of Tokyo University recognized that a chemical he had isolated from a type of seaweed enhanced the flavor of certain foods. Scientists then sought ways to extract the substance from natural foods, generally those rich in carbohydrates. A process of extraction was used for many years and was finally replaced by a process of fermentation. Most MSG manufactured in the U.S. was produced by fermentation.

In 1968 American housewives and food manufacturers purchased about 43 million pounds of MSG. Total world consumption was 180 million pounds.

The question of the chemical's safety was first brought up in July by five medical scientists who told a Senate committee that monosodium glutamate was potentially harmful and nutritionally unnecessary. The same charge was made July 15 by consumer advocate Ralph Nader. Nader told the Senate Committee on Nutrition and Human Needs that MSG had caused considerable concern among competent nutritionists. Spokesmen for baby food manufacturers that added MSG to their products denied the charge July 28, claiming that MSG was harmless to human beings.

DES banned as cattle feed. The FDA Aug. 2, 1972 banned all further production of the livestock growth hormone DES (diethylstilbesterol) for use in cattle feeds but allowed cattlemen to continue using DES in feed until Jan. 1, 1973. (The ban was overturned in 1974.)

FDA Commissioner Charles C. Edwards said he acted under requirements of the 1968 Delaney amendment to the Food, Drug and Cosmetic Act, which banned all substances in foods that caused cancer in humans or animals, although, he said, "no human harm has been demonstrated in over 17 years of use."

The order permitted continued implanting of DES pellets in cattle and sheep. The pellets, which contained one-thirtieth the amount of DES in direct feed supplements, had not been known to leave detectable residues. DES, which was fed to most commercial cattle in the U.S., had been known to cause cancer in laboratory animals.

Secretary of Agriculture Earl L. Butz said Aug. 2 he regretted the FDA decision, which he said could add $3\frac{1}{2}¢$ a pound to consumer beef prices.

A subcommittee of the Senate Health Committee approved an immediate ban on DES in feed and pellets Aug. 3. Edwards had opposed the bill in a July 21 hearing of the subcommittee. The FDA, he said, believed "piecemeal legislation directed at any given substance" was not "appropriate for making regulatory decisions that are to be based on scientific evidence," since "DES will not be the only substance to generate these kinds of issues."

Sen. Edward M. Kennedy (D, Mass), who chaired the hearing, noted that 21 countries, including Argentina and Australia, the leading beef producers, had banned DES.

Edwards had announced June 16 a formal proposal for a DES ban, in order to set in motion machinery for a public hearing, but at that time he repeated his belief that the hormone was "safe when used as directed." The FDA announcement noted that a ban would ultimately cost consumers $300 million–460 million in meat prices, because of increased feed requirements.

Six days earlier, Department of Agriculture inspectors reported they had found residues of DES in 1.9% of 1972 samples of beef and lamb liver, up from .5% in 1971, before new regulations on DES use went into effect. Rep. L. H. Fountain (D., N.C.) said June 16 Edwards was acting contrary to his December 1971 pledge to a House subcommittee to ban DES if the new rules proved ineffective. A further increase in the rate of contamination to 2.27% was reported by the Agriculture Department July 20.

In a July 10 Washington Post interview, National Cancer Institute Director Frank J. Rauscher asked for a complete ban, saying "anything that increases the carcinogenic burden to man ought to be eliminated from the envirnoment if at all possible, and in this case it is possible."

In an earlier action, announced Jan. 4, 1972, the Agriculture Department had tightened regulations for the use of DES in food animals.

Starting Jan. 8, no DES could be fed cattle or sheep within seven days of slaughter, compared with two days under the old rule, and animals brought to slaughter would require certification of compliance.

It was then reported March 10 that the FDA had banned the use of DES in liquid form in cattle and sheep feed.

The ban on DES in cattle feed was reaffirmed by the FDA April 25, 1973, and Agriculture Secretary Butz reiterated that this would mean higher beef prices for consumers.

Ban voided—The U.S. Court of Appeals in Washington ruled Jan. 24, 1974 that the FDA had acted illegally in 1972 and 1973 in banning DES. The court said that the drug could be marketed again until the FDA held the required hearings or the secretary of health, education and welfare concluded that "such marketing constitutes an imminent hazard to public health."

The court said the FDA had used "scare tactics" instead of sound regulatory procedures in banning the drug without hearings. Noting that "most drugs are unsafe in some degree," the court said that in light of the "acknowledged value" of DES in enhancing meat production, the FDA should consider the possibility of "meaningful restrictions" on the consumption of DES residues rather than an outright ban of the drug.

The FDA said Jan. 28 that it would not appeal the decision but would set hearings to consider the possibility of new restrictions.

Certification was reinstituted by the Agriculture Department Feb. 11, 1975 for livestock producers using DES as a fattening agent. Effective immediately, they would be required to certify that DES was withdrawn from feed at least 14 days before the animals were sold to slaughter, by which time it would have been eliminated naturally from the animal's body.

The certification period, before DES was banned from livestock feed in 1973, had been seven days.

Poultry drug withdrawn—In 1959, Arthur S. Flemming, then secretary of health, education and welfare, had announced Dec. 10 that the poultry industry had agreed voluntarily to stop selling chickens treated with stilbestrol, a synthetic sex hormone that had caused cancer in test animals and—in rare cases—in human beings. Manufacturers of stilbestrol agreed to stop selling the hormone for use in poultry. Stilbestrol had been used to fatten chickens sold mainly in New York and Los Angeles. It had been used on only 1% of chickens marketed in the U.S. Flemming said that in tests, residues of the chemical had turned up in the skin, liver and kidneys of the treated chickens. (He said stilbestrol was used to fatten beef cattle, sheep and lambs also but that tests up until then had showed no traces of the drugs in those animals.) The FDA had approved stilbestrol's use in 1974.

Nitrates & nitrites. Ralph Nader's Center for the Study of Responsive Law filed suit in U.S. district court in Washington, D.C. May 3, 1972 to prohibit the use of nitrates and nitrites as food coloring additives in cured meat products, after the Agriculture Department had rejected a petition seeking a ban.

The additive, which Agriculture authorities said was an effective preservative and antibotulism agent, had been known to combine with amines in foods to produce small amounts of nitrosamine, known to cause cancer in animals. Other evidence suggested that the additives could affect the brain, or lead to anemia in infants and aged persons if consumed in large quantities.

The Agriculture Department Aug. 23 ordered that nitrates and nitrites be listed on labels of cured meat packages pending determination of safe and necessary levels.

Four major public-interest organizations submitted a statement to the FDA protesting its decision against an immediate ban on the use of sodium nitrate and nitrite as color and shelf life preservatives of cured meats and other foods, it was reported Jan. 6, 1973.

Consumers Union, the Environmental Defense Fund, the Center for the Study of Responsive Law and the Consumer Federation of America said the chemicals were not needed to prevent botulism, and could help produce a cancer-producing substance in the stomach.

A panel of experts appointed by the Agriculture Department recommended Sept. 9, 1974 that, because of their cancer-potential, sodium nitrates and nitrites be banned.

The panel said nitrates should be banned from most foods but recommended a temporary exemption for certain sausages and dried, cured products pending completion of further research. Nitrites would be permitted in most products, but only at levels necessary for botulism protection.

Food color banned. The FDA said April 5, 1973 that it was banning the use of Violet No. 1, the food coloring used by the Department of Agriculture for grade labels on meats, and by industry in a variety of food products, because of preliminary Japanese studies indicating that large quantities of Violet No. 1 may have been carcinogenic in laboratory rats.

The substance had been used for 22 years, and had been confirmed as safe by an independent panel nominated by the National Academy of Sciences in 1972. The Agriculture Department said April 5 it would switch to yellow, orange and green stamping colors.

Nutrition, Labeling & Advertising Deception

Cereals industry scored. The breakfast cereals industry was accused of marketing dry cereals with "empty calories" among 40 of its 60 leading brands. The charge was made by Robert B. Choate Jr., a former government consultant on hunger, in testimony before the Senate Commerce Committee's consumer subcommittee July 23, 1970.

Using detailed charts identifying the brands of the industry and a TV monitor to display a series of children's TV commercials for the cereals, Choate illustrated his accusation that major cereals companies were concentrating their advertising on their less nutritious brands, especially to children.

Company executives and industry nutritionists appeared before the subcommittee Aug. 4 to refute the charges leveled by Choate. The industry witnesses testified that Choate lacked specialized training in nutrition and presented their own set of charts to show that cereal and milk contained more nutritive value for less money than other foods. Dr. Frederick J. Stare, chairman of the Department of Nutrition at the Harvard School of Public Health, argued that the charts submitted by Choate had ignored the energy and protein value of the combination of cereal and milk.

In the third day of hearings Aug. 5, the subcommittee's chairman, Sen. Frank E. Moss (D, Utah), submitted a letter from Dr. Jean Mayer, a Harvard nutrition expert, which urged the FCC to monitor any television advertising that was directed at children if it appeared to pertain to their health and nutrition.

Another nutritionist, Prof. Michael C. Latham of Cornell University, testified that there was less nutrition to the dollar in cereals than in bread, hominy grits, spaghetti, baked beans or pizza.

Coca-Cola cleared on Hi-C ads. Coca-Cola Co.'s advertising for its Hi-C fruit drinks was challenged by the Federal Trade Commission (FTC) Sept. 28, 1970. The FTC charged that the ads made false claims that the drink was nutritional and economical as a source of Vitamin C. It said the Hi-C trademark should be banned as misleading. The complaint also cited Marschalk Co., the New York advertising firm that prepared the ads. After more than three years of litigation, however, the FTC Nov. 7, 1973 dismissed the charges.

In a statement issued Sept. 28, 1970, Coca-Cola had refuted the FTC's charges by noting that the Food and Drug Administration considered 30 milligrams of Vitamin C to be "a significant contribution to the diet." The company said every six-ounce serving of Hi-C contained the necessary 30 milligrams.

(The FDA June 4, 1971 announced a voluntary compact whereby citrus growers and producers of diluted orange beverages agreed to label products according to the percentage of pure orange juice in the drinks. Products called "orange juice drink" would have to contain at least 35% pure orange juice, "orange drink" at

FOOD

least 10% and "orange flavored drink" less than 10%.)

Cranberry corrective ads. Ocean Spray Cranberries, Inc. agreed May 5, 1972 to a consent decree with the FTC by which it would run corrective advertisements for one year to clarify nutritional claims for its "cranberry juice cocktail" which the commission had charged were false.

The company agreed to include a message in all its ads for one year, or devote one quarter of its advertising budget to disseminate the message, which read in part: "If you're wondering what some of our earlier advertising meant when we said Ocean Spray Cranberry Juice Cocktail has more food energy than orange juice or tomato juice, let us make it clear: We didn't mean vitamins and minerals. Food energy means calories. Nothing more."

The company also agreed not to label any diluted product as "juice," but the FTC allowed the company to use the label "juice cocktail" for such products.

Baby-food nutritional labeling. In 1970 the FDA acted to give consumers more adequate knowledge of the nutrition they could expect from baby foods.

The FDA ordered the makers of speciality baby foods Oct. 28 to label the nutritional value of their products. The order, to take effect in 30 days, applied to foods such as infant formulas intended as human-milk substitutes. Labels of products that fell below FDA specified protein levels would have to state that the food should not be used as the sole source of protein in a baby's diet. Added material, such as vitamins, minerals and fats, would have to be shown on the labels. In the case of cows' milk and evaporated milk, the labels would state that a baby's diet should include added amounts of vitamins and iron.

In a related action, the FDA proposed that baby foods such as strained meats, fruits and vegetables be labeled as to name and origin of each ingredient.

Baker's ads scored. The FTC March 16, 1971 charged ITT Continental Baking Co. Inc., headquartered in Rye, N.Y., and its advertising agency, Ted Bates & Co. Inc. of New York City, with false and deceptive advertising in their promotion of Wonder Bread, Hostess Snack Cakes and Profile Bread.

The agency issued a proposed consent order to bar the company from making false nutritional statements for Wonder Bread and Hostess Snacks and false weight loss claims for Profile Bread. The agency claimed that Wonder Bread was no better than other standardized enriched breads and, contrary to advertisements, provided only eight of the 17 required nutrients. The FTC said Profile Bread was only about five calories less than regular bread and that eating two slices before lunch and dinner would not result in weight loss without rigorous dietary measures. The agency charged that Hostess Snacks' main nutrient was sugar, which the company neglected to signify.

Among requirements demanded in the consent order: abolition of Profile trade mark as deceptive, disclosure in future ads of all three products for a period of one year the fact of the deceptive advertising charges, elimination of claims of uniqueness without disclosure of distinctions and similarities with competing brands that were closely identical, and inclusion of the percentage content of sugar in cakes and pies for children.

ITT Continental Baking replied to the FTC charges with the statement that it had been "a pioneer in bringing nutrition to the public." In a detailed and lengthy denial of the charges, the company said it would fight the case.

The company agreed July 5 to run "corrective" ads for Profile Bread, but later it filed a denial of the charges covering the other two products.

In order to ward off an FTC ban against its Profile trademark, ITT Continental became the first company to accept an FTC consent order calling for corrective advertising.

The FTC ruled Nov. 5, 1973 that the advertisements for Wonder Bread had for a decade falsely implied that the bread was "an extraordinary growth-producing food" and ordered that such claims be halted. In the same ruling, the commission dismissed its other charges of numerous false nutritional claims for Wonder Bread and Hostess Snack Cakes. The FTC also ruled that the company would not have to run corrective advertising on the Wonder Bread claims.

The original FTC complaint had been seen as a test case on the legality of advertising "uniqueness" for products that were basically the same as competing brands. But the FTC declined to decide the issue, ruling that the question had not been clearly defined in the case and that ITT Continental had not expressly claimed nutritional superiority for Wonder Bread.

Corrective sugar ads. The Wall Street Journal reported Aug. 21, 1972 a provisional FTC consent agreement which would require two sugar trade associations to run ads correcting previous advertisements which the FTC had charged were misleading.

This was the first FTC decision which required corrective advertising and specified the language to be used in the correction and where the ad would run. In the past, delinquent companies were allowed the option of not advertising at all for a certain period of time, according to the Journal.

Sugar Association Inc. and Sugar Information Inc. agreed to take full page ads in seven national magazines saying they could not substantiate prior claims that sugar aided weight loss.

Rule on fat content. The FDA June 13, 1971 issued a regulation that FDA Commissioner Charles C. Edwards said was designed to "help consumers identify the amount, source, and type of fat in the foods they buy." The fat-labeling rule would compel processed-food manufacturers to list the source of animal or vegetable fat in a product.

The fat-content regulation, adopted after a 90-day period for comment, would also allow labels to cite the percentage of unsaturated fats. But the agency refrained from endorsing the disputed view that saturated fats contribute to heart disease. Edwards said, "We are not recommending changes in American dietary habits."

FDA sets label changes. The FDA June 20, 1972 issued labeling rules for seafood cocktails as the first step in a program to conform labels to ingredients in certain types of packaged foods. The rules would require products containing more than one variety of seafood to be called "seafood cocktail," and allow only those products containing solely one variety to be so designated, as shrimp or crabmeat cocktail. The percentage of each seafood ingredient would be listed on the label.

The agency said "complaints from consumers and others" had convinced the FDA that "labeling of some food products suggests that those products have more of a specified ingredient than is actually present." Some shrimp cocktails, spokesmen said, contained only 40% shrimp.

Other products that the agency was investigating were table syrup, fruit salad, juices and pies. Some 400 foods whose ingredients were standardized, such as bread and peanut butter, would not be affected.

Label reform. The FDA Jan. 17, 1973 issued a set of proposed or final regulations that would ultimately insure full and uniform nutrition labeling on most packaged foods, and impose content and labeling restrictions on food supplements. (The FDA March 13 set Dec. 31, 1975 as the deadline for implementing the new rules.)

The rules, which FDA Commissioner Charles C. Edwards called "the most significant change in food-labeling practices since food labeling began," were generally approved by the food processing industry and by consumer groups, although some of the latter criticized the voluntary nature of some of the proposals.

All food products for which any nutritional claim was made on labels or in advertisements would have to carry labels showing the number of calories, the number and size of servings, the amount of protein, fat and carbohydrate, and the percentage of recommended daily allowance (RDA) of protein, Vitamins A and C, thiamin, riboflavin, niacin, calcium and iron. Labels could also carry listings for other vitamins and minerals. The label would generally have to appear just to the right of the brand name.

As a concession to the food industry, the rules would allow manufacturers to omit listing on the label any nutrient present at less than 2% of the RDA, along with a disclaimer for the omitted substances. The RDA, which replaced the former, generally lower minimum daily requirement as the nutritional standard, was the amount found by the National Academy of Sciences to be required by 95%-99% of the normal, healthy population.

Edwards said competitive pressures would force 75%-90% of all food products to eventually conform to the standards.

One rule permitted labels, for the first time, to list cholesterol and fatty acid content, but would prohibit claims that "the product per se will be sufficient to modify fat intake or will help prevent coronary heart disease." Edwards said the FDA "is not taking a position on the controversy" over cholesterol and heart disease.

A series of rules would regulate food supplement and health food labeling. Vitamin and mineral products, if sold as food supplements with claims of nutritional value, would have to contain between 50% and 150% of the RDA of five specified vitamins or five specified minerals, or all 10 substances, with further additions optional. Preparations with less than 50% would have to be marketed as foods, and those with over 150% would be classified as drugs, and have to undergo correspondingly tougher regulation. As a result, some fortified breakfast cereals would have to be sold as food supplements.

Health claims for supplements, and for organic or health foods, would be limited. No product label or advertisement could claim the product was sufficient to prevent, treat or cure disease. The rule would prohibit claims or implications that ordinary diets lacked adequate nutrition, or that the soil in which a food was grown, or the process of distribution, could deprive food of nutrition, or that vitamins derived from natural sources were superior to synthetic vitamins.

Another group of rules would regulate the labeling of artificially enhanced and imitation products. A food substitute with equal nutritional value to a natural food would not have to be labeled as an imitation.

The FDA March 13 issued an additional set of food-labeling rules.

The agency proposed to begin a program of voluntary guidelines for recommended protein, vitamin and mineral content of various types of food. As a first step, frozen dinners that contained the requisite amount of nutrients would be allowed to indicate on their package labels that they met U.S. government standards. Excess nutrients, which could sometimes be damaging to consumers, would disqualify a product from carrying the approval label. The FDA hoped competitive pressures would force most processors to comply. Guidelines for breakfast cereals, breakfast drinks and convenience food dishes were being developed.

The FDA issued a final order implementing labeling requirements on orange juice beverages and seafood cocktails.

Among the new proposals, the FDA asked that labels of noncarbonated juices that contained neither fruit nor vegetable extracts list the missing natural ingredients that the product imitated. The agency also proposed that main course enhancer products, like chickenless "chicken casserole" and steakless "pepper steak" clearly state that the meat must be added by the consumer.

The FDA also proposed that products labeled "frozen dinner" must indicate on their labels what foods should be added to complete a nutritionally balanced meal.

The March 13 new proposals were made final Aug. 1, 1973.

Meat rules set. The Department of Agriculture June 1, 1973 issued labeling and ingredient rules under which processed meats such as frankfurters and other sausages would have to be labeled to closely reflect their contents.

Labels would be required to show whether a product was made of one or more types of meat and to indicate the presence of meat by-products or variety meats. Non-meat binders, such as milk solids and cereals, would be allowed as long as they were described in labels.

The USDA had ruled Aug. 28, 1969 that the content of hot dogs could be 15 per cent poultry without the special labeling then required for "chickendog" products. The ruling also applied to the use of chicken or other poultry products in federally inspected cooked sausages, including frankfurters, knockwurst and bologna.

Nutrient rules. The FDA June 12, 1974 issued regulations and guidelines could be added to foods. The latest proposal continued the FDA's series of regulations designed to improve nutritional quality, labeling and promotional practices.

The new rules, which took effect after a 60-day period for comment, would establish a set of general principles for nutrient additions, including guidelines for certain classes of foods, restoration of nutrients lost in processing and safeguards against overfortification and exaggerated nutritional claims.

The proposals included nutritional quality guidelines for an initial five classes of foods: ready-to-eat breakfast cereals, hot breakfast cereals, "main dish" products, "formulated meal replacements" such as diet aids and snacks, and breakfast beverage products.

As examples of the guidelines, the FDA said the Vitamin C level under which "breakfast beverages" could be labeled as such would be 60 mg. per six-ounce serving, approximately the same as in natural orange juice; for the ready-to-eat cereals, appropriate levels of protein, vitamin and mineral content would be set, and over-fortified products would have to be labeled as containing nutrients regarded to be "unnecessary and inappropriate."

The FDA also proposed standard labeling requirements for textured vegetable proteins, such as soy, which were widely used as extenders or replacements for meats and other protein foods. Under the requirement, labels would have to state the amount and source of the substitute protein.

The FTC Nov. 7 issued regulations requiring advertisers to support claims about nutritional value with substantial information, including a food's vitamin, protein and caloric content.

According to the new regulations, food advertisers making no nutritional claims about their products would not be required to reveal the information, although the FTC staff and most consumers groups had supported mandatory nutritional statements on all food ads.

An FDA regulation, to take effect June 30, 1975, would require that food companies making nutritional claims on labels disclose the proportion per serving of the recommended daily allowance of protein, vitamins and other nutrients.

The labeling regulations were to have taken effect Jan. 1, 1975, but the FDA announced a six-month delay Nov. 25 in response to President Ford's directive to weight the impact of government regulations on inflation.

The FTC Sept. 4, 1975 issued a set of new advertising and labeling rules for protein diet supplements that would inform consumers the supplements were unnecessary for most of them. Almost all Americans had adequate intake of protein from regular food, the agency found, and protein supplements cost from two to 10 times as much as comparable amounts of protein found in many common foods. The supplements, largely distributed through health-food stores, brought annual sales of about $100 million.

The proposed label requirement would carry a warning for protein supplements deriving more than 50% of their calories from its protein content that improper use of the product could cause serious illness in certain cases, such as if used for feeding infants or persons with acute liver or kidney disease.

The agency proposed to stop such deceptive descriptions of the supplements as a source of quick energy, or a weight-reducing aid, or retarder of aging.

FOOD

Price Gouging Charged

The poor pay more. The House Government Operations Committee reported Aug. 10, 1968 that supermarket chains in New York, St. Louis and Washington charged higher prices for inferior food in ghetto neighborhoods. The report indicated that its investigations, although confined to only 3 cities, found evidence that the same practices probably existed in other major cities.

The report was signed by a majority of the 35-member committee, but 11 of the 15 committee Republicans disputed the majority findings. Their minority report contended that high-income and low-income areas appeared to be treated equally by the grocery chains.

The majority charged that the supermarkets sold "to low-income consumers . . . food items of lower quality than are available in [their] outlets located in middle and upper-income areas" and that "evidence . . . that shoppers pay higher prices at food chain stores in poverty areas, though not conclusive, is sufficient . . . to warrant immediate attention by the responsible federal agency."

The majority report said: Federal agencies had paid too little heed to "recurring reports of consumer injustices and grievances in America's low-income areas." The FTC should "scrutinize food retail operators in low-income areas" and take legal action against chains that falsely advertise uniform prices and quality. "There is considerable evidence to support the case" that ghetto stores raise their prices on days when welfare checks are delivered.

Rep. Fletcher Thompson (R., Ga.) warned in his minority report that "by improperly asserting that discrimination exists, this report may very well offer justification to some for additional riots, burning, looting and destruction in the ghetto areas, and those guilty may try to cite this report as an excuse for such action."

Sources close to the committee told newsmen that the supermarket industry had lobbied to have the report suppressed or modified.

The Agriculture Department June 17 had released a study of food prices in 6 cities; it reported "no identifiable pattern of differences between sample stores of the same chain operating in high and low-income areas."

(The FTC reported July 8 that low-income buyers in the District of Columbia were "frequently confused and deceived" by the deceptive practices of some ghetto merchants. "Bait-and-switch" advertising, advertising low-priced products as "bait" with the intention of selling more expensive goods, was found to be the most frequent deceptive practice; it accounted for 41% of the complaints investigated.)

Low-price curb upheld. The Supreme Court Feb. 18, 1963 had upheld a section of the Robinson-Patman Act barring businesses from selling at "unreasonably low prices for the purpose of destroying competition." The company involved was the National Dairy Products Co., which had been charged with reducing prices in the Kansas City area to force small dairies out of business. The majority opinion, written by Justice Tom C. Clark, held that the law applied to below-cost prices if they had been set in order to destroy competition or did not further legitimate business aims. Justices Hugo L. Black, Potter Stewart and Arthur J. Goldberg dissented on the ground that the decision should have been based on a 1921 decision barring unreasonable rates or charges.

2-label pricing barred. The Supreme Court Mar. 23, 1966 held it was a violation of anti-trust law for a company to base a difference in price of the same product on a difference in labels. The 7–2 decision upheld FTC action against the Borden Co. for charging a higher price for canned milk bearing the Borden label than for the same product without the label.

Milk & bread price rises. The FTC Jan. 3, 1968 confirmed its preliminary findings, released Oct. 25, 1966, that the mid-1966 increases in retail milk and bread prices were justified and that there was no evidence of price-fixing by processors. The FTC conclusions, based on an in-depth study of milk and bread prices in 6 cities, were sent to Agriculture Secy. Orville Freeman, who had requested the investigation in Aug. 1966. The new report confirmed that the 1966 prices reflected processors' costs and predicted that the prices nationally would "peak out" and decline, as they did in New York, Baltimore, Dallas and Denver. "Many wholesale bakers [prior to mid-1966] had been under a severe profit squeeze, in some cases because of depressed prices resulting from price wars," the report said. The report predicted a gloomy future for independent wholesale bakeries that competed with supermarkets' private-label bread.

Cereal monopoly charged. The FTC voted 3–2 Jan. 24, 1972 to accuse the nation's four largest manufacturers of breakfast cereals of illegally monopolizing the market, preventing "meaningful price competition" and forcing consumers to pay "artificially inflated" prices.

The FTC said the four companies—Kellogg Co., General Mills Inc., General Foods Corp. and the Quaker Oats Co.—comprised 91% of the ready-to-eat cereals market.

The proposed complaint did not charge the firms with conspiracy, but accused them of individually violating Section 5 of the Federal Trade Commission Act which prohibited restraint of competition. They were charged with "proliferation of brands and trademark promotion; artificial differentiation of products; unfair methods of competition in advertising and product promotion; restrictive retail shelf space control programs and acquisitions of competitors."

The complaint was signed by Chairman Miles W. Kirkpatrick and Commissioners Paul R. Dixon and Mary Gardiner Jones. Commissioners Everette MacIntyre and David S. Dennison Jr. dissented.

A commission staff study estimated that cereal prices would be 20%–25% lower in a competitive market.

A&P guilty on meat prices. A federal jury in San Francisco July 24, 1974 found the Great Atlantic & Pacific Tea Co. (the A&P supermarket chain) guilty of conspiring to fix wholesale and retail beef prices. The jury awarded actual damages of $10.9 million to six livestock producers, and the damages were automatically trebled under antitrust law.

The verdict came in a suit filed in 1968, in which the plaintiffs accused A&P of conspiring with other major food chains to set high, noncompetitive retail prices and low wholesale prices paid to packers. The suit had also charged that A&P conspired to restrain trade by allocating geographical territories to preclude competition.

Two other defendants, Safeway Stores Inc. and Kroger Co., had settled out of court in 1973, agreeing to pay only plaintiffs' attorneys fees.

The damages covered the 1964-68 period, although the plaintiffs had contended that the practices continued through early 1973.

Another suit charging A&P and Safeway with conspiring to fix meat prices had been filed in Lincoln, Neb. federal district court June 10. The plaintiff, Loren Schmit—a cattleman and Nebraska state senator—filed the suit as a class action for other state meat producers and claimed $507 million in actual damages.

ITT baking unit fined as monopoly. Reversing lower-court decisions, the Supreme Court Feb. 19, 1975 ruled, 5–4, that ITT Continental Baking Co. pay daily civil penalties for the acquisition of three other bakeries in violation of a Federal Trade Commission (FTC) antitrust consent order.

In 1962, Continental Baking Co. had settled an FTC antitrust complaint by signing a consent order that prohibited it for 10 years from acquiring other bakeries without FTC permission. In 1968 the government sued ITT Continental Baking—Continental had merged with International Telephone & Telegraph Corp. (ITT) earlier in the year—charging that Continental's acquisition of assets in three companies had violated the 1962 order. The government sought, among other things, civil penalties of $1,000-a-day for each acquisition, as well as divestiture of the three companies.

Subsequently, the U.S. 10th Circuit Court of Appeals ruled that the consent order had barred only the acquisition. Consequently, the appellate court said, ITT Continental was liable for a single penalty of $5,000 for each violation and did not have to divest itself of the three companies.

In reversing the appellate court, the Supreme Court concerned itself only with the matter of penalties. The appeals court decision would undermine the deterrent effect of the penalty, the court said, and convert it "into a minor tax upon a violation which could reap large financial benefits to the perpetrator." The court also decided that the 1962 consent order had included both purchase and retention of the assets.

In a Dec. 10, 1974 complaint, the FTC had accused ITT Continental of trying to monopolize the wholesale bread baking industry. ITT was also charged with joining in "most or all" of the anticompetitive practices alleged against ITT Continental.

According to the FTC, ITT Continental and its predecessor, Continental Baking Co., had tried since 1952 to monopolize regional and local bread markets by selling bread below cost in areas where there was serious competition, while subsidizing the losses incurred by marking up bread prices in areas where there was little competition. Most of these predatory pricing practices were still in use, the FTC charged.

The FTC contended that ITT Continental's alleged anticompetitive practices had driven 43 wholesale baking concerns out of business since January 1972 and caused closure of 80 wholesale bakery plants.

In its complaint, the FTC said it would seek to force ITT Continental to divest itself of wholesale baking assets in some areas of the country.

ITT Continental, which had been acquired by ITT in 1968, was the "world's largest bread baker," according to the FTC. The firm had operations in 30 states. In 1973, its net sales of bread totaled about $475 million, up 47% from 1968 and 50% greater than its nearest competitor.

Sugar charges. Six U.S. sugar firms were indicted Dec. 19, 1974 by a federal grand jury in San Francisco on charges of fixing prices in 23 West and Midwest states.

Two criminal indictments and two companion civil suits, filed by the Justice Department, accused the defendants of engaging in separate price fixing conspiracies in two regional markets on the West Coast and in the Midwest. Named as defendants were Great Western Sugar Co.; American Crystal Sugar Co.; Holly Sugar Corp.; California and Hawaiian Sugar Co.; Amalgamated Sugar Co.; and Consolidated Foods Corp.

A third civil suit, filed against Utah-Idaho Sugar Co. and the National Sugar Beet Growers Federation, alleged a similar conspiracy in Western and Mountain states.

Justice Department spokesmen said the charges grew out of an 18-month investigation into pre-1973 pricing practices of the $2.5 billion U.S. sugar market, and were not related to the current high price of sugar.

According to the government, sales of refined sugar in the California-Arizona market totaled $268 million in 1972. The defendants accounted for 69% of this market.

In the Chicago-West regional market, the Justice Department said, sales totaled $770 million in 1972, with the defendants accounting for more than half of that figure. In the mountain state area, the defendants shared 86% of the market, in which sales totaled about $50 million, according to the government.

The two indictments alleged that "purchasers of refined sugar have been deprived of free and open competition in the sale of refined sugar" and that competition for sugar sales "has been restricted, suppressed and restrained."

The Wall Street Journal reported Dec. 24 that three class action suits had been filed in U.S. District Court in San Francisco against the various defendants named in the federal charges. The suits were brought on behalf of food processors and eating establishments which had bought sugar from the defendants.

Hazardous Products

Government Action & Inaction

Nader charges inaction. Ralph Nader charged Jan. 31, 1975, in an address before the annual convention of the Consumer Federation of America, that government agencies have a poor record in protecting consumers from hazardous products.

Citing what he described as "a few typical examples [that] reveal the unseemly pattern," Nader said:

"Congress passed the Child Protection & Toy Safety Act in 1969, but the Food & Drug Administration did virtually nothing to implement it for three years. Finally, after being sued by consumers, FDA did ban several dangerous toys a few days before Christmas 1971, too late to keep them out of the hands of thousands of children.

"In the face of evidence that about 5,000 deaths and 200,000 injuries result each year from burns associated with flammable fabrics, Congress strengthened the Flammable Fabrics Act of 1967. The Commerce Department, charged with administering this law, took no action under it for four years. Finally, the agency issued the only clothing standard that has been issued to date, setting flammability standards for children's sleepwear up to size 6X. Manufacturers were given a two-year grace period before their products could be sold only if they met these standards. There are still no flammability standards for any clothing over size 6X...."

Hazardous products listed. In a preliminary step before setting mandatory safety standards, the Consumer Product Safety Commission (CPSC) Sept. 29, 1973 listed the consumer product categories that it said "appeared to pose the greatest threat of injury to the public."

The list, based on reports from hospital emergency rooms, ranked 369 categories according to frequency and severity of injuries. Bicycles and related equipment were listed as the most dangerous category, followed by stairs, ramps and landings, doors other than glass doors, and cleaning agents and caustic compounds.

The primary list included only products over which the commission had jurisdiction. Supplementary lists were issued covering products over which it had no jurisdiction or had questionable or shared jurisdiction. Among these were automobiles, motorcycles, firearms and drugs, all of which the commission said would rank high on its "hazard index."

Chairman Richard O. Simpson said most of the CPSC's activities in setting safety standards would be based on the list. However, he conceded the inadequacy of the data sample, since many hazards would not be reflected in emergency room

Dangerous Toys

Safety law. In 1969 a bill (S1689) to broaden the protection of children from hazardous toys was approved by the House Oct. 23 and Senate Oct. 27. It was signed by President Nixon Nov. 10. Federal jurisdiction was extended to toys containing electrical, mechanical or heat hazards. Previous legislation covered toys that were too flammable, too pressurized or chemically hazardous.

The Department of Health, Education and Welfare was empowered under S1689 to suspend without formal hearings the sale of toys deemed hazardous. A manufacturer was permitted to appeal the secretary's decision. A permanent ban would require formal hearings.

Dangerous toys banned. With three days left in the 1970 Christmas sales season, the Food and Drug Administration (FDA) banned 39 toys as dangerous Dec. 21. The agency said manufacturers had been informed and were expected to notify retailers to remove the toys from the shelves. The ban was the first under the Toy Safety Act that went into effect a year before.

The ban followed an action Dec. 11 when the FDA ruled that five "mechanically hazardous" types of toys should be removed from the market. The types were: rattles that could break and cause punctures or that had parts that could prove dangerous if swallowed; dolls or stuffed animals with sharp parts inside; noisemakers (balloons with whistles) with parts that could be inhaled and swallowed; dart toys with sharp edges; and caps or toy guns with noise levels of 138 decibles or above.

Warning against 'clackers.' The FDA Feb. 10, 1971 issued a warning against the "clacker," a popular new toy consisting of two plastic balls connected by a cord. The agency said the toy, intended to clack together rhythmically as the balls swung like pendulums, could cause bodily injury since the plastic balls could shatter on impact.

The FDA said four cases of injuries to the eyes and face had been confirmed. It said the toys were being tested to determine velocity and shatter potential before the agency would decide whether to ban the product, which was produced by at least a dozen companies.

150 toys banned. The FDA reported Oct. 31, 1971 that it had prohibited about 150 toys and obtained modifications on 60 others during 1971.

Edward M. Swartz, consumer advocate specializing in toys, called on the FDA the same day to publicize the banned products. The agency had contended that publicity would cause consumer confusion due to multiple brand names and an inability to ascertain on sight whether the product in question had already been modified.

(The Wall Street Journal had reported Oct. 12 that FDA aides had minimized publicity to preserve industry cooperation.)

The Public Health Service estimated that 700,000 children were injured by toys each year, according to an Oct. 1 report.

Chicago bans unsafe toys—The Chicago city council outlawed the sale or possession for sale of unsafe toys, in the first such move by a municipality, it was reported Nov. 16, 1972. It set a $500 fine for each offense, and defined unsafe toys as those with toxic paint, sharp edges, small parts or dangerous heat or electrical components.

200,000 toys banned. The FDA announced June 29, 1972 that more than 200,000 toys considered dangerous had been recalled since November 1971, with over 90% already removed from retail outlets.

The toys included varieties of squeeze dolls, toy lawnmowers, rattles, musical balls, musical typewriters and wooden soldiers.

FDA failures seen. A private Washington research group charged Dec. 1, 1972 that the FDA had not enforced its rulings and regulations on toy safety.

The Washington Public Interest Research Group said a November survey of stores in 19 metropolitan areas had uncovered 382 toys being sold that had been banned as unsafe by the FDA.

An FDA spokesman said in reply that the agency had "removed millions of dangerous toys from the market, and countless others have been made more safe" as a result of FDA action. He said efforts to remove the toys in question were continuing.

The FDA had banned 30 toys during September, it announced Nov. 9, for a total of 803 banned toys.

Bicycle safety standards set. The Consumer Product Safety Commission (CPSC) July 2, 1974 set mandatory safety standards for bicycles sold in interstate commerce after Jan. 1, 1975.

All bicycles distributed before the effective date could still be sold, but a CPSC label would distinguish those meeting the standards.

Under the regulations, bicycle frames, steering systems, wheels and brakes would be tested for safe construction, strength and performance. The rules would also require protected edges and coverings for protruding parts, chain guards, locking devices for certain parts and improved reflector systems.

Sleep Products

Flammable sleepwear ban. Commerce Secretary Maurice H. Stans announced rules July 28, 1971 to ban the sale of flammable sleepwear for children by July 1973. The regulations were the first affecting clothing since the department gained increased powers under 1967 amendments to the Flammable Fabrics Act.

The rules, applicable to sleepwear in sizes for children up to six years of age, required garments that failed fireproofing tests by June 1972 to be labeled as not meeting government standards. The sale of such garments would be prohibited the following year.

Stans said, "An earlier mandatory compliance date . . . would only create shortages of goods." Sen. Frank E. Moss (D, Utah), chairman of the Senate Commerce Consumer Subcommittee, criticized the regulations as "too little, too late."

Health, Education and Welfare Department statistics estimated that 3,000–5,000 deaths and 150,000–250,000 injuries each year resulted from burns due to flammable garments and indoor furnishings.

Mattress, fabric fires curbed. The Commerce Department adopted a new mattress flammability standard that would require all mattresses produced after May 31, 1973 to be 99.9% resistant to cigarettes, it was reported June 1, 1972. The Department said current mattresses ignited 50% of the time when exposed to burning cigarettes.

The department announced at the same time that no delay would be permitted in children's sleepwear flammability requirements, despite manufacturers' protests that flame-resistance technology was lacking for some fabrics. Garments not meeting the standard would be barred from sale after July 29, 1973.

Crib curb set. The FDA proposed new rules to eliminate safety hazards in baby cribs that it said had killed 133 infants since 1970, it was reported April 1, 1973.

The rules, which took effect after a 60-day comment period, would limit the space between vertical slats and require safety locks for drop sides, among other modifications.

Chemicals & Poisons

Lead in pottery. The FDA warned Feb. 8, 1971 that some pottery imported from Italy contained high levels of poisonous lead that could be absorbed by food and drinks on contact and could cause serious injury. The pottery included small mugs, pitchers, dishes and bowls distributed by Holt Howard Inc. of Stamford, Conn., which was recalling the products.

Lead danger widespread. A 1971 Public Health Service survey of 27 cities, made public June 14, 1972, found that as many as 75% of housing units built before 1950 had hazardous levels of lead in exposed interior surfaces accessible to children. The survey also found that a greater percentage of black children seemed to have high levels of lead in their blood than whites in similar environments, with 33% of blacks and 11% of whites showing elevated levels.

The November issue of the magazine Consumer Reports had reported that 400,000 children a year contracted lead poisoning, of whom 200 died, usually after eating 30-year-old paint from peeling slum walls.

Lead in paint curbed. In separate actions in 1972, the FDA and the Department of Housing & Urban Development (HUD) acted to curb the use of lead in paints.

It was reported Jan. 8 that HUD had banned all paints containing over 1% lead by weight from all uses in all properties owned or insured by the department, as of Jan 1.

The FDA March 10 ordered lead content in all household paints, for interior or exterior surfaces, toys and other articles limited to no more than .5% after Dec. 31, and to no more than .06% after Dec. 31, 1973. FDA Commissioner Charles C. Edwards said March 10 that the American Academy of Pediatrics had persuaded the agency that its earlier proposed limit of .5% would not protect children one to three years old.

Dr. Merlin K. DuVal, an assistant secretary of health, education and welfare, told a Senate subcommittee March 10 that 50,000–100,000 children a year required treatment for lead paint poisoning, which caused 200 deaths annually and could cause brain damage.

A U.S. district judge ordered HUD Jan. 24, 1973 to remove all lead-based paint in the 1,200 homes it owned in Philadelphia before selling them.

The City-Wide Coalition Against Childhood Lead Paint Poisoning had brought the suit, charging that 89 children in the area had died of lead paint poisoning since 1950. Removal was estimated to cost $400–$500 per house. HUD owned about 50,000 homes throughout the country.

In a related development, the New York City Health Services administrator said that the number of cases of lead poisoning in the city had dropped 70% since 1970, and attributed the decline to educational efforts among parents, it was reported Feb. 1.

Paint poisoning prevention. 1970 legislation to prevent poisoning from lead-based paint was extended by Congress Oct. 24, 1973. The Senate approved the measure extending the program Oct. 16, the House Oct. 24. The President signed it Nov. 9. The program was authorized $63 million in each of fiscal 1974 and 1975. Lead content in interior paints was required to be limited to .5% by weight. In 1975, the limit would drop to .06% unless another level was demonstrated as safe.

Detergent makers remove NTA. Surgeon General Jesse L. Steinfeld and William D. Ruckelshaus, head of the Environmental Protection Agency, announced Dec. 18, 1970 that detergent manufacturers had agreed to remove nitrilotriacetic acid (NTA) from their products because the chemical could be hazardous to humans, particularly pregnant women. The action was described as a "preventive measure," and the officials said there was no evidence that people had been harmed by use of NTA, which had been developed as a substitute for phosphates in detergents.

After reports that federal authorities might drop their opposition to the use of NTA in laundry products, the Department of Health, Education & Welfare (HEW) May 5, 1972 released a new study that found that the possibility of harm to human beings had not been disproved. Leading detergent manufacturers agreed to abide by the opinion,

HAZARDOUS PRODUCTS

although they reiterated their belief that the product was safe.

News columnist Jack Anderson had charged April 5 that White House aides had been pressuring HEW to approve the renewed use of NTA. Soap and chemical manufacturers had reported losses of over $20 million when they suspended use of the product in 1970. Laboratory tests had disclosed cancer and birth defects in rats fed large amounts of the chemical.

Procter & Gamble Co., Monsanto Co. and W. R. Grace & Co. were all reported May 7 to have reluctantly agreed to withhold NTA from the domestic detergent market, although Grace continued to sell the product to textile and agricultural firms.

Enzymes removed—Union officials at a Procter & Gamble plant in New York said Feb. 11, 1971 that all enzymes were being removed from Tide, the largest selling detergent. The Lever Brothers Co. said Feb. 12 that it had stopped using enzymes in its Drive detergent Feb. 4. Another leading detergent manufacturer, Colgate-Palmolive Co., said Feb. 12 that the company "has been reducing and will continue reducing enzymes" in its detergents.

Phosphate-free detergent seized—About 50,000 pounds of two kinds of laundry detergents, widely advertised as safe for the environment, were seized March 8, 1971 by U.S. marshals in actions in New York and in Landover, Md., outside Washington. A spokesman for the FDA said the seizures were made because laboratory tests showed the products to be "extremely dangerous."

The detergents, Ecolo-G Controlled Suds and Bohack No-Phosphate Controlled Suds Detergent, were both manufactured by the Ecolo-G Corp., a subsidiary of North American Chemical Corp. in Paterson, N.J.

Fred S. Halverson, an FDA official, said some of the chemicals in the products, used as a substitute for phosphates, "may all have direct physical dangers." He said: "They're toxic, corrosive to intact skin and produce, on contact, a severe eye irritation." He said the seizures came as part of an FDA investigation into about 10 different "pro-environment" detergents.

The seizures were made under a charge that the products failed to have adequate labels warning that they were dangerous. An FDA spokesman said the products were sold nationwide and that the seizure would act as a warning to grocers to remove the products or face suits for damages if customers were injured.

In 1972, the FTC agreed Feb. 23 to accept a consent order under which the North American Chemical Corp. agreed not to advertise that its caustic detergent, Ecolo-G, was "unconditionally approved throughout the U.S.A." The order required that all future ads "conspicuously disclose the required cautionary statements" which the product's label had carried since a 1971 consent order.

In another development, the FTC decided to suspend its investigation of possible toxic effects of enzymes in detergents, it was reported Feb. 24. The commission concluded that the evidence was "insufficient to warrant any action at the present time."

Caustics questioned—Undisclosed HEW tests showing that detergents containing caustics had caused blindness in laboratory animals were reported by the Washington Post April 9, 1972.

While other detergents were known to cause eye irritations in young children, only the caustics, introduced as a substitute for water-polluting phosphates, threatened irreversible blindness, even if rinsed away minutes after contact. The study had been conducted by the National Institute of Environmental Health Sciences at the request of Surgeon General Jesse Steinfeld.

The Post reported that some HEW scientists had complained that the FDA had not sufficiently warned consumers of the risks involved.

'Child-proofing.' The FDA said June 9, 1971 that liquid drain cleaners that contained more than 10% lye would be banned in 60 days unless sold in a government-approved "child-proof" package. The action followed reports of at least 271 incidents of children swallowing drain cleaners in the last four years, with 114 hospitalizations and three deaths. A spokesman said most manufacturers had already reduced lye content below 10% in reaction to a standard proposed in November 1970.

In a similar development reported Sept. 7, the FDA proposed a rule requiring furniture oil polishes containing 10% or more petroleum distillates to be sold in child-proof packages. FDA Commissioner Edwards said that between 1965 and 1970, 54 children died after swallowing furniture polish.

Malcolm W. Jensen, director of the FDA Bureau of Product Safety, said July 23 that he had urged Colgate-Palmolive Co. to withdraw a detergent packaged in a milk-type carton. He said he had acted to seek the removal of Crystal Clear, a lemon-scented detergent, under the Hazardous Substances Act, which stated that a hazardous substance could not be sold in a "container which is identifiable as a food, drug or cosmetic container."

Jensen said the agency would move against other non-food products packaged in milk-type containers, including fertilizer, mothballs, insecticides and others.

The FDA was reported Oct. 16, 1972 to have extended its child-proof package requirements to several new categories of household products.

The rules, which prohibited packages that could be opened by more than 15% of a test group of 200 children less than five years old, would now cover products containing at least 10% liquid turpentine, 4% liquid methanol, 10% dry sodium or potassium hydroxide or 2% nondry sodium or potassium hydroxide. The products affected were paint thinners and solvents, automobile anti-freeze, and drain and oven cleaners. Earlier rulings had covered aspirin, habit-forming drugs, liquid furniture polish and methyl salicylates.

Razor blade ads. The FTC said March 12, 1971 that it would seek an injunction to bar Philip Morris Inc. from distributing sample razor blades in Sunday newspapers. The FTC said it was taking the case to court because of complaints received by the agency of injuries to children. Although the agency is permitted by federal law only to seek injunctions specifically against false advertising of foods and drugs, the FTC said it would argue the case on grounds of "imminent danger to health and safety."

The immediate purpose of the FTC court action was to prevent insertion of Personna blades, a product of Philip Morris subsidiary, American Safety Razor Co., in Sunday newspapers of 11 cities March 21.

The razor company March 14 canceled distribution of the Personna blades scheduled for March 21. In a letter to the FTC, the company said the blades were withdrawn "because of our desire to still any fears, however unfounded they may be." The company argued that it had not been negligent in regard to public safety, having asked over 200 people of all ages to test the packages for toughness.

The Wall Street Journal reported Dec. 4, 1972 that the FTC had secretly renegotiated its consent order with Philip Morris and had amended the ban to permit special packaging of the blades.

PCB curbs. The FDA March 17, 1972 published new regulations on the use of the PCB group of chemicals (polychlorinated biphenyls).

Under the new regulations, PCBs could not be used in plants processing food, animal feed, or food packaging, and would be banned from recycled paper. Temporary limits on "unavoidable" PCB residues would be set for dairy and poultry products, fish, baby foods and animal feed.

The chemicals, which do not occur in nature, and like DDT tend to persist in the environment and become absorbed in the food chain, had been linked to skin irritations, liver damage and birth defects.

Rep. William F. Ryan (D, N.Y.), who had introduced legislation to ban PCBs from interstate commerce, March 17 welcomed the FDA move but called

HAZARDOUS PRODUCTS

it incomplete. Ryan, a leading critic of the chemical's use, had conceded Sept. 29, 1971 that there was no acute PCB hazard yet but had warned of long-term environmental effects.

FDA Commissioner Charles C. Edwards had said Sept. 29, 1971 that use of the industrial chemical, employed primarily as a coolant, was "a potential but not immediate health hazard."

Hexachlorophene curbs. Curbs on the use of the germicide hexachlorophene were imposed in 1972.

The FDA Dec. 12, 1971 had first proposed that cleansers containing over 3% hexachlorophene, commonly used for bathing babies and other antiseptic purposes, display labels warning against "total body bathing."

The chemical, present in lesser quantities in some soaps and deodorants, had been found to cause brain damage in monkeys, and possibly cause toxic skin reactions.

Edwards reported that the Monsanto Co., the only U.S. producer of the chemical, would restrict sales to "essential closed-system uses, with no use in food or feed plants." A complete ban, he said, was "not feasible."

The FDA Jan. 5, 1972 proposed severe curbs on the use of hexachlorophene.

The agency's restrictions would prohibit the use of hexachlorophene in cosmetics, except when it was needed in minute amounts as a preservative. Products with more than .75% of the antibacterial chemical would be limited to hospitals and prescription sales.

A cautionary label would be required on soaps and other products with less than .75% hexachlorophene. The label would read: "Caution: Contains hexachlorophene. For external washing only. Rinse thoroughly."

FDA spokesmen said the proposed curbs were advanced because of recent studies that had raised questions about the safety of hexachlorophene. The spokesmen stressed, however, that the agency was not aware of any harm to humans resulting from the use of hexachlorophene under recommended or normal conditions.

An FDA statement Feb. 2 advised hospitals to resume careful bathing of infants in 3% hexachlorophene solution when faced with outbreaks of staphylococcus infection in nurseries. Since its December 1971 warning about the chemical, 22 hospitals had reported such outbreaks.

The FDA repeated that it had specifically supported the practice of hexachlorophene hand-washing by personnel, which had been dropped by some of the hospitals later infected. The agency also reported that some hospitals had discontinued hexachlorophene bathing without ill effect, and others had staph problems while using the product.

More stringent rules curbing the use of hexachlorophene were issued by the FDA Sept. 22, 1972 on learning that 39 babies had died in France in August after being dusted with talcum powder containing an accidently high 6% level of hexachlorophene.

The new order would ban all production or shipment of 400 categories of over-the-counter products containing less than .75% of the chemical, a dose widely considered ineffective as a germicide. The ban would not apply to products already on retail shelves, or those containing minute amounts of hexachlorophene as a preservative.

The January proposal would have permitted the sale, with a cautionary label, of these over-the-counter products, which included deodorants, soaps, shampoos, toothpastes, cosmetics and cleansers with annual sales of about $200 million.

Medical products containing over .75% hexachlorophene, used mostly to treat skin outbreaks and dandruff, would continue to be sold, but only by prescription. But all baby powders containing the chemical were recalled, "because they are not rinsed off, are applied repeatedly and are covered by diapers."

The FDA said the action was taken because "under certain circumstances and at higher concentrations hexachlorophene is a very, very potent neurotoxin," although there was no evidence that products containing limited amounts of the chemical were health hazards. The order would serve to ban unnecessary exposure "to assure continued safe use of this effective germ fighter" in special cases.

New label for Shell pesticide ordered. The Agriculture Department, acting at the request of the Food and Drug Administration, told the Shell Chemical Corp. Aug. 8, 1970 to change the label of its "No-Pest Strip" or lose its registration. The department ordered the following put on the household pesticide: "Do not use in kitchens, restaurants or areas where food is prepared or served." The FDA had found the product left unacceptable pesticide residues.

Aerosol sprays. The Center for Concerned Engineering charged Dec. 2, 1972 that the makers of aerosol cans had for 20 years suppressed development of safety devices which could defuse an exploding can. The group urged that the government provide triple damages for victims of the pressurized containers. Manufacturers termed the report "alarmist."

In several actions Aug. 20–28, 1973, the Consumer Product Safety Commission (CPSC) ordered the removal from the market of a total of 13 brands of aerosol spray adhesives, all manufactured by the 3-M Co. of St. Paul, Minn. and the Borden Co. of Columbus, Ohio. The adhesives, used mostly in arts and crafts hobbies and photography, had been linked to genetic damage in adults and resultant severe birth defects.

The CPSC also urged that couples who had been exposed to the adhesives consider postponing having children until more information was available.

The Goodyear Tire and Rubber Co. announced Sept. 12 that it was discontinuing production of a spray adhesive which had not been banned.

The CPSC Aug. 16, 1974 ordered a ban on the use of vinyl chloride as a propellant in household aerosol sprays. The CPSC said the gas was not currently being used in newly-manufactured aerosols, but that some produced several months earlier might contain it. The CPSC ban primarily affected paints and paint removers, adhesives and solvents.

In a series of actions April 3-24 involving other aerosol products containing vinyl chloride, the EPA and FDA ordered recalls and banned further sales of some brands of cosmetics, medicinal products and deodorants (FDA), and 29 brands of indoor pesticides (EPA). The EPA added five more pesticides to the banned list, it was reported May 29.

The FDA announced Feb. 25, 1975 that new warning labels would be required of the cosmetics industry for aerosol products and feminine deodorant sprays.

A caution against improper storage and disposal of pressurized containers was required for the aerosol label. Sprays with halocarbons or hydrocarbons were to carry an additional warning against deliberate inhalation. Labels on feminine deodorant sprays were to caution users to keep the product at least eight inches from the skin, not to apply it to imperfect skin area, to discontinue use if imperfection resulted and to seek medical advice if problems persisted.

A label that "the safety of this product has not been determined" was required for products with any cosmetic ingredient not fully tested for safety.

Ingredient labeling on cosmetic products was required under the regulations issued Feb. 25. Two of these requirements—a listing of color additives and declaration of ingredients on packages too small for ingredient labeling—were subject to formal hearing if industry objections continued.

The new requirements were to be effective for all labeling for aerosols, cosmetics and feminine deodorants produced after March 3, 1976.

The FDA May 29, 1975 issued a proposal to halt the marketing of aerosol antiperspirants containing zirconium until proof of safety and effectiveness could be established by the manufacturer. Such sprays were considered a potential health hazard because zirconium had been shown to cause lung disease in test animals when inhaled.

Food and Drugs Commissioner

HAZARDOUS PRODUCTS

Alexander M. Schmidt took the action after an advisory panel concluded that the benefit from such sprays was insignificant when compared with the risk. The panel also found that such antiperspirants were not more effective than non-aerosolized antiperspirants containing zirconium or aluminum, which were not affected by the proposed restriction.

A recall of the products was not anticipated since the health hazard involved repeated exposure over a prolonged period.

The products affected by the proposed marketing halt were Procter & Gamble Co.'s Sure and Secret sprays and Carter-Wallace Inc.'s Arrid XX. Both companies defended their products as safe.

The CPSC July 14, 1975 rejected a petition for a prohibition on marketing aerosol sprays because of reports they were harmful to the atmosphere. By a 3–2 vote, the panel decided there was insufficient evidence available for a ban. The petition was filed by the National Resources Defense Council.

Other Products

Plastics ad accord. The Federal Trade Commission (FTC) announced July 29, 1974 that 25 chemical companies and their trade association—the Society of the Plastics Industry Inc.—had agreed to stop claiming that cellular plastic products were non-burning or self-extinguishing and to inform the public of fire hazards associated with the products. The agreement was the result of a class action complaint filed in 1973.

The products, primarily foamed polyurethanes and polystyrenes, were widely used in construction, furniture and airplane interiors.

Under the agreement, the companies would: cease use of misleading terms about the products' performance under actual fire conditions; attempt to notify all purchasers since Jan. 1, 1968 of fire hazards and take advertisements in popular and trade magazines warning of dangers; and establish a $5 million program for research into improving safety of the products.

The FTC withdrew its complaints against one manufacturer and a testing organization, the American Society for Testing and Materials, but announced a new investigation of the testing company's procedures for certification and standards-setting.

The FTC said that once ignited, the plastics often created greater fire hazards than conventional materials by producing dense smoke, faster spreading of flames, extreme heat and toxic or flammable gases. The Federal Aviation Administration had found such gases to be the possible cause of death in airplane crashes. The plastics were also cited as the source of lethal gases in the overheated Skylab space station.

The FTC contended that the industry had known of the hazards as early as 1967 but had continued to promote them as safe on the basis of small-scale tests by the American Society for Testing and Materials. The manufacturers and the trade group—the Society of the Plastics Industry, Inc.—had helped set the testing standards, the commission alleged.

FTC authority in the case was limited to acting against "unfair and deceptive" marketing practices. Regulatory power over the products themselves rested with the new Consumer Product Safety Commission.

Microwave oven rule. The FDA ruled April 10, 1973 that all microwave ovens must be equipped with back-up switch-off devices, to guard against radiation exposure if the primary switch-off device failed.

The Consumers Union had reported March 7 that 15 leading models of microwave ovens it had tested had shown "measurable radiation leakage."

The FDA June 25, 1975 issued a warning about possible radiation hazards from 12,500 General Electric Co. microwave ovens. Owners were cautioned not to use them until they were inspected and, if needed, repaired by the company. A similar warning had been issued in May involving 5,300 ovens.

Color TV dangers. The FTC and Public Health Service Sept. 5, 1969 warned owners of color TV sets to sit no closer than six feet from a set to avoid possible radiation danger. The FTC said that the effects of low radiation doses were not known.

In another development, the National Commission on Product Safety said Oct. 31 that up to 10,000 fires a year start without warning in the nation's 20 million color TV sets. Arnold B. Elkind, chairman of the commission, said the fire danger was "a uniquely unreasonable" hazard in which the consumer was "entirely at the mercy of the manufacturer." He said, however, that the industry was undertaking a "crash program" to make fireproof sets in the future.

The Consumer Product Safety Commission said Dec. 3, 1973 that over 93,000 portable color television sets had been found to have fire and shock hazards. The CPSC said the problem was probably design defects caused by reduction in size of components to fit compact models.

The largest TV set recall ever made was announced by the FDA Jan. 10, 1975. The recall went out for more than 300,000 color TV sets that, it was reported, could emit five to 25 times the maximum allowable radiation. The manufacturer was the Matsushita Electric Corp. of America, whose parent company was based in Japan.

Shipping hazardous items. The House Dec. 19, 1974 completed legislative action on a bill to restrict the shipment of hazardous materials on passenger aircraft. The transportation secretary would have increased authority to set safety regulations. The bill would prohibit shipment by passenger aircraft of any hazardous or radioactive materials except short-lived isotopes used for research or medical purposes.

The bill also mandated increased railroad safety enforcement and set the National Transportation Safety Board in an independent position outside the Transportation Department. The Senate had approved the bill Oct. 7.

Other Consumer Issues

Reports Released

Shopper guide urged. Ralph Nader Sept. 21, 1969 released a report made by a Presidential task force during the last weeks of the Johnson Administration recommending that the government's research on consumer goods be used as a basis for a public shopping guide. The report was presented to President Johnson under an "administratively confidential" stamp Dec. 9, 1968.

The report said the federal government, as both tester and purchaser of hundreds of consumer goods, had compiled comparisons of brand-name items and additional research on product categories. The task force suggested that the government's list be released to the public to insure better knowledge about products on the market. The report said the "consuming public rarely had sufficient information to make fully rational decisions about the products they purchase."

Though the report was made available to the Nixon Administration, none of the panel's suggestions had been adopted. Nader charged that the report's findings had been "ignored or actively opposed" by the Nixon Administration.

The report conceded that release of the government's consumer data would raise many practical and political problems. But the panel said some information should be released due to what the panel called the "woeful" state of consumer knowledge.

The study group suggested that the General Services Administration, within the first year of the proposed program, release ratings on several of the 98 products it rates. The panel also recommended that the Army release information on the commercial drugs that do not meet its specifications and proposed that the Veterans Administration (VA) release test results on wheelchairs and hearing aids.

The VA agreed Oct. 29 to release all its test data and the ratings it assigned to various brands of hearing aids. The VA had previously refused to release such information on the grounds that it would reveal trade secrets and violate assurances of secrecy to bidders who submitted their products for testing.

FDA failings. A research panel of the FDA reported Aug. 7, 1969 that the agency was ill-equipped to protect the American consumer from faulty products. The panel's study concluded that lack of legal authority and a shortage of funds prevented the FDA from protecting the consumer from shoddy merchandise.

The task force was assembled May 1 under a directive by FDA Commissioner Dr. Herbert L. Ley Jr., to define the objectives of the agency and to identify the shortcomings of the FDA. Dr. Ley also instructed the panel to advance suggestions to remedy deficiencies.

The report said the FDA was severely handicapped by legislation, manpower shortages and finances and said the increasing complexity of the consumer market made it increasingly difficult for the FDA to guarantee the reliability of all products. The report added that because of these conditions the FDA "had been unable to develop the kind of concerted and coordinated efforts needed to deal adequately and simultaneously with problems" related to goods on the consumer market.

Advertising & Selling Practices Under Scrutiny

False TV ads barred. The Supreme Court ruled by 7-2 April 5, 1965 that it was illegal for an advertiser to show on TV a mock test, experiment or demonstration intended to prove a claim—even a valid one—about a product. The court ruled in the case of TV commercials, prepared by Ted Bates & Co., Inc., that showed what appeared to be sandpaper being shaved but actually was Plexiglas and sand. The "sandpaper test" was designed to support the beard-softening claims made for the Colgate-Palmolive Co.'s "Rapid Shave" shaving cream.

'Free' merchandise guidelines. The FTC March 19, 1969 issued guidelines on merchandise promotions that made use of such offers as "free," "two-for-one sale," "half-price sale," "one-cent sale" and "one-half off" in advertising. Under the proposed guidelines: advertisers would have to avoid "any possibility that consumers will be misled or deceived by such offers"; free offers could be used to introduce new products, but repetitious use of such offers would have to be avoided; the prices on which half-price and other offers were based would have to be the regular prices of the seller's own products and not another seller's prices.

Dance schools curbed. The Arthur Murray, Inc. dance schools had consented in 1960 to an order that they end deceptive sales practices through which "innocent, unwary and unsuspecting" persons allegedly were induced to buy expensive dance lessons. The FTC's March complaint had named the company and Kathryn and Arthur Murray.

Deception charged. The FTC Nov. 25, 1970 announced charges of deceptive advertising against the producer of the second largest selling car antifreeze and against two leading toy manufacturers. The three firms said the commission's charges were without foundation.

The agency challenged E.I. du Pont de Nemours & Co. ads for Zerex antifreeze claiming that a TV demonstration of the product was "invalid" and that the antifreeze could clog car radiators and interfere with operation of a car's cooling system.

The toy companies charged by the commission were the Topper Corp. (Elizabeth, N.J.), makers of Johnny Lightening cars, and Mattel Inc. (Hawthorne, Calif.), makers of Hot Wheels cars and Dancerina Dolls. The FTC said advertising for the toys contained false claims or misleading camera or sound techniques and "unfairly exploits" the gullibility of children.

The commission published formal complaints and proposed cease-and-desist orders against the three companies.

Du Pont agreed June 16, 1972 to disclose to consumers when auto damage might result from use of its products and also not to market products without first testing for damage results.

The FTC June 21, 1962 had ordered the Regina Corp., manufacturer of electric floor polishers and vacuum cleaners, and Giant Food, Inc., retail food chain selling small consumer appliances, to end the

OTHER CONSUMER ISSUES

practice of quoting "suggested list prices" that were higher than prices usually charged by other distributors. "Where the advertised 'manufacturers suggested list price' is not in fact the usual or regular price generally prevailing in the area, the public may be misled," the FTC said.

The FTC announced Jan. 6, 1971 that it had agreed provisionally to accept a promise by Irma Shorell Inc. of New York that it would not falsely advertise a facial cream costing $27.50 a jar. The claim to which the FTC objected was that the product, Irma Shorell Contour/35, "will rejuvenate and restore youth to the skin, is equivalent to and may be used instead of surgical face lifting, and will have a permanent or lasting effect."

The FTC accused Popeil Brothers, Inc. of Chicago Jan. 7, 1971 of falsely advertising a food cutting product, Veg-o-Matic. The commission also announced similar charges against the Telex Corp. for its hearing aid promotion.

In a proposed consent order, the FTC said Veg-o-Matic TV ads contended that the cutter would slice raw carrots, tomatoes and other products but that instructions on the packages read: "Don't slice raw carrots, raw beets, lemons, ripe or overripe tomatoes. Veg-o-Matic is not intended to slice these foods."

The proposed Telex order charged that contrary to advertised claims, the hearing aids were not new inventions and were not invisible when worn. The FTC also challenged Telex's claim of the product's value in distinguishing sounds in group conversations or against background noise. In addition the agency said the ads created the "false impression" that people could send for a free book on hearing disabilities with no strings attached. The commission said names of people responding were distributed to dealers who would send door-to-door salesmen.

FTC Chairman Miles W. Kirkpatrick said Jan. 8 at the opening session of the International Newspaper Advertising Executives convention that he personally had found advertising "insulting to good judgment and taste," irrelevant, shoddy, tawdry and uninformative. The chairman acknowledged that the matter of taste was not within the scope of the FTC, but he said the quality of advertising reflected badly on American business practices. He also noted that poor sales and service policies had hurt business in the eyes of the consumer.

The FTC Jan. 11 proposed new rules to combat "wide abuse" in the advertisement of radios, phonographs and other home audio equipment because of variant power output ratings used for amplification equipment. The agency proposed industry-wide adoption of a single standard, the continuous power method (sometimes called RMS), as the uniform rating system of power output.

The FTC, challenging ads for a surgical hair-replacement system, sought a federal court injunction Jan. 15, 1971 against Medi-Hair International of Sacramento, Calif. The commission asked the court for a temporary restraining order against advertisements for the system, which failed to disclose alleged medical risks.

FTC general counsel Joseph Martin said it was believed to be the first time in about 10 years that the FTC had sought such an injunction. Martin added, "It is my belief that the commission will use this approach increasingly in such cases whenever it appears necessary, particularly when medical and health dangers to the public may be involved." In recent years, the FTC had acted through consent orders or cease-and-desist orders, often involving lengthy court proceedings if the orders were challenged.

In an "informational" advertising program started June 10, 1971, the FTC Aug. 24 ordered 11 air conditioner manufacturers and four electric shaver producers to supply supporting evidence for more than 40 air conditioner claims and 14 electric razor ads.

The FTC Dec. 2, 1971 published complaints against the sugar trade associations, Sugar Information Inc. and Sugar Association Inc., in connection with magazine ads suggesting that consumption of sugar before meals could help weight reduction. The FTC charged that the ads implied that eating sweets before meals would result in lower daily caloric intake when in fact it "may result in increased" daily intake. The commission proposed that the two organizations be required to run advertisements admitting the weight loss claims were inaccurate.

The FTC Dec. 2 accused the Sun Oil Co. of using advertisements falsely claiming that its Sunoco gasolines provided more engine power than other brands with similar octane ratings. Sun Oil issued a statement in Philadelphia that the FTC had ignored "extensive documentation" submitted by the company that "the Sunoco custom blending system does in fact enhance automobile engine performance."

(An FTC administrative judge ruled July 22, 1974 that between 1969 and 1972 Sun Oil had made false performance claims for its Sunoco gasolines.

(While ruling that Sun's claims of extra engine power for Sunoco gasoline were improper, the judge said corrective advertising would not be necessary since engine power was "no longer the theme of gasoline promotions.")

The FTC March 3, 1972 charged Sterling Drugs, Inc., manufacturer of Lysol spray, with false advertising practices. The FTC said that although Lysol did kill surface germs, it did not eliminate airborne germs and viruses and thus did not fulfill its claim of preventing colds and flu.

In a proposed cease and desist order, which the company said it would oppose, the FTC called for "corrective advertising" to inform consumers that use of Lysol would not significantly prevent or reduce the incidence of colds and flu.

In a complaint May 2, 1972, the FTC said that three major computer training school chains had engaged in deceptive advertising practices. The FTC asked the schools to disclose the percentage of their graduates placed in computer jobs, the names of employers and starting salaries.

The FTC claimed that the companies had advertised that graduates of the $1,000–$2,500 courses were assured of jobs, that many graduates earned $6,500–$11,000 a year, and that programming jobs did not require a college degree. In fact, the commission charged, fewer than 50% of the graduates found computer jobs, and during recession periods the courses were "virtually worthless."

The companies: the Electronic Computer Programming Institute, Inc. of New York, the Control Data Corp. of South Bloomington, Minn. and Lear Siegler, Inc. of Santa Monica, Calif.

FTC Chairman Miles W. Kirkpatrick, testifying May 16 before the Senate Subcommittee on Consumer Affairs, said that 60% of the data submitted by 32 companies to support 282 advertising claims was either inadequate or "so technical in nature" that neither consumers nor the FTC staff could judge its validity.

The companies, manufacturers of automobiles, television sets, air conditioners and electric shavers, had been ordered in 1971 to file reports supporting claims that the FTC considered could be factually verified. The commission planned the program to aid consumer choice, and to encourage manufacturers to contest exaggerated claims by competitors.

When the claims were analyzed by FTC staff, about 30% raised "serious questions" about adequacy of supporting material, and at least an additional 30% could not be verified. Kirkpatrick said, however, that the staff finding did not in itself constitute grounds for charges of deceptive advertising.

Similar data had also been submitted by manufacturers of cold remedies and dentifrices.

The FTC May 25 ordered 18 automobile tire manufacturers and distributors to document their advertising claims for 75 brands of passenger car tires and on June 28, the FTC ordered 22 manufacturers and distributors of soap, detergents and cleansers to provide information backing up advertising claims made for 59 products.

Spiegel, Inc. was ordered to stop advertising amounts-off and free trial offers in its catalogues without also informing consumers of the restrictions placed on those sales, the FTC announced July 3.

OTHER CONSUMER ISSUES

The FTC charged July 27, 1972 that the nation's largest chain of food stores, the Great Atlantic & Pacific Tea Co. (the A&P), had engaged in deceptive advertising practices on sale items.

In its proposed consent agreement, the FTC said it would require A&P to maintain adequate stocks of sale products and to fire store managers knowingly violating the proposed order.

E. J. Korvette, Inc. was accused of using false quality, price and guarantee claims and scare tactics in its sale of home improvements, under a proposed FTC complaint released Aug. 17.

An evaluation of FTC advertising data, performed by the engineering firm of Bolt Beranek & Newman, Inc. and released Oct. 6 by Consumers Union, indicated that 65% of the documentation submitted to the federal agency by auto makers was irrelevant and inadequate.

The FTC moved against nine car makers and advertisers and air conditioner makers Oct. 12, charging that their ads were "misleading and unfair."

Named in the action, which culminated a 15-month campaign to obtain substantiation for advertisements, were General Motors Corp., Volvo of America Corp., Fedders Corp. and Whirlpool Corp.

The FTC also acted Dec. 14 to order the four U.S. car makers and eight foreign manufacturers of autos to submit documentation for their advertising claims on late model cars.

Other industries ordered to provide the FTC with proof of advertising claims were:

■ 14 soap and detergent makers, ordered Sept. 20 to comply with a second challenge to their advertisements by the government.

■ 12 pet food makers, who were ordered Nov. 24 to provide substantiation.

Those charged with "false and deceptive" advertising were:

■ The Firestone Tire & Rubber Co., which was accused Oct. 6 of falsely claiming that its Wide Oval tires stopped quicker, were free of defects and were safe under all conditions. Corrective advertisements were not ordered because Firestone had not manufactured the tires "for several years," according to company spokesmen, who said a court appeal would be filed in the case.

■ Three pesticide manufacturers, who were charged Nov. 1 with misrepresenting the hazards of bug killers.

■ W. T. Grant Co., which was accused Dec. 7 of falsely promoting its credit plans.

The FTC Nov. 27, 1972 proposed six guidelines for preventing deceptive advertising and product endorsements.

The proposed rules, which were intended to discourage what FTC officials termed "substantial" use of misleading advertisements, would enable the agency to issue cease and desist orders in the event of violations.

A public interest law group at Georgetown University charged in a Dec. 3, 1972 report that TV set advertisers failed to substantiate nearly 70% of their ads questioned by the FTC.

The group, using 1971 data from 10 manufacturers and two retailers supplied by the FTC under a campaign aimed at verifying the claims of advertisers, found that 41 of 59 ads could not be substantiated by the advertisers. Of the 18 ads which were documented, only four had a legitimate basis in claiming that features of their television sets were "unique."

Advertising "promises, misleads and tempts, but it does not do much in the way of informing the public," the report concluded.

The FTC July 10, 1974 accused Sears, Roebuck & Co. of using "bait and switch" advertising and sales techniques for major home appliances. The FTC charged that the company would lure consumers to a store with advertisements for a relatively inexpensive model; the "switch" involved a salesman's urging the customer to buy a more expensive model by such techniques as saying the advertised model was unavailable or making disparaging remarks about the cheaper model. The FTC also said the company's compensation system encouraged salesmen to use such techniques.

The FTC accused three major auto manufacturers July 31, 1974 of misleading advertising on gasoline mileage. Most of the advertising had appeared during fuel shortages earlier in the year.

In complaints against Ford Motor Co. and Chrysler Corp., the FTC charged that ads claiming high fuel mileage, while not necessarily false, lacked sufficient explanatory detail and in Chrysler's case were unfairly derogatory against a General Motors Corp. product.

Regarding General Motors' ads, the FTC tentatively accepted a consent order under which the company agreed to stop making misleading mileage comparisons with other companies' products. Some of the comparisons, the FTC said, had been based on misleadingly selective use of government fuel economy testing data.

The FTC ruled Dec. 18, 1974 that the Standard Oil Co. of California had engaged in false advertising by claiming that the F-310 additive in its Chevron gasoline significantly reduced air pollution from auto exhausts. In issuing a cease and desist order against Standard and the company's advertising agency, the FTC reversed a 1973 decision by a staff law judge who recommended the case's dismissal. The FTC had entered the complaint in 1970.

FTC issues advertising guidelines. The Federal Trade Commission announced new guidelines for advertising endorsements and testimonials May 20, 1975. Experts would have to be bona fide and their expertise used in evaluating the product, the commission decided, and endorsements by organizations must represent "the collective judgment of the organization."

The FTC proposed guidelines requiring an endorsement to reflect the honest view of the endorser and the endorser to be a "bona fide user of the product." Other distortion by the advertiser would be barred.

Among other things, the proposals would require identification as actors of those impersonating "actual consumers" and disclosure of any connection between an endorser and the seller of the product that might affect "the weight or credibility" of the endorsement. If an atypical performance were depicted for a product, the typical performance in the same circumstances would have to be disclosed.

Mail sale system challenged. The FTC May 13, 1970 proposed to outlaw, as "inherently unfair," a direct-mail sales technique used by most major book and record clubs.

The rule would ban plans in which subscribers were sent computerized cards informing them that they would receive and be billed for merchandise unless they returned the card declining the goods by a specified date. The FTC said such practices were unfair because they exploited subscribers' natural preoccupation with "more important or pressing personal affairs" and took advantage of "uncertainties of postal service" and possible computer errors. The commission also suggested that some sellers failed to allow sufficient time to respond, failed to fully disclose details of the plan and failed to respond to subscribers complaints of computer-billing errors.

■In its first action against unsolicited, mailed ads, the FTC April 9, 1970 had charged Metromedia Inc., a major seller of mailing lists, with sending "misleading" questionnaires to about four million people in order to compile mailing lists for direct-mail firms. The FTC allowed the company to settle with a consent order. The agency said that Metromedia, a diversified New York firm with large radio and TV interests, induced persons to fill out form letters by offering "an opportunity to win fabulous gifts" when, in fact, the information was sought for the express purpose of compiling lists for marketing use. A Metromedia spokesman denied the allegation and said the challenged questionnaire was "clearly for commercial purposes."

'Cooling off.' The FTC Sept. 30, 1970 issued a draft regulation to protect consumers from high-pressure door-to-door sales techniques. The regulation would require a three-day "cooling-off" period during which a buyer could cancel any agreement to buy goods or services costing $10 or more.

Publishing companies charged. The Federal Trade Commission (FTC) and

OTHER CONSUMER ISSUES

the Justice Department took separate actions against Cowles Communications Inc. for deceptive practices in the sale of magazine subscriptions. Cowles and five of its magazine sales subsidiaries were fined $10,000 each Jan. 18, 1971 on pleas of no contest in a Des Moines, Iowa federal district court to 10 criminal and civil counts of mail fraud. The FTC said Jan. 21 it had filed formal complaints against Cowles and the Hearst Corp., also for deceptive sales practices.

Both actions charged that door-to-door salesmen and telephone callers had misrepresented to prospective customers the cost and terms of the magazine subscription contracts.

In the federal court action Jan. 18, Cowles and its five Des Moines-based subsidiaries agreed to a permanent injunction barring them from continuing the fraudulent practices cited. The five subsidiaries were Home Reference Library Inc., Home Readers Service Inc., Mutual Readers League Inc., Civil Readers Club Inc. and Educational Book Club Inc.

Cowles and the five subsidiaries June 21, 1972 accepted a consent order barring door-to-door magazine sales with misleading free or reduced-price subscription offers.

In a preliminary action June 1, 1970, the FTC had accused Cowles, Hearst, Time Inc. and Perfect Film & Chemical Corp. and their sales agencies of using deceptive practices to sell subscriptions.

The agency said that because the magazine companies received revenues arising from deceptive sales practices, the firms must accept responsibility for the deceptions even though selling was done by franchised companies or independent contractors.

The FCC said customers were misled into signing subscription contracts at regular rates that could not be canceled although the salesmen indicated the subscriptions were cut-rate and could be canceled. The commission also said salesmen misrepresented contracts as guarantees or route slips and charged that the companies harassed customers who refused to pay after signing unfair contracts.

Rep. Fred B. Rooney (D, Pa.), who had waged a campaign against deceptive magazine sales, said June 1, 1970 that the FCC action encompassed every major area of "consumer trickery" that he had urged the commission to consider. "In some respects the order goes beyond my greatest expectations," he said.

Attorney General Slade Gorton of Washington state said in a Jan. 28, 1970 announcement that Washington state consumers had won a "landmark" case against two marketing subsidiaries of Grolier Inc., a New York publishing firm. An order, filed in Spokane County Superior Court, authorized Washington residents to cancel purchases and have their money refunded in connection with any purchases of books between June 15-Nov. 3, 1969 involving misrepresentation by salesmen of Spencer International Inc. The other subsidiary, Grolier Interstate Inc., voluntarily agreed to discontinue five sales practices that had aroused complaints from the public.

Pyramid sales ban. The FTC ruled Aug. 21, 1974 that pyramid sales plans, under which distributors got bonuses for recruiting others to join the plan, were potentially fraudulent by nature and should be banned.

Although the 4-0 decision dealt with only one company—Symbra'ette Inc., a California apparel marketer—it was seen as setting a new policy under which a company could be closed if was proved to be a pyramid. The decision stated that any plan involving "unlimited recruitment" and extracting "a valuable consideration from individuals in return for the opportunity to participate in it, threatens severe injury."

Accord on enzyme detergents. The FTC March 3, 1971 announced agreement by the three largest U.S. detergent manufacturers to halt advertising that misled consumers into believing enzyme detergents removed all stains. Under terms of the agreement contained in a consent order provisionally accepted by the agency, Procter & Gamble Co., Colgate-

Palmolive Co. and Lever Brothers Co. Inc. accepted FTC proposals for advertising and packaging their enzyme products.

Without admitting guilt, the three companies agreed to implement the following requirements after nine months: (1) disclosure on the packages of the types of stains the product can and cannot remove, (2) acknowledgement in their media advertising that all types of stains will not be removed by the products and (3) elimination of claims that an additive in a product removed stains when in fact the product could have done the job alone. Products affected by the FTC action included Drive, Amaze, Punch, Axion, Ajax, Gain, Biz and Tide.

Promotional Contests

Coca-Cola suit dismissed. A $200 million class action suit, charging Coca-Cola Co. and Glendinning Cos. with deception in Coca-Cola's "Big Name Contest," was dismissed in San Francisco Oct. 19, 1970.

U.S. District Court Judge Gerald S. Levin said he dismissed the suit, brought by five private citizens, because precedent "makes it clear" that no "private rights of action" had been established under Section 5 of the Federal Trade Commission Act cited by the suit. The suit had followed an announcement by the Federal Trade Commission in July that it planned to file a complaint against Coca-Cola and Glendinning, a Westport, Conn., sales promotion company, for deceiving contest participants.

Oil company charges dropped. The FTC dropped a proposed complaint against Glendinning Cos. and the Shell Oil Co. Aug. 3, 1970 after it received pledges of the two companies that they would voluntarily comply with FTC rules in connection with games of chance promotions. The FTC had previously charged that games of chance used to promote gasoline sales had violated new agency rules for "clear and conspicuous" disclosure of contest rules and prize distribution. It also said the contests had not met rules for the random mixing of winning and nonwinning pieces.

Reader's Digest accused. The FTC Dec. 29, 1970 accused Reader's Digest Association, Inc. of deception and misrepresentation in 11 "sweepstakes" contests held between 1966 and 1969 to promote magazine and book and record club subscriptions.

The FTC said the Digest had awarded only 39% of the prizes in numbers and 45% in dollar value in connection with the 11 contests. Of the 699,293 prizes valued at $5,645,000, the FTC alleged that only 274,282 prizes worth $2,350,700 were awarded. In response, a Reader's Digest spokesman said that under company policy at the time awards were made only to winners who claimed prizes. (The FTC noted that even before the public received the contest tickets, winning and losing tickets had already been picked.) The spokesman said the company had given out during 1963–1969 $3,792,000 in prizes (40% of the total prizes) to 306,577 winners.

The Digest was accused of misrepresentation by not disclosing prior to the contest conditions that would be imposed on the winners: first and second prize winners had to submit to an interview by a private detective; an affidavit was required from third and fourth prize winners. The complaint also challenged the contests' implication that participants had a reasonable opportunity of winning by having been "selected" or "one of the few people invited to participate," when in fact millions had been solicited.

The Supreme Court April 23, 1973 rejected by refusing to hear an appeal by Reader's Digest against a Washington state ruling against the magazine's use of mailed sweepstakes to advertise books and magazines. The state claimed the publication was in violation of a law prohibiting lotteries in Washington.

In another case, however, the court ruled that the magazine had not violated

OTHER CONSUMER ISSUES

the constitutional rights to privacy of persons whose names were used in promotional mailings without their knowledge. This practice was discontinued in January 1972 on an FTC order.

McDonald's agreement. In an announcement March 3, 1971, the FTC said that McDonald's Corp., a nationwide hamburger chain, agreed to abandon deceptive practices in promotional contests and to adopt certain FTC requirements.

Without admitting guilt in connection with its 1968 "Sweepstakes" contest, McDonald's accepted the FTC's consent order requiring it to award all prizes offered in future promotions, insure that each winner receives his prize and disclose the number and exact nature of each prize and the odds of winning.

In addition to accepting the provisional consent order from McDonald's, the FTC tentatively accepted a separate order agreed to by McDonald's Restaurants and D'Arcy Advertising Co. of St. Louis. No settlement with D. L. Blair Corp. of New York City, the company which prepared and operated the sweepstakes, was announced.

Credit Practices

Mailed credit cards banned. The Federal Trade Commission (FTC) banned the mailing of unsolicited credit cards effective May 18, 1970, it was reported March 17. The ruling prohibited the mailing of a credit card to any party without prior consent or request, which, however, did not have to take written form. Although banks, airlines and other regulated "common carriers" were technically exempt from the rule, their cards would be subject to FTC scrutiny on an individual case basis.

Compromise legislation restricting the mailing of unsolicited credit cards was later passed by the Senate Oct. 9 and by the House Oct. 12 and was signed by the President Oct. 26.

Following the first FTC action under the new law, the FTC announced March 27, 1972 that the BP Oil Corp. had agreed not to distribute unsolicited credit cards.

The FTC complaint said BP was sending cards to customers who had charged their BP gasoline on other credit cards. The sales slips signed by those customers included a box that said: "Please issue me a BP credit card. Strike out if card not desired." The FTC said the box was not conspicuous and did not constitute an application as required by law.

Truth-in-lending action. In 1970 the FTC began action against alleged violations of the truth-in-lending law.

The FTC filed a formal complaint April 1, charging the Zale Corp., the country's largest jewelry retailer, with violating the truth-in-lending act. The complaint, the first of its kind to be issued under the act since it went into effect in July 1969, accused the corporation and a wholly owned subsidiary of 10 violations involving failures to inform customers properly and fully of finance charges on articles sold on credit.

In a related development, the FTC provisionally accepted a settlement in truth-in-lending charges against Chrysler Corp April 29. The company, a wholly owned subsidiary and their advertising agency agreed to a consent order that prohibited them from advertising amounts of monthly installment payments unless car dealers customarily arrange for those payments. The FTC Jan. 11, 1971 announced Chrysler's agreement to cease alleged truth-in-lending violations in its advertising of Simca and Sunbeam cars. The agency charged that Chrysler's advertisements cited monthly installment rates not usually used by dealers selling Simcas or Sunbeams and did not publish legally required credit information. The FTC accepted Chrysler's agreement to stop advertising installment payments unless commonly offered by dealers and to henceforth disclose the car's cash price, the down payment required, the number of payments and the interest rate.

Credit rules proposed. The FTC Oct. 8, 1970 proposed a series of regulations designed to protect consumers in dealing with computerized credit accounts. The proposal, which the agency said was the result of "thousands of letters from consumers" complaining of unfair billing practices, was made applicable to banks, retailers, oil companies and other issuers of credit cards. The creditors would be barred from reporting adverse credit information to credit bureaus or other businesses without first supplying the customer with a copy of the report and the names of intended recipients.

The new regulations would bar the creditor from including charges disputed in writing on future bills without investigating the customer's claims and making an explanation "in clear and definite terms." If a dispute were resolved in the customer's favor, interest or service payments on the disputed item would have to be credited to the customer.

Rules regarding billing practices were designed to give the customer recourse to challenge disputed charges, time enough to make payments before interest could be charged, prompt crediting of payments and the option of receiving refunds or credits on overpayments.

Stolen-card rules. New rules went into effect Jan. 25, 1971, making it more difficult to use a stolen credit card and limiting a card owner's liability for goods purchased on a stolen card. The rules, to be administered by the FTC, were mandated by the October 1970 truth-in-lending act amendments.

Immediately effective, when the amendment was signed into law, was a provision making it illegal to mail unsolicited credit cards. The newly effective rules required all new credit cards to bear some type of certain identification, such as a signature or color picture.

The rules also provided that a card holder could not be held responsible for more than $50 of unauthorized purchases made on a lost or stolen card. Companies had to inform card holders of the liability and had to provide self-addressed, prestamped notices to be returned if a credit card was lost or stolen.

FTC vs. mail order houses. The FTC accused two of the nation's largest mail order retailers Feb. 10, 1971 of deceptive advertising and violation of the Truth-in-Lending Act. The companies accused were Montgomery Ward & Co., Inc. and Spiegel, Inc.

The commission said both companies misled consumers about their methods of computing finance charges. In addition, the FTC said Spiegel advertised free trial offers and reduced prices without disclosing that customers had to satisfy credit requirements before products would be shipped. The commission said Spiegel also sold credit life insurance to new customers without requests by the customers.

The FTC accused Montgomery Ward of insufficient disclosures concerning liens placed on the property of home owners as security for home improvements.

'Holder-in-due-course' abuses. The FTC Jan. 21, 1971 issued a proposed rule to protect consumers in "holder-in-due-course" situations. This involved retail customers who buy products or services on installment-credit plans in cases when contracts were transferred to finance companies or other third parties for collection. Under the rule, the sales agreement would state that the holder of the contract was "subject to all defenses and claims" that a consumer could legally raise against the retailer.

The customer's legal "defenses" included the right to refuse payment or bring suit in case of fraud or a defective product. The proposed regulation would define as unfair and deceptive the transfer of an installment payment contract without protection of the consumer's claims against the original retailer.

A state act giving consumers similar protection in New Jersey cases was signed into law by Gov. William T. Cahill Jan. 11, 1972.

OTHER CONSUMER ISSUES

The bill gave greater legal recourse to consumers buying on installment plans whose contracts were sold by merchandise sellers to collection companies or agents. It gave the consumer the same legal recourse against the new holder of the note that he would have been entitled to against the seller.

The law also absolved the consumer of debt still owed at the time he filed a complaint and permitted him to recover whatever payment or deposit he might have already made.

Credit data abuse. The FTC Dec. 18, 1973 accused Retail Credit Co., the U.S.' largest credit reporting agency, of improper practices in both the gathering and use of data on individuals.

According to the FTC, the company used quota and salary systems which required its investigators to find a certain percentage of adverse information and put "a premium on the number of reports gathered at the expense of their accuracy." Company investigators, the FTC said, were allowed to gather information under "false pretexts," such as posing as insurance company representatives.

Stores kept money. The FTC charged Sept. 11, 1974 that five major department store chains had over the past five years retained more than $2.8 million in unclaimed credit balances owed to charge account customers. The proposed complaints were filed to set the stage for possible consent agreements halting the practice.

According to the FTC, customers who established credit balances would, over several months, receive statements showing the amounts in their favor. But unless the customers requested refunds or made offsetting purchases, the stores eventually cleared the accounts and kept the money. The FTC said the amounts owed individual customers were relatively small.

The five chains and amounts involved were: Gimbel Brothers Inc., $1,158,000; Genesco Inc., $740,000; Carter Hawley Hale Stores Inc., $509,740; Associated Dry Goods Corp., $405,275; and Rapid American Corp., $75,000.

Interest-rate data sought. Two consumer organizations sued Sept. 14, 1973 in federal district court in Washington against the Federal Reserve Board to force public disclosure of information related to interest rates charged on various types of consumer loans.

Consumers Union of the U.S. and San Francisco Consumer Action sought to publish the information so that consumers could compare costs before taking out loans. The Federal Reserve contended that release of the data would violate the Freedom of Information Act, which protected "trade secrets and commercial or financial information."

Consumer finance industry studied. The National Committee on Consumer Finance presented 85 recommendations Jan. 3, 1973 for making credit more available to the public and at more competitive prices.

The nine-member group, created by Congress in 1969 to undertake a $2 million study of the consumer credit industry, urged changes in federal and state laws to stimulate competition and provide consumer safeguards.

"Widespread instances" of discrimination against women were reported in the granting of credit. While disclaiming charges of racial discrimination, the report stated that "evidence does suggest that creditworthy consumers living in poverty areas have severe problems in obtaining credit."

Minnesota banks end rate-fixing. Eighteen Minnesota banks agreed, in consent judgments filed in U.S. District Court in Minneapolis Feb. 11, 1964, to end alleged rate-fixing practices. (The rates were the interest charges to smaller banks, and these rates determined consumer interest rates.) Three civil anti-trust suits had been filed against them by the Justice Department Feb. 8, 1963. Seventeen of the banks entered pleas of no contest Feb. 11

and were fined a total of $253,000 in parallel criminal cases filed by the department Feb. 11. The criminal cases were the first such actions brought against commercial banks under the anti-trust laws.

The three cases involved: (1) these 10 banks (fined a total of $126,000)—Northwestern National Bank, First National Bank, Midland National Bank and Marquette National Bank, all of Minneapolis; First National Bank, Northwestern National Bank, American National Bank, St. Paul; Stock Yards National Bank of South St. Paul; Northern City National Bank, First American National Bank, Duluth. (Criminal charges against an 11th bank, the Midway National Bank of St. Paul, were dismissed.) (2) These five banks and the First Bank Stock Corp., all of St. Paul (fined $70,000)—First National Bank of St. Paul, First Grand Avenue State Bank, First Security State Bank, Northwestern National Bank of St. Paul, Commercial State Bank. (3) These four Duluth banks and the Duluth Clearing House Association (fined $57,000)—First American National Bank, Northern City National Bank, Northwestern Bank of Commerce, Duluth National Bank.

Bank advertising rules—New standards for advertising rates of interest paid to depositors by banks and savings and loan associations were promulgated Dec. 18, 1966 by the Controller of the Currency, the Federal Deposit Insurance Corp., the Federal Home Loan Bank Board and the Federal Reserve Board. Among the rules: (a) The rate must be stated in terms of the simple annual rate of interest; (b) the word "profit" was barred from descriptions of interest on deposits; (c) it must be stated whether the rate advertised was payable only on accounts of a specified size or duration.

Price Manipulation

Electrical manufacturers guilty. Twenty-nine electrical equipment manufacturers and 44 of their officials, charged with rigging price bids during 1956–59 in the annual sale of over $1¾ billion worth of electrical goods to U.S. government agencies and others, changed their pleas Dec. 8, 1960 to guilty or to nolo contendere. They pleaded before U.S. District Judge J. Cullen Ganey in Philadelphia. Westinghouse Vice President W. C. Rowland was the only defendant to plead not guilty. The government dropped charges against General Electric Vice President Arthur F. Vinson on the ground that it lacked evidence of his participation in the alleged bid rigging.

The 19 companies pleading guilty to one or more indictments: GE, Westinghouse Electric Corp., Allis-Chalmers Manufacturing Co., Federal Pacific Electric Co., I-T-E Circuit Breaker Co., Clark Controller Co., Cutler-Hammer, Inc., Square D Co., Ingersoll-Rand Corp., Foster-Wheeler Manufacturing Co., Worthington Corp., McGraw-Edison Co., Southern States Equipment Corp., H. K. Porter Co., Allen-Bradley Co., Wagner Electric Co., Schwager-Wood Corp. and Maloney Electric Co. All except Schwager-Wood, Allen-Bradley, Clark Controller, Ingersoll-Rand, Wheeler, Worthington and Foster-Wheeler also pleaded nolo contendere in other cases.

The 10 firms pleading only noto contendere to one or more charges: Carrier Corp., Sangamo Electric Co., Ohio Brass Co., Cornell-Dubilier Electric Corp., Porcelain Insulator Co., Lapp Insulator Co., Joslyn Manufacturing & Supply Co., A. B. Chance Co., Hubbard Co., Kuhlmann Electric Co.

The 29 companies and 44 officials were fined a total of $1,924,500 (the company share was $1,787,000) by Ganey Feb. 6–7, 1961. In addition, seven of the officials were sentenced Feb. 6 to serve 30-day jail terms starting Feb. 13. Twenty-three others were given suspended 30-day terms Feb. 6–7 and were put on five years' probation. The penalties were imposed under 20 separate indictments.

Ganey, in a pre-sentence statement, pointed out that "virtually every large manufacturer of electrical equipment in the industry" had been implicated. "This is a shocking indictment of a vast section of our economy," he said. He held that "the real blame is to be laid at the doorstep of the corporate defendants and those [top corporation officials] who guide and direct their policy."

General Electric, the heaviest-penalized

corporate defendant (fined a total of $437,000 under 19 indictments), denied in a Feb. 7 statement that the actions of its 17 indicted officials conformed with GE's "corporate policy." Their acts were "in deliberate violation of General Electric directive policy," the statement said.

The Senate Antitrust & Monopoly Subcommittee held hearings, during April, May and June 1961, under the chairmanship of Sen. Estes Kefauver (D, Tenn.), in an inquiry into the electrical price-fixing conspiracy.

George E. Burens, ex-General Electric vice president who had been fined and jailed after conviction in the Philadelphia price-fixing trial, testified Apr. 25 that GE Board Chrmn. Ralph J. Cordiner had known about the conspiracy at least as early as 1952. Burens said a GE executive vice president, the late Henry V. Erben, had told him in 1952 of a conversation Erben had had with Cordiner about agreements with competitors to help stabilize prices. Burens testified that Erben had said he had asked Cordiner not to stop him from reaching such agreements and had promised that Cordiner "would never hear about it." (Cordiner Apr. 25 issued a statement calling Burens' testimony about him "false.") Burens also testified that former GE Pres. Robert Paxton had once told him he could "see no reason in the world why you can't meet with these people [competitors] and do business with them."

Clarence Burke, former general manager of GE's Switch-Gear Division at Pittsfield, Mass., testified Apr. 25 that Paxton had suggested to him in 1946 that he get the competitors "to agree to eliminate stocks [inventories] the same way as you get them to agree on prices." Paul Hartig, ex-general manager of GE's insulator department, had testified Apr. 20 that Paxton had been aware of the price-rigging conspiracy at least a year before the Philadelphia trial. Hartig said "it was part of the job" to attend secret price-fixing sessions with competitors in 1955.

(Paxton Apr. 25 issued a statement saying the Justice Department "neither charged nor claimed" that he had any "knowledge of" activity in the price-fixing conspiracy.)

Burens and Burke testified that they had conferred with GE Vice Pres. Arthur F. Vinson to argue against continuing the meetings with competitors because the competitors were making "suckers out of" GE and "double-crossing" on agreements. Burke said Vinson's reply was that he had "'the assurance of Mr. Monteith [vice president] of Westinghouse that from now on it will work'." (Vinson sent Kefauver a letter in which he denied knowledge of the illegal practices.)

Among highlights of the hearings:

Apr. 17—Donald Ray Jenkins, sales manager for Westinghouse Electric Corp.'s medium turbine production, testified that in 1956-58 he had attended 18 meetings at which competing companies decided which would submit the lowest bids for contracts.

Apr. 18—GE officials John Peters, 42, and R. B. Sellers testified that the bickering between companies and foreign competition had prompted the decision to end illegal meetings to fix turbine generator prices. The meetings took place from 1951 to 1959, Peters said.

Apr. 19—L. B. Gezon, engineering manager of GE's low-voltage Switch-Gear department in Philadelphia, testified that Frank E. Stehlik, who was named in the Philadelphia indictment, had become his boss in 1956 and immediately ordered the competitors' meetings ended. But, Gezon continued, Stehlik, apparently reluctantly, had ordered the meetings resumed in 1958. "I presume he had orders from above," Gezon said. He testified that there were many complaints about "chiseling" and "fudging" on the rigged bids during biweekly sessions with GE's 4 chief competitors.

Apr. 26—George E. Burens and H. Frank Hentschel, both of whom had been fired by GE after being convicted at the Philadelphia electric price-fixing trial, testified that GE Vice Pres. Arthur F. Vinson had ordered price-fixing meetings with competitors in 1957 or 1958.

Apr. 27—Vinson, accompanied by counsel Gerhard Gesell, testified that prior to the fall of 1959, when the Philadelphia grand jury had been called, he had not been aware of price-fixing collusion with competitors.

Vinson was questioned about a 1958 Philadelphia luncheon at which, Burens, Hentschel, Clarence E. Burke and Frank E. Stehlik had testified, Vinson had ordered and approved their price-fixing activities. Vinson testified that "there was no such luncheon."

Committee Chrmn. Estes Kefauver (D., Tenn.) interrupted Vinson's testimony to call ex-GE divisional Vice Pres. Raymond W. Smith. Smith testified that Vinson had met in Boston in June 1958 with ex-GE Pres. Robert Paxton and Westinghouse Electric Corp. Pres. Mark W. Cresap and Vice Pres. A. C. Monteith. Smith said Vinson had told him afterwards that an "acrimonious" discussion of the general price situation had taken place but that Paxton had "cleared the air" by warning Cresap that Westinghouse's "price-cutting" was "the main upsetting factor in the market" and that GE "was willing to be more than competitive" if it continued. Smith said it was his impression that the meeting had resulted in a decision to renew the temporarily discontinued price-fixing meetings. He said he never had doubted that Vinson had been aware that he and other GE managers had been meeting with competitors.

Recalled to the stand, Vinson said the Boston meeting had had nothing to do with prices but had been a social meeting. Westinghouse spokesmen also denied the meeting had been anything but social. Vinson said Smith's "impression" was a "misunderstanding." "I may be naive, but I'm sure I'm telling the truth," he added.

May 2—Ex-GE Vice Pres. William S. Ginn, who also had been fired after his conviction at the Philadelphia trial, testified that GE Board Chrmn. Ralph J. Cordiner and Paxton had had no part in the conspiracy. Ginn said he had started to meet with competitors illegally in 1946, that the meetings had ended in 1949 but had resumed in 1950 on orders of the late ex-GE Vice Pres. Henry V. Erben. Ginn said Erben cautioned him not to tell Paxton of the meetings because Paxton did not understand "these things." Ginn said Cordiner's advice to him in 1954 to comply with antitrust laws had "lasted about as long as it took me to get . . . to Mr. Erben's office." Ginn said he complied with the advice when it was reoffered by Cordiner in 1957.

May 3—Paxton testified that he had been "pretty damn dumb" not to have known more about the conspiracy. "If I had," he said, GE's recent history "might have been very different." "I contented myself," he continued, "with telling them I was unalterably opposed to this monkey business and that they were to have no truck with that sort of thing. . . . It never occurred to me that a man under me was doing what I told him not to do."

He said the company in May 1946 had forbidden sales executives from membership in the National Electric Manufacturing Association. Paxton said he "was aware that the company wanted to minimize the risk [of price-fixing meetings] and to that extent I was aware" of such meetings. He testified that in 1947 he had told his subordinates "to make damn sure there was no misunderstanding—that there were to be no meetings with competitors." Ginn, he said, had questioned his order, saying "I didn't see you wink." Paxton said he gave him specific instructions not to meet with competitors. "But," he said, "I didn't concern myself with what he had been doing in the past." Paxton testified that after he had transferred Ginn away from sales activities, "I said to him, 'I hope you haven't compromised yourself' and he said, 'I'm afraid I have.' I said to him, 'I think you're a damn fool.'"

He had not reported the incident, Paxton said, because it was "out of my jurisdiction." "If there had ever been any transgression by Ginn or anybody else who worked for me," he said, "I would have reported it."

Paxton and Kefauver clashed over testimony concerning a meeting at which Raymond Smith, in the presence of Paxton, Vinson and a GE counsel, had pointed his thumb at Vinson when the counsel asked him if any company officials had been aware of the price-fixing conspiracy. Smith then left the room, and Vinson categorically denied his accusation. Paxton said Smith's answers had been evasive when he questioned him about the accusation several days later. Kefauver accused Paxton of "trying to cover up for Vinson" and said "any 2-bit lawyer would have known to get immediately at the accusation but everyone remained silent until the accuser had gone." Paxton shouted that "there has never been any need to cover up" for Vinson.

May 4—Landon Fuller, manager of Westinghouse Electric Corp's East Pittsburgh (Pa.) Switchgear Division, and J. T. Thompson, a sales manager who worked for Fuller, testified that they had participated in secret price-fixing meetings with competitors "on and off" since the 1930s because they had wanted to protect the company against "sharp purchasing practices," keep workers employed during slow periods and ensure continuation of costly research programs. Fuller said his illegal activity had been "entirely on my own" without orders from superiors. Both men had been convicted at the Philadelphia trial.

Thompson said he had "squared" his conscience by telling himself that the meetings, albeit illegal, were "not criminal" and that he was not "damaging someone." "I still don't think we overcharged anyone," he added.

General Electric Pres. Ralph J. Cordiner testified June 5 that GE was not proud of its history of anti-trust violations, but that he did not "acquiesce" with Chrmn. Estes Kefauver's (D., Tenn.) description of that record as "corporate disgrace." He said the knowledge of GE's involvement in the conspiracy was "humbling," and he accepted "my share of responsibility" for it "even though I did not know of these secret violations of the law or condone such acts."

Cordiner told the Senators June 6 that GE had rejected a Justice Department proposal that GE and other major electrical equipment manufacturers join in a consent decree banning "unreasonably low prices" in the industry. Westinghouse Electric and other big manufacturers were reported to have agreed with GE. The Justice Department's stand was that excessive price cuts could decrease competition by ruining small firms.

Westinghouse Electric Corp. Pres. Mark W. Cresap Jr. testified May 17-18 that his management assumed responsibility for his company's rôle in the conspiracy and was not trying to make "scapegoats of a few." He said the company had created an advisory board—"to review our procedures and counsel us"—composed of Harvard Law School dean Erwin N. Griswold, Yale Law School dean Eugene V. Rostow, Prof. S. Chesterfield Oppenheim of Michigan Law School and a Brookings Institution economist, Dr. A. D. H. Kaplan. Cresap insisted that "competitive price pressures" rather than "conspiracy" often caused identical prices and bids.

John K. Hodnette, Westinghouse's executive vice-president, testified May 10 that top management was unaware of the conspiracy and had failed in its responsibilities in not instructing its employes about the anti-trust laws.

OTHER CONSUMER ISSUES

Describing these laws as "the foundation of the free-enterprise system," he opposed changing them. He said the company's new "living policy . . . to get compliance all the way down the line" included (a) legal orientation programs for pricing officials, who would be required to sign (every 3 months) certificates disavowing collusion, (b) periodic examinations by certified public accountants. He said employes were notified that antitrust violations were acts "of disloyalty" to Westinghouse.

Allen-Bradley Co. (Milwaukee) Pres. Fred Loock and I-T-E Circuit Breaker Co. (Philadelphia) Pres. Max Scott conceded May 11 that they had met in the past with competitors to fix prices and synchronize increases. Loock, who had been fined on conviction in the Philadelphia indictment, said the increases often were made to "recover cost increases." Scott, who had not been indicted, testified that he had met with former GE division manager George E. Burens about 3 years previously and had refused Burens' request that I-T-E raise its selling prices to catalog levels.

Frank Roby, Federal Pacific Electric Co. (Newark, N.J.) president, testified May 16 and denied Scott's testimony that Roby had told him he thought GE Executive Vice Pres. Arthur F. Vinson was 100% "involved" in the conspiracy. Roby said he had never attended a price-fixing meeting with Vinson and had never heard of Vinson attending one.

Former GE department manager William F. Oswalt told the probers May 17 that he had phoned Westinghouse employes to try to avert a "devastating price war" in direct-current electric motors in 1958 and 1959.

(GE counsel Gerhard A. Gesell notified the subcommittee June 6 that GE had rejected, as "unreasonable, excessive and burdensome," Kefauver's request in May that GE submit detailed financial data for the subcommittee's probe into "administered" pricing. Westinghouse Electric rejected a similar request.)

FCC bans limit on low private-line rates. The Federal Communications Commission (FCC) ordered the American Telephone and Telegraph Co. and Western Union June 12, 1970 to extend to all private line users the firms' special Telpak rates, a discount package applying to customers with large private-line demands.

The commission said that existing Telpak privileges "are unduly discriminatory because they permit, without justification, certain private-line service users to combine their requirements for the sole purpose of obtaining the benefits of volume rate discounts, while the same sharing privileges are denied to all other private-line users."

FCC drops AT&T study—The FCC announced Dec. 23, 1971 its decision by a 4-2 vote to drop a full-scale investigation of the American Telephone & Telegraph Co. (AT&T), for lack of staff and funds.

The investigation would have determined whether the FCC should accept AT&T's expense figures in ruling on a requested long distance rate increase. The investigation would have covered prices and profits of Western Electric Co., an AT&T subsidiary, investment practices and overall efficiency.

Dissenting Commissioner Nicholas Johnson charged "the FCC has not been regulating the Bell System [AT&T] as the law and common sense requires it to do."

The FCC would now accept AT&T's own cost estimates.

Sohio accused of price fixing. The Justice Department filed suit in Cleveland Sept. 18, 1970 against the Standard Oil Co. (Ohio), charging the company with fixing prices at arbitrarily high levels on gasoline and other products sold under the Sohio label. It accused the company of conspiring through secret agreements with service stations not owned by the company and operated by commission managers to set prices for Sohio products. The alleged agreements required these stations, regarded by the Justice Department as independent businesses, to use the same prices as Sohio-operated stations.

The company said it would not discontinue its commission manager station operations, which it had used for a number of years and regarded as a "proper method of marketing."

Gasoline & oil price-fixing charged. Among 1974's price cases:

In New York, seven major oil firms pleaded not guilty Sept. 5 to criminal charges that they had conspired to fix gasoline prices during 1972 with the aim of driving independent gasoline dealers out of business. Named as defendants were Exxon, Mobil, Gulf, Texaco, Amoco, Shell and Sun.

It was alleged that they "refrained from competing among themselves in terms of price in areas where independent marketers were not a significant competitive factor, while concentrating discriminatory rebates in areas where independent marketers were a significant competitive factor."

Three of the oil firms—Exxon, Gulf and Mobil—were also accused of agreeing to thwart "competition in public bidding for contracts for the sale of gasoline to" the state and New York City.

A civil complaint had been filed by the state against the same seven defendants in 1973.

The attorney general of Kansas filed suit Oct. 8 against 12 large oil companies. They were charged in federal district court with controlling prices and eliminating competition from smaller, independent rivals. "These companies are organized in a manner which enables them to control the flow of petroleum and its derivatives from the well-head through a multilevel system to the eventual consumer at the pump," the suit charged.

Oil firms accused of restraint on accessories. The FTC Oct. 31, 1974 accused four major oil firms—Exxon Corp., Standard Oil Co. (Ohio) Standard Oil Co. (California) and Amoco Oil Co., a subsidiary of Standard Oil Co. (Indiana)—of eliminating competition among themselves by conspiring to offer a common line of tires, batteries and other automobile accessories.

The antitrust charges in the FTC's proposed complaint related to their joint ownership in the Atlas Supply Co. According to the agency, the four oil firms agreed that at least 50% of the auto accessories sold in their gasoline stations would be Atlas brands. Officials of the four companies were also accused of jointly setting prices for the Atlas items. The FTC said that they also agreed on the types of products that would be allowed to use the Atlas name, and on advertising and guarantees provided for Atlas products. Atlas products were sold exclusively by the four oil companies.

The FTC sought divestiture of the oil companies' interests in Atlas or asked that three of the four sell Atlas to the highest bidder among them.

15 oil firms roll back prices. Fifteen oil companies agreed to price rollbacks totaling about $77 million to correct alleged overcharges to customers, the Federal Energy Administration (FEA) announced Dec. 17, 1974. The FEA also disallowed about $375 million in "banked" costs claimed under a controversial agency ruling, since revised, permitting the oil industry to make a double recovery on costs. These expenses could have been passed on to consumers.

The FEA ordered price rollbacks of $10 million from Standard Oil Co. (Ohio), $6.9 million from Exxon Corp. and $600,000 from Mobil Oil Corp.

The remaining adjustments were settled voluntarily or through consent agreements:

Kerr-McGee Corp., $12.8 million in rollbacks, $2.9 million in cost reductions; Skelly Oil Co., $6.2 million cost reductions; Murphy Oil Corp., $1.4 million cost reductions; Phillips Petroleum Co., $31.7 million cost reductions, $215,000 rollbacks; Amerada-Hess Corp., $6.7 million cost reductions; Texaco Inc., $25.5 million cost reductions; Delta Refining Co., $157,000 cost reductions; Sun Oil Co., $700,000 refund to identifiable customers; Getty Oil Co., $300,000 rollbacks and $940,000 cost reductions; Shell Oil Co., $1 million cost reductions; Charter Oil Co., $4 million rollbacks; and Atlantic-Richfield Co., $1.5 million rollbacks and $8.1 million cost reductions.

The FEA revised its price regulations Nov. 6 to limit the amount of "banked" costs that oil companies could pass on to consumers in any single month to 10% of the total costs that they had delayed

OTHER CONSUMER ISSUES

passing through by Oct. 31. The action was designed to protect the public from sudden large price increases in any one month. For competitive reasons, oil companies had been accumulating banked costs and postponing recovery of these expenses.

Oil refiners indicted for price-fixing. A federal grand jury filed an indictment March 19, 1975 in federal court in Los Angeles charging six oil refiners with conspiracy to fix wholesale gasoline prices in five Western states. The government also filed a companion civil suit against the refiners.

The indictment said the alleged conspiracy had brought to "artificial and noncompetitive levels" the wholesale price of "rebrand gasoline"—the kind sold in service stations under a trademark or brand name not owned or controlled by an oil refiner—in 1970 and 1971 in California, Oregon, Washington, Nevada and Arizona.

Those named as defendants were Phillips Petroleum Co. of Oklahoma; Douglas Oil Co., of California, a subsidiary of Continental Oil Corp., of Texas; Powerline Oil Co., of California; Fletcher Oil & Refining Co., of California; Golden Eagle Refining Co., Inc., of California, a subsidiary of Ultramar Co., Ltd., of London, England; and MacMillan Ring-Free Co., of New York.

FTC charges soft drink firms. The Federal Trade Commission (FTC) attacked a system of exclusive area franchising in drafts of complaints against seven major soft-drink companies Jan. 15, 1971. The complaints, the result of an investigation of corporate franchising and licensing, charged that the companies kept retail prices artificially high and curbed competition by restricting the sales territories of local bottlers handling the same brands.

The companies cited in the proposed complaints were the Coca-Cola Co. (Atlanta), PepsiCo Inc. (Purchase, N.Y.), Royal Crown Cola Co. (Columbus, Ga.), Seven-Up Co. (St. Louis), Crush International Ltd. (Toronto-based but with offices in Evanston, Ill.), National Industries Inc. (Louisville) and Dr. Pepper Co. (Dallas). The seven companies and their 3,000 franchised bottling companies made up more than 70% of the nation's soft drink sales.

8 dye makers fined. Eight chemical companies which had pleaded no contest to federal antitrust charges were fined a total of $360,500 by U.S. district court in Newark, N.J. Dec. 15, 1974. They had been accused of conspiring to fix dye prices.

Two of the defendants, E. I. du Pont de Nemours & Co. and Verona Corp., were fined $50,000 each. Fines imposed on the other six defendants ranged from $40,000 to $45,000 each. The companies assessed the latter fines were: Allied Chemical Corp.; American Cyanamid Co.; BASF Wyandotte Corp.; CIBA-GEIGY Corp.; Crompton & Knowles Corp.; and GAF Corp. A ninth defendant, American Color & Chemical Corp., pleaded not guilty Oct. 18.

According to the one-count indictment, du Pont officials discussed a "proposed across-the-board increase in the price of dyes with each of the other defendants." By the end of 1970, all had agreed to a price increase. Du Pont initiated the action in January 1971, announcing a 10% across-the-board price rise, which was quickly followed by similar announcements from each of the other defendants.

Sales of dyes totaled about $480 million in 1971, with the defendants accounting for about $300 million of those sales.

Engineers guilty of price fixing. The National Society of Professional Engineers was convicted Dec. 19, 1974 of violating federal antitrust laws by prohibiting its 69,000 members from bidding competitively for contracts.

Judge John L. Smith Jr. of U.S. District Court in Washington ruled that a provision in the group's code of ethics banning competitive bidding was "in every respect a classic example of price fixing in violation of the Sherman Act."

The ban had been enforced by the society since 1964. In defending the practice, the engineers had contended that they were not engaged in trade or commerce, but in a "learned profession," which was exempt from antitrust action because it was state regulated.

Judge Smith rejected the argument, saying, "It would be a dangerous form of elitism, indeed, to dole out exemptions to our antitrust laws merely on the basis of the education level needed to practice a given profession, or for that matter, the impact which the profession has on society's health and welfare."

Uniform legal fees barred. The Supreme Court ruled 8-0 June 16, 1975 that the setting of uniform minimum fee schedules by lawyers was price fixing and a violation of U.S. antitrust laws. Chief Justice Warren E. Burger, author of the court's opinion, called the fee schedules "a classic illustration of price fixing" and "a pricing system that consumers could not realistically escape."

The classic argument, Burger said, that professions could not be considered "trade or commerce" lost "some of its force when used to support the fee control activities involved here." Although the court rejected the contention that Congress had intended to exempt all "learned professions" from antitrust regulation, it cautioned against interpreting the ruling too broadly. "It would be unrealistic to view the practices of professions as interchangeable with other business activities, and automatically to apply to the professions antitrust concepts which originated in other areas," Burger wrote in a footnote to his opinion.

The ruling stemmed from a suit originally brought by a Reston, Va. couple, who discovered they could not find a Fairfax County, Va. attorney to conduct a title examination search for their home for anything less than $522.50, the minimum 1% of the value of their $50,000 home, which was the fee "suggested" by the county bar association. Ruth and Lewis Goldfarb, the homebuyers, subsequently brought a class action suit against the Fairfax and Virginia state bars on behalf of home purchasers in their area who had been charged title-examination fees in accordance with a fee schedule.

Two gypsum makers plead no contest. Flintkote Co. and Kaiser Gypsum Co. Inc. pleaded no contest Jan. 16, 1975 to price-fixing charges and were fined the maximum amount, $50,000 each, by U.S. District Court Judge Hubert I. Teitelbaum. Seven individual defendants also pleaded no contest: three were fined $40,000, given six-month suspended jail sentences and placed on probation; four others were fined $20,000, given 30-day suspended sentences and also placed on probation.

Four other gypsum makers and three executives pleaded not guilty to the government's charges that over a 14-year period they had conspired to fix and stabilize gypsum prices and set the terms of sale and packaging gypsum board.

Clothiers fined after pleading no contest. A judge in U.S. District Court in New York Feb. 27, 1975 imposed the maximum antitrust fine on three New York City clothing stores accused of fixing the prices of women's clothing.

The stores, Saks Fifth Avenue, Bergdorf Goodman and Genesco Inc., which operated Bonwit Teller, had entered not guilty pleas before the court in November 1974, but filed a motion to change the pleas to no contest the following month. (Increases in maximum antitrust penalties took effect during December 1974. Alleged price-fixing conspiracies carried on before that period were subject to the previous maximum fine.)

In fining each defendant $50,000, Judge Harry F. Werker said that the stores' management had "bilked" the public, adding that "it seems to me that [the public's] patronage may have been misplaced."

The defendants had all been indicted Oct. 7 by a federal grand jury after a two-year investigation. They were charged with conspiring since the late 1960s to fix retail prices for women's ready to wear clothing by adopting uniform mark up lists. They were also accused of compelling clothing manufacturers to use the same mark up lists in devising their "suggested retail prices," thereby forcing other retailers to maintain the same high prices.

Revlon cleared of price fixing charges. U.S. District Court Judge Inzer B. Wyatt March 7, 1975 ruled Revlon, Inc. not guilty of federal antitrust charges filed in 1962. Revlon had been accused of conspiring to fix prices in restraint of trade.

However, Wyatt granted the government's request for an injunction barring the cosmetic maker from restricting the rights of beauty products jobbers and retailers in reselling its products. Until 1963, Revlon had limited the jobbers' sales territory and set conditions on resale.

The case had been tried without a jury in 1967.

Car-rental price accusation. The Federal Trade Commission June 12, 1975 accused the nation's three largest car rental firms of having conspired to monopolize automobile rentals and keep prices artificially high at airports throughout the U.S.

The companies specified in the FTC complaint were Hertz Corp., a subsidiary of RCA Corp.; Avis Rent-A-Car System Inc., a unit of Avis Inc.; and National Car Rental System Inc., subsidiary of Household Finance Corp.

According to James T. Halverson, an official of the FTC, the three companies named had developed since 1968 a "highly concentrated, non-competitive market structure" which forced U.S. consumers "to pay substantially higher prices for the rental of passenger automobiles." The arrangement allowed the firms to obtain "profits and returns on investment substantially in excess of those they would have obtained in competitively structured" markets. Halverson said the three firms, which in 1968 controlled 99% and in 1973 96% of a market now believed to exceed $500 million a year, had submitted to airports common bid specifications and contractual provisions designed to exclude their smaller competitors. They were able, for example, he said, to get airports to require that car rental concessionaires have a national reservation network and credit card arrangements. In addition, each company was charged with having entered into an "exclusive arrangement" for advertising subsidies with the three major automobile manufacturers—Hertz with the Ford Motor Corp., Avis with Chrysler Corp., and National with General Motors Corp.—although the auto makers were not named as respondents in the complaint. Halverson said one of the rental firms had received subsidies from Detroit of up to $5 million a year.

Other Developments

Movers' rules tightened. The Interstate Commerce Commission March 5, 1975 issued new rules to govern the interstate shipment of household goods. The regulations dealt with such practices as underestimation of moving costs and delays in pickup and delivery that had generated 5,000–6,000 complaints a year to the agency by consumers.

Despite requests by the industry for hearings and delays, the new regulations went into effect May 1. The Defense Department, the largest user of moving services in the U.S., had also requested a delay because it feared chaos in the industry. The department said, however, that it supported the rules.

Under the regulations, movers could not demand cash-on-delivery payment of more than the amount estimated in advance plus 10%. The householder would have 15 days in which to pay any charge in excess of the estimated cost. In the past, householders complained that movers had demanded cash payments several hundred dollars in excess of costs estimated previous to the move. If the householder was unable to produce the additional cash, he was charged waiting rates until he could pay, or goods were put in storage at the customer's expense until the full bill was paid.

Under the new rules on prompt delivery, a mover was required to pick up and deliver goods on dates promised or within a period specified to the customer or else promptly notify the householder of a delay and arrange for a new date. Violators would be subject to a $500 fine, and movers who made false or incomplete representations to the customer would be subject to a $5,000 fine.

(The ICC Jan. 4, 1973 ordered the Allied Van Lines, Inc., the nation's largest movers, to pay $20,000 in fines and suspended the company's operating rights to move nonhousehold goods for 15 days.

(The disciplinary action was taken after customer complaints that the movers had violated several consumer protection rules, such as providing estimates, reporting underestimates and delivering goods on schedule.)

Mail insurance curb. The Supreme Court ruled, 6-3, March 28, 1960 that the federal government could regulate insurance companies doing interstate business by mail even if the companies were located in states that had insurance regulation laws. The decision upheld an FTC order to the Travelers Health Association of Omaha, Neb. to inform prospective customers more clearly of certain policy provisions. Travelers, licensed in Nebraska and Virginia, also mailed circulars to residents of other states. When it appealed the order, the U.S. 8th Circuit Court of Appeals refused to enforce the FTC order on the ground that the 1945 McCarran-Ferguson Act deprived the FTC of jurisdiction over unfair insurance practice cases in states (such as Nebraska) with laws regulating such practices.

Raiders score small plane safety. As part of a continuing investigation of government agencies, consumer advocate Ralph Nader's group, Nader's Raiders, charged that small-plane manufacturers were producing "the most lethal of the major forms of transportation in the U.S.," it was reported Jan. 22, 1970. The report charged the Federal Aviation Administration (FAA) with inadequate supervision of the industry.

The report, compiled by Princeton University engineering graduates James T. Bruce and John B. Draper, said the 125,000 private aircraft in operation lacked many crash-surviving features of cars. It said 1,400 fatalities involving small planes had occurred in 1968. The report said accident statistics suggested that at least 70% of the small planes then in production would eventually have an accident.

According to the report, FAA only recently began making shoulder harnesses mandatory in new private plane models. It said FAA in 1964 and 1965 had rejected suggestions by the Civil Aeronautics Board (CAB), then responsible for air safety, to require harnesses. The report asserted that FAA had failed to require two auto safety regulations—padded instrument panels and limited rearward movement of the control wheel or strong seat belts. Other weaknesses cited involved strapping down cargo that might strike the pilot or passengers in a crash and rules on airplane structure strength. According to the report, Beech Aircraft Corp. had taken steps in the 1950s to provide shoulder harnesses, but had given up its efforts because of insufficient market acceptance.

Airline damages to Nader. A federal court in Washington Oct. 18, 1973 ordered Allegheny Airlines to pay consumer advocate Ralph Nader $25,010 for "bumping" him from a scheduled flight from Washington to Hartford, Conn. in April. Nader had held a confirmed reservation but was denied a seat because the flight had been oversold.

Because of the incident, Nader was prevented from addressing a rally sponsored by the Connecticut Citizens' Action Group. The group was awarded $25,051 in punitive damages.

The airline carried out bumping practices "wantonly ... and with malice," the court ruled. According to Nader's attorney, Allegheny had bumped nearly 16,000 passengers within the last three years and 944 in April.

In a related development, Nader and his aviation consumer action project filed suit Oct. 26 against Alexander P. Butterfield,

OTHER CONSUMER ISSUES

administrator of the Federal Aviation Administration (FAA). Nader asked federal district court in Washington to prohibit the FAA's use of X-ray security checks at airports.

Because the FAA had failed to consider the environmental impact of such an operation, had failed to set minimum standards for X-ray machines, and had failed to allow an adequate period for public comment on the proposed practice, Nader contended that millions of airline passengers and personnel were being exposed to a health hazard.

Octane rating rule issued. The Federal Trade Commission (FTC) issued a regulation Dec. 30, 1970, effective June 28, 1971, that would require the posting of octane ratings on gasoline pumps in 80% of the nation's gas stations. The commission said the rule would cover all but independently owned service stations, exempt because of uncertainty over their status under interstate commerce.

Octane ratings on gasolines, which varied from 91 to 95 for regular gas and up to 101 for premium gas, would be used to determine the antiknock quality of various products. The higher the rating, the greater the protection against engine knocking, which could cut efficiency and cause damage. However, the FTC said the average motorist paid $50 to $75 extra a year for gas with unnecessarily high octane ratings.

The FTC added that "the use of a gasoline which is either too high or too low in octane rating for that particular automobile tends to create excessive emissions which contribute to air pollution."

Cosmetic industry rules. The FDA accepted in principle a proposal by the cosmetic industry for voluntary filing of product ingredients for disclosure to doctors, it was reported April 9, 1972.

The proposed regulations, according to the New York Times April 10, said "mandatory regulations could result in lengthy litigation that would seriously delay FDA from obtaining the type of information expected." The agency was considering requirements for "labeling of sensitizing ingredients," but ruled out mandatory listing of all ingredients on labels.

A manufacturer requesting confidential treatment of any filed statement would have to justify its request under the proposed rules, with FDA making the final decision. The agency warned that if the voluntary procedure failed to provide adequate enforcement of the Food, Drug and Cosmetic Act, compulsory rules might be imposed.

An estimated 60,000 cosmetic reaction injuries were incurred by Americans annually.

The FDA issued a ban on using mercury in cosmetics, with the exception of those used near the eye, it was reported June 30.

Mercury was used in concentrations of up to 3% in skin-lightening creams, and at lower levels as a preservative in other types of cosmetics. The element was known to cause neurological damage.

Eye-area cosmetics would be permitted to contain low levels of mercury, which was an effective preventative against a harmful bacteria that could cause blindness.

After less than 10 months of experience with voluntary ingredient disclosure, the FDA proposed Feb. 7, 1973 that, except for trade secrets, all cosmetic ingredients be listed on package labels. The final order was issued Oct. 11, 1973. The FDA acted after the Consumer Federation of America had filed a petition urging full disclosure.

The FDA also directed manufacturers to report consumer complaints to the agency twice a year to determine the need for further regulatory action against possible hazards from adverse reactions.

The effective date of the rules was delayed until March 31, 1975 to allow companies to clear out existing stocks.

The FDA June 4, 1975 announced final regulations to require the testing of cosmetics sold with claims that they had low incidence of allergic reactions.

To be labeled "hypoallergenic" and carry the claim that it is "less likely to cause adverse reactions than some competing products," the agency said, the product must be backed by scientific studies showing that it caused significantly fewer adverse reactions in human test volunteers than a competing product having at least 10% of the market. The agency said the test data would be made available to the public.

Such products currently on the market would be given a two-year period for testing. New products would be required to meet the new rules.

Land promotion curbs set. The Department of Housing and Urban Development (HUD) Sept. 4, 1973 announced regulations designed to prevent deceptive promotional practices in land sales in interstate commerce. A HUD spokesman said the regulations, effective Dec. 1, would apply to the 2,700 developers registered with the department who had 300 or more lots or more than $500,000 in annual sales.

One key rule required that the property report given to prospective buyers include a notice that the buyer could revoke a sales contract within 48 hours after signing. A document waiving the revocation right would have to be separate from the contract, ending the industry practice of placing the waiver in the body of the contract.

Sellers would also be required to provide audited and certified statements of their financial condition, as well as more detailed information and timetables on promised property improvements.

Refunds—The FTC March 26, 1974 announced tentative acceptance of a consent order setting refunds and barring deceptive sales practices by GAC Corp., a major land developer based in Miami. The FTC said it viewed the settlement as a possible pattern for other agreements in its nationwide investigation of deceptive land sales.

Under the refund plan, involving purchases since July 1968 in Arizona and Florida, GAC would return $2.85 million to purchasers who had defaulted on contracts later challenged by the FTC and forfeited their rights. The company would also offer land worth about $14 million to some 11,000 other purchasers of allegedly worthless land.

According to the FTC complaint leading to the agreement, GAC had misrepresented the degree of development of many tracts. The FTC said some customers had bought land sight unseen and found later that their land was under water. The company also often overstated transportation and utilities accessibility and investment value of land, the FTC charged.

Under the consent order, which technically did not constitute an admission of wrongdoing by GAC, deceptive promotional practices would be stopped, contracts would include warnings to buyers and a 10-day cancellation period.

Charges—The FTC March 17, 1975 announced separate complaints against two major land companies charging "unfair and deceptive practices" in the sale of lots from large tracts in five states. The companies named were the Horizon Corp. of Tucson, Ariz. and Amrep Corp. of New York City. The properties involved covered 900 square miles in Arizona, Florida, Missouri, New Mexico and Texas, where approximately 215,000 customers had purchased property since the 1950s at prices ranging from $2,000 to $5,000 a lot.

The complaints charged misrepresentation about the "all-inclusive" purchase price of lots and about development of sites. The FTC proposed an end to such practices, a "cooling-off" period in which purchasers could cancel contracts without penalty and a limit on a buyer's liability in event of default. It also sought contract warnings in bold-face, for example, that certain lots should not be considered as an investment since there was virtually no resale market for the land.

Both companies named defended their business practices as legal and proper.

Condominium abuses seen—The State of Florida filed charges against a developer of condominium apartments Sept. 5, 1974 in an effort to break long-term recreation leases which were reportedly costing consumers millions of dollars and providing windfall profits for developers.

The state contended that buyers were required to sign leases for recreation fa-

OTHER CONSUMER ISSUES

cilities for terms up to 99 years and had to pay fees whether or not the facilities were used. Failure to make recreation payments was a ground for foreclosure on a residence.

The attorney general's office said the action was a test case designed to ban a practice applying to most of the estimated 250,000 condominium units in the state.

Reacting to widespread complaints about the condominium industry, the Federal Trade Commission had announced July 4 that it was launching a nationwide investigation of alleged unfair and deceptive practices. But the inquiry was discontinued in 1975. The decision, by a 3-2 vote March 24, was confirmed by an agency spokesman, who cited budgetary considerations and a duplicate study by the Housing and Urban Development Department. A proposal to make the decision public also was rejected by 3-2 vote.

Suit seeks AT&T breakup. The Justice Department filed an antitrust suit Nov. 20, 1974 against American Telephone & Telegraph Corp. (AT&T), the world's largest privately owned corporation.

AT&T and two other defendants—Western Electric Co., Inc., AT&T's wholly owned subsidiary, which manufactured telecommunications equipment for the Bell System, and Bell Telephone Laboratories, Inc., the nation's largest industrial laboratory and owned equally by AT&T and Western Electric—were accused of combining and conspiring to monopolize telecommunications service and equipment in the U.S., in violation of the Sherman Act.

The suit, which was filed with U.S. District Court in Washington, asked the divestiture of Western Electric by AT&T and the division of Western Electric into two or more competing firms, if necessary, to assure competition in the manufacturing and sale of telecommunications equipment.

The government also sought to promote competition with its request that "some or all" of AT&T's Long Lines Department, which handled long distance calls, be separated from "some or all" of the 23 local Bell Telephone Operating Cos., which together with the three defendant firms made up the Bell System. The local Bell companies were named co-conspirators in the antitrust suit.

Under the divestiture plan submitted by the government, the Long Lines Department could be divested from the Bell System, or some or all of the Bell Operating Companies could be divested by AT&T as separate and independent firms.

According to a government spokesmen, the suit did not challenge the concept of exclusive franchises for the provision of local exchange telephone service.

The Justice Department said that "in terms of assets," the antitrust suit was the largest ever filed by the government, surpassing the 1911 suit that led to the breakup of Standard Oil Co., and the 1969 suit against International Business Machines Corp.

The Bell network and its dominance of the telecommunications field were without parallel. AT&T, with assets of $67 billion, had annual revenues of $23.53 billion in 1973; Western Electric's sales in 1973 totaled more than $7 billion. With earnings of $315 million, Western Electric was one of the 12 largest manufacturing firms in the nation. The 23 Bell operating subsidiaries served 112.3 million telephones, about 80% of the nation's total. (There were 1,705 independent phone companies, but none of them competed directly with AT&T for phone customers, because like the AT&T subsidiaries, they operated within specific geographic areas under a monopoly franchise.)

AT&T's Long Lines Department transmitted more than 90% of the nation's long distance telephone calls, and the Bell System transmitted most of the nation's data, television shows and other communications. Western Electric manufactured most of the nation's telecommunications equipment and was the largest maker of telephone equipment in the world, producing about 11 million units in 1973.

The government had filed another antitrust suit against AT&T in 1949, also seeking the divestiture of Western

Electric. A consent judgment was finally accepted in 1956, but the Bell System was left intact. Critics of the settlement charged that the consent decree was a mere "slap on the wrist" for the giant company. AT&T settled the suit with an agreement that Western Electric would be restricted to the manufacture of telephone equipment, and would relinquish units that produced nontelephone equipment, such as railroad dispatch machinery and movie gear. AT&T also agreed to license all of its existing patents.

It was later revealed during 1958 House subcommittee hearings that Herbert Brownell, attorney general in the Eisenhower Administration, had given AT&T's vice president and general counsel, T. Brooke Price, a "little friendly tip" on how to settle the case. The "tip" was that AT&T should examine its operations and tell the Justice Department about "practices that we might agree to have enjoined with no real injury to our business."

AT&T officials had testified at the Congressional hearings that the patent licensing requirement would greatly reduce its dominance in the telephone business.

AT&T's competitors won a landmark victory with the "Carterfone" decision in 1968 when a small company won the right to sell a device, a cradle-like apparatus called the "carterfone," that connected a mobile radio into the phone network. The ruling allowed makers of non-Bell equipment to hook into the Bell system. In a 1971 ruling, the Federal Communications Commission, created a new classification of specialized common carriers licensed to provide interstate communications facilities on a private line basis, thereby allowing customers to bypass the Bell dial network.

Competing firms which attempted to take advantage of these rulings later charged that AT&T impeded their efforts. Antitrust suits were pending to decide whether AT&T could require non-Bell equipment makers to use a Bell-produced, installed and leased interface to hook into the Bell network. In regard to the 1971 FCC ruling, a court had recently ordered that Bell provide its private line rivals with linkage service necessary to connect non-Bell interstate customers to the non-Bell interstate system.

AT&T official comments—John D. deButts, chairman of AT&T, said Nov. 20, "We are confident that we are not in violation of the antitrust laws and are astonished that the Justice Department would take its present action with apparent disregard for its impact on the public."

"By its present action, the Justice Department would destroy a unique national resource, the value of which has been repeatedly proved not only by its contributions to the betterment of communications, but also by its unparalleled record of technological innovations vital to national defense and space exploration," deButts said.

Divestiture "could lead to fragmentation of responsibility for the nation's telephone network," deButts warned. "If that happens, telephone service would deteriorate and cost much, much more." The government had contended that cheaper phone rates might be an eventual consequence of greater competition in a field dominated by AT&T.

DeButts defended AT&T's monolithic structure, saying "the telephone network, to work efficiently must be designed, built and operated as a single entity." That structure, he added, "is in very large measure responsible for the advanced development of telecommunications in this country and its low cost."

According to deButts, AT&T's structure "has been repeatedly examined" by Congress, the courts and regulatory bodies, and "every time its appropriateness has been confirmed." He cited the 1956 consent judgment as proof of the government's approval of AT&T's operations.

Funeral practice rules proposed. The Federal Trade Commission proposed Aug. 28, 1975 to ban several funeral home practices it said inflicted "economic and emotional injuries" on customers.

The prohibition would extend, among other things, to embalming corpses without family permission, requiring a casket in cases of immediate cremation and

OTHER CONSUMER ISSUES

refusing to make available inexpensive cremation containers. The proposed rule also would require itemized price sheets for customers and a fact sheet stating the legal requirements for embalming, caskets and burial vaults.

The FTC announced at the same time a consent order with Service Corp. International, the largest funeral-home operator in the country, under which the company would refund more than $100,000 it charged customers in excess of crematory costs since Jan. 1, 1971. The company was ordered to end overcharging practices.

Carpet standards. The Housing & Urban Development Department announced Feb. 26, 1975 that minimum performance standards would be put into effect March 1 for carpeting in homes with mortgages insured by the Federal Housing Administration (FHA). Although such carpeting comprised only about 5% of the total sold in the U.S., carpet makers used FHA standards on a much higher percentage of their output. The standards covered minimum weights, or fiber content, and color maintenance against light and water.

Companies wanting to state that their product met the FHA standards were required to register in a certification program, which consisted of pretesting by FHA-approved laboratories and subsequent spot-checking by independent laboratories.

Consumerism

> *The consumer protection movement of the 1960s–70s achieved the quasi-status of an "ism"—consumerism. As such, it was the subject of study by the White House's National Goals Research Staff. The results of this study, originally presented as a chapter in the 1970 report entitled "Toward Balanced Growth: Quantity With Quality," are presented below.*

American business prides itself on its ability to create a growing stream of mass-produced new products, thanks to new technology, efficient organization, and a diligent effort to discover and to serve new needs. But the success of U.S. business—exceeding all other nations in its flow of goods and services—has bred a reaction. There is now a movement called "consumerism" which claims that the consumer's ability to make an "informed choice" is eroded and that we can no longer rely on "consumer sovereignty" to police the marketplace. Proponents of this movement complain that the vast flow of new products leaves the consumer bewildered, that the technological complexity of many products makes it impossible for him to evaluate them, and that many products have dangerous side effects. It is further alleged that the marketing skill and power of American business, long a matter of pride, leaves the consumer helpless before our large corporations.

The current consumer movement has distinctive features arising from our affluence. Previous waves of consumerism featured protection of the consumer from monopolistic control over prices, from dangerous products, and from false and misleading business practices. Such issues persist into the present and in some instances—e.g., product safety—have been accentuated. But what distinguishes the present consumer movement from those in the past is the outcry against the "flood" of new products and their technological complexity, the alleged power of large corporations to "manage" the market, the difficulties associated with buying with freely available credit, and the plight of the poor consumer left out of the mainstream of affluence. In addition, the new consumerism is much wider in scope, aiming at health services, public utilities, transportation, and automobile safety, and urging consumer representation, consumer education, and antipoverty programs. Also it may be said that the present movement is spurred by an affluent level of aspiration.

Previous waves of consumer interests raised issues of safety, deception, and so on that affect both rich and poor. The new movement has added a different flavor. Only an affluent society, where most people's basic material needs already are met, would raise the issues of reliability, quality, fullness of information, uses of credit, purity, and trust, as they are now discussed in the consumerism movement. And only a society whose material needs were assuaged could produce a generation of young people who would revolt so strongly against material success. (This is not to deny that concerns for abuses affecting the poor persist, and have even increased.)

The variety of goods in the marketplace and the high expectations of the consumer are two aspects of our affluence and the consumerism spawned by that affluence.

The variety of the American marketplace means that today's consumer is able to buy, enjoy, use and discard more types of goods and services than was ever before possible. The problem this creates for the consumer is illustrated by today's appliances. While the individual appliance may be better than ever before, and may be less likely to break down, the total number of appliances in the house has grown so rapidly in the last two decades that the aggregate repair problem probably has grown larger. Thus, for some people, things may seem worse today simply because there are more items in the marketplace.

Things may also seem worse to some consumers today because they expect more. The widely heralded advances of American technology lead the consumer to expect a great deal. He knows that American industrial prowess can produce a better article than those he buys. As prices rise, the consumer expects increased quality.

Like the other movements discussed in this report, modern-day consumerism may to a large extent be interpreted as an attempt to redirect the forces that helped produce "success" by earlier and different criteria. After all, we have succeeded in our goal of producing a vast flow of goods and services. The movement has enlisted powerful political support—a somewhat unusual circumstance since the "consumer" has none of the characteristics of the traditional American pressure groups. Consumerism is a diffuse public interest, much like the environment issue. While consumers may not be completely organized, they now have organizations and spokesmen for long-range recognition of consumer rights. Consumerism's main thrust has been to assert through legislation the right of consumers to be safe, to be informed, to choose, and to be heard. New laws give retail buyers more protection against fraudulent and deceptive business practices, and unsafe or unreliable products and services. Such industries as automobile manufacturing, food processing and packaging, drugs, and banking and finance have already felt the impact. Opinion surveys show that the public overwhelmingly favors laws to protect their health and safety, and that they react strongly against products they feel give little value. Consumerism can also be seen in the programs of States, counties, and municipalities as well as corporations, trade associations, and voluntary groups.

Previous Periods of Consumer Unrest

The present era of consumerism, while it has certain unique features, follows two similar periods, the early 1900's and the 1930's. Each of the three periods occurred during a time of rapid social change. In each period journalistic exposés alerted the public concerning dangers to health and safety. And in each period, new laws came only after an aroused public overcame governmental inaction.

Economic life changed rapidly in the last four decades of the 19th century. Industrial output and employment increased fivefold. The population doubled, and the urban portion rose from 20 to 40 percent. Completion of the nationwide rail network created the possibility of national markets. Trademarked goods began to be advertised in the new mass-circulation magazines. But the new urbanism and industrialism yielded new and unfamiliar problems—urban poverty, tenement housing, immigrant ghettoes, municipal corruption, hazardous working conditions, sweat shops, child labor, and a variety of consumer problems.

By the 1870's, some of the abuses and excesses of rapid industrialization led some States and the Federal Government to enact laws to regulate them. But by then the Supreme Court had begun to interpret the Constitution to invalidate the regulation of business. *Caveat emptor* (let the buyer beware) was the law of product sales, and this interpretation was retained and extended as the courts took a strict, hands-off policy towards private contracts, no matter how unfair or oppressive the terms.

The basic posture of the law began to change in the last two decades of the 19th century. The Sherman Antitrust Act (1890) was a forerunner of a new wave of consumer-oriented laws. When the Clayton Act was added to antitrust legislation in 1914, the Government's role as protector of the public domain was confirmed. Joining the procession of early consumer legislation were the Food and Drug Act (1906), the Federal Trade Commission Act (1914), and the Federal Power Commission Act (1920).

These pieces of legislation came about because consumer advocates, trade unions, journalists, and the executive branch clamored for them before a reluctant Congress. The first Consumers' League of middle- and upper-class advocates, formed in 1891, led to establishing the National Consumer League in 1898. The leagues joined with other groups including the National Child Labor Association, the League of Women Voters, and the labor unions, and got laws passed and enforced affecting safety and working conditions, maximum hours, child labor, and minimum wages.

Muckraking journalists exposed corruption in business and government and thereby stimulated public opinion to demand consumer legislation. The muckrakers attacked such industries as oil, meatpacking (a new national industry opened up by the new railroads and refrigerated freight cars), and patent medicines. Upton Sinclair's 1906 exposé, *The Jungle*, rescued the Food and Drug Act from burial in a House committee and brought pressure on Congress to pass the 1906 amendment to the Meat Inspection Act.

Perhaps the most important result of the first era of consumerism was recognition by American society that the consumer had a valid interest which was not always served by the existing market mechanisms.

Consumerism ebbed during World War I, but not before courts had begun to be consumer conscious. The rule of *caveat emptor* began evolving toward *caveat venditor* (let the seller beware)—a rule applied against powerful industries, such as utilities and insurance.

The depression of the 1930's ushered in the second phase of consumerism. During the 1920's educators had developed guidelines for consumer education. Consumer discontent with new and unfamiliar consumer durables found expression in *Your Money's Worth* (by Chase and Schlink) in 1927. Consumers' Research, Inc., was formed (1929) to meet the inquiries about products, which flooded in on the heels of the bestseller. By 1933, people were eager to examine critically the issues of brand proliferation, unwise spending, and misleading advertising as discussed in *100,000,000 Guinea Pigs*, by Kallet and Schlink (1933). A spate of similar books followed. The National Recovery Act (1933) gave the first formal recognition to the consumer interest in Federal law by providing labor and consumer advisory boards in the codemaking process. In 1935, consumer groups formed Consumers' Union, which fought for recognition of consumer interests throughout the years to World War II.

Consumerism Enters a New Phase

Consumerism in America began to move into its third phase at the end of the 1950's. Again, the resurgence of consumerism was sparked by

CONSUMERISM

journalistic criticisms from such authors as Rachel Carson, Vance Packard, David Caplovitz, and Maurine Neuberger, each of whom wrote one or more books on topics related to consumerism.

On March 15, 1962, President John F. Kennedy sent to the Congress a special message on protecting the consumer interest. His central thesis was that consumers "are the only important group in the economy who are not effectively organized, whose views are often not heard."

As a result of the message, a Consumer Advisory Council under the aegis of the Council of Economic Advisers was formed. In 1964, President Johnson established the President's Committee on Consumer Interests, under the chairmanship of Mrs. Esther Peterson, Assistant Secretary of Labor, and later Executive Secretary of the Consumer Advisory Council. She was subsequently named Special Assistant to the President for Consumer Affairs. Mrs. Peterson was succeeded by Miss Betty Furness.

As public interest grew in consumerism issues, Congress passed the Fair Labeling and Packaging Act (truth in packaging) in 1966 and the Credit Disclosure Act (truth in lending) in 1968. Congress also approved legislation on poultry and meat inspection, pipeline safety, fraudulent land sales, and hazardous appliances regulation.

Mrs. Virginia Knauer, current Special Assistant to the President for Consumer Affairs, can now deal directly with the heads of corporations and businesses to help consumers with their problems. She is working with the States to improve consumer protection laws and is advocating a Consumer Register—a translation of the Federal Register into language easily understood by the layman so that consumers can comment knowledgeably on proposed Federal regulations.

In addition, a consumer education office has been instituted and is now planning a set of guidelines for all grades in the public schools beginning with kindergarten, and has been authorized to deal directly with consumer complaints.

One of the major research projects her office deals with is the problem of disclosing for public use the expertise gained by Government testing and purchasing agencies in order to give to the consumer a better set of standards in his buying decisions.

In his Consumer Message of October 30, 1969, President Nixon offered a "Buyer's Bill of Rights:"

> I believe that the buyer in America today has the right to make an intelligent choice among products and services. The buyer has the right to accurate information on which to make his free choice.
>
> The buyer has the right to expect that his health and safety is taken into account by those who seek his patronage.

The buyer has the right to register his dissatisfaction, and have his complaint heard and weighed, when his interests are badly served.

Complaints of Consumers

Many issues of past waves of consumerism have persisted into the present. Consumers still complain of deceptive practices, product failure, product dangers, lack of competitive pricing, and the plight of poor people in the marketplace. Added to these accusations are complaints about package shapes and sizes that confuse or deceive the buyer. The old issue of product unreliability is compounded by the difficulty of getting adequate repairs for complex appliances.

Consumer movements always have been concerned with the marketplace problems of the poor. Not only do the poor lack money, but they frequently lack information and understanding, and must buy and borrow money under disadvantageous circumstances. The present consumer movement has been especially concerned with minorities in the ghetto. In addition to the traditional marketing problems of the poor, ghetto residents have suffered from discrimination in access to housing, and until recently in access to some services.

However, there are certain new features of consumerism that stem from the development of the economy. In recent years the emphasis of American business has shifted from production to marketing, with the latter occupying an increasing role in the total job of producing and delivering goods and services. The change reflects the fact that ability to produce products was mastered earlier than was the ability to detect new needs and then to design, distribute, and promote new products. But many people see production as an honest activity while marketing is a nonproductive activity—virtually by definition. This is not the place to analyze this assumption, but rather to record its persistance into an era in which marketing has assumed enormous importance. This negative evaluation of marketing represents an essential ideological difference between much of today's consumerism movement and current business practices.

Crucial for our understanding of modern marketing is the fact that the means for satisfying man's basic needs for food, shelter, transportation, warmth, and clothing were developed long ago. We now are concerned with improving the distribution of these necessities, and then with better ways of satisfying these basic needs, and with comfort, convenience, esthetics, and social and psychological needs.

To the modern businessman the detection and serving of new and subtle needs is a legitimate and challenging activity. The businessman sees himself as improving the quality of American life, but to his critics,

CONSUMERISM

many of these activities are suspect. To the critic, these subtle needs are nonexistent until the marketer creates them. A characteristic reaction is that of Dorothy Sayers:

> A society in which consumption has to be artificially stimulated in order to keep production going is a society founded on trash and waste, and such a society is a house built upon sand.

The two contrasting notions of what a market is, or should be, place different meanings on the concept of a product. For the critic of modern marketing, a product is—or should be—a commodity that is one of a class of relatively undifferentiated items which serve some primary need. An automobile, for instance, serves man's need for transportation. But the modern marketer sees a product as something much more complex; in the marketer's view, the product serves as many purposes as he or the consumer can imagine. The automobile, for instance, is seen not merely as a means of transportation but as a symbol of status and potency, a token of self-indulgence, and even as a means of making oneself attractive to the opposite sex. If a product attribute, such as its appearance, is communicated by advertising, the product is said to gain as much utility as it might if it were actually redesigned. While the modern marketer will concede that some consumer behavior is irrational or socially undesirable, his view of what a product is makes it very difficult to establish clear criteria of rationality or desirability. The marketer must regard as legitimate any need that is not antisocial, whether the consumer already is aware of it, or if he responds to it only when it is called to his attention.

A similar dilemma involves the modern marketers' view of what constitutes "information." In the traditional view, a product is seen as basically a commodity serving a single well-defined purpose, and information is that which tells the consumer about how that purpose is served, and which warns him about the dangers that might be risked in using the product. The preferred choice process is seen as rational in the common-sense use of that term. If, however, the product is seen in the modern marketer's view as serving many needs, some of them quite subtle, the process of choice is viewed as too complex to be described by any simple notion of rationality. Thus, anything that influences a consumer's choice may be considered as information. In this latter view, the association of a product with a favorable mood (e.g. depicting a food as creating a harmonious family atmosphere, or a toiletry as attracting the opposite sex) is seen as informative, just as is technical information.

Clearly, the modern marketer's view makes it exceedingly difficult to draw clear boundaries between what is proper and what is improper—except in obvious cases of overt deception, or the invocation of socially undesirable appeals. The marketer argues for "consumer sovereignty," declaring that the consumer is, by and large, an adequate defender of his own interests. But, the current consumer movement charges that the conditions of the modern market make "informed choice"—the fundamental basis of the doctrine of consumer sovereignty—extremely difficult. Consumer advocates say the consumer is helpless in the face of the marketing power of large corporations. The ordinary consumer, it is said, cannot evaluate modern products due to the extremely rapid rate with which new, slightly differentiated products are introduced and the highly technical content of modern products. At the very least, the variety and technical complexity of the new products breeds the requirement for more and different information than the consumer has had in the past.

One point of contention in the current controversy is the assertion that there is a growing imbalance between producer and consumer because of the rise of the "corporate state." The group of academicians, journalists, and consumer advocates holding this view maintains that the entire relationship between the corporation and the individual needs to be reexamined in order to remedy the vast bargaining power of big business. The economy is said to be dominated by a few hundred giant corporations which shape a future in which the whole society will have to live. These large corporations are viewed as unresponsive to the needs of the consumer. Instead, they use their marketing power—aided with massive advertising—to "manage the market," that is, to persuade the consumer to buy essentially whatever products they choose to put on the market.

This view of the marketing power of the large corporations ignores their efforts to determine consumer wants by market research, and the innumerable new products which are rejected by the market (e.g. the Edsel), or halted in the development stage by the prospect of consumer rejection even before they are brought into the market.

Extreme notions of how large corporations "manage" the market may be dismissed as exaggerations, but there is no doubt about the reality of the concern in some quarters about the power of large corporations over the consumer. There also is little doubt that many marketers of consumer goods have paid less attention to health and safety than they have to design and styling. It is not clear whether this latter circumstance should be regarded as a manifestation of callousness on the part of the business firm, or as a failure of the market mechanism in which the aggregate of individual choices in favor of styling failed to produce a socially desirable result, or both. Regardless of which interpretation one prefers, these failures have resulted in vigorous and, to a large extent successful efforts to have the government intervene and/or to make large corporations more responsive.

Linked to concern over the power of large corporations is what has been called the "impersonal" nature of the modern market. The consumer shops in larger and larger stores, with increased emphasis on self-service. He buys more and more and more prepackaged goods, almost all of which have originated farther and farther from the point of purchase. Whereas previously he got much of his information from a sales person with whom he may have been well acquainted, now he gets it from advertising in the mass media or from labels developed by the manufacturer. The message is not tailored to his particular needs, but to those of broad groups of people. He must place his confidence in an unknown corporate entity rather than in an individual he has learned to trust.

All in all, the consumerism movement of today is in large part a result of the way in which the American business system has developed. There have been sufficient abuses to stir up consumer anxiety, and there are problems that warrant corrective action.

Some consumer complaints contain an element of irony. American business has long prided itself on its ability to produce a vast flow of new products. Now consumers complain about the vastness of the flow and the sophistication of the products.

The recent increase in product offerings in the U.S. market has become part of the business folklore. The number of items on the average supermarket shelf is said to have been 1,500 in 1950 and 8,000 today. The spate of new automobiles introduced into the market in recent years show a widening spectrum, ranging from standard models to compacts, subcompacts, and "personal" cars.

Traditionally, one would have thought that the introduction of many new products would strengthen the consumer's hand by increasing his range of choice. Presumably, the more items he can choose among, the more precisely he can meet his own needs, and the more precisely he can discipline the firm to serve him with what he wants. But, for some people, it seemingly has not turned out this way. One of the charges of the consumerism movement concerns the "proliferation" of new products. Aside from the difficulty of judging products of high technical complexity, the products appear on, and disappear from, the market with such rapidity that the consumer may have insufficient opportunity to become familiar with them. Consumer advocates also argue that differences among products are so trivial as to make any choice difficult.

It would be difficult indeed to document what portion of consumers are confused and to what extent by the sheer volume of new products. It would be even more difficult to balance the cost of their confusion against the benefits of the availability of new products. But, once more a precise estimate of the objective situation is not what is at stake. The fact is that enough consumers perceive themselves as being confused to make this a live issue. It has produced a demand for better product information.

The promotion and buying of so many varieties of new items has also contributed to the ideological revolt against "materialism," of which the flow of new products is a visible manifestation.

Largely ignored by spokesmen for consumer protection are the manufacturers' difficulties in recognizing unfilled consumer wants. In a market in which all primary needs are served by existing goods and services, the unfilled needs must be increasingly subtle (convenience, comfort, esthetics, prestige, ego enhancement) to the point where it is often questioned whether such needs are real or legitimate or created. Whether or not such needs are real or merely represent opportunities for the creation of needs may be debated, but the needs unquestionably are difficult to determine. The difficulty is compounded by the changing nature of the market. New products enter all the time, and consumer preferences constantly change, and at the same time there is a long lead time in developing, producing, and introducing a new product.

While a need may initially have been correctly perceived, it may have disappeared or been considerably modified by the time a product is ready for the market. The manufacturer is then confronted with the choice of either scrapping the product or trying to sell it by a vigorous and skillful marketing effort—what the theorists of the corporate state call "managing the market." In such a situation, advertising may alter the consumer's choice toward a product that does not really suit his needs. This state of affairs naturally is undesirable for the consumer, but it is equally undersirable for the manufacturer. At best, he can compensate in selling effort for what the product lacks in intrinsic appeal. More likely, his product will fail.

The difficulty of the manufacturer in detecting consumer needs is probably not in itself a matter for public policy. But it becomes a matter of public concern when it produces inefficiency in the economy.

Increased technological sophistication enables American industry to develop synthetic fabrics, processed foods, novel appliances, and other new products, but it also makes products more complex and therefore harder to evaluate. The buyer of a generation ago could do a better job of estimating the probable performance of an icebox than can today's buyer confronted with a refrigerator. The buyer of fresh fruit can judge its quality, but the buyer of a processed food can hardly anticipate the long-range consequences of the additives it contains, or even to assess the nutritional changes which may have occurred in processing.

Moreover, when a complete analysis of a purchase is too technical or time consuming, consumers tend to shortcut their decision making. For example, consumers often equate tire safety with tire life or clothes cleanliness with whiteness and brightness. In some instances, the con-

CONSUMERISM

sumer may virtually abandon rational decision making, and choose almost blindly.

One consequence of the outpouring of technically complicated products is that the consumer's decision increasingly is delegated. The transfer of responsibility may be partial, as in the use of consumer rating services that judge products on several dimensions (e.g., radios on tone, sensitivity, selectivity, ease of repair, and so on) and leave the consumer to decide which attributes he values most. It should be noted that some "delegation" is done *de facto* by setting of standards. However, the setting of standards of quality may deprive a consumer of the right to buy an inferior product at a lower price. Or, the delegation may be at some stages total, as in the screening of prescription drugs by the FDA. Here it has been decided that even the average professional cannot make an informed choice. There seems little doubt that the range of products and services for which consumers will need technical assistance is likely to increase, as are those for which part or all of the decision is delegated.

At this point, the consumerism movement overlaps the field of technology assessment, covered in another chapter of this report. All the questions raised there are pertinent here. Who shall decide on what bases which product will be assessed? Where shall this function be located? How are costs to be weighed against benefits?

In short, there is reason to believe that the consumer feels he needs more protection and information as a result of changes in business practice and in the volume and nature of new products. Evidence for this need is the fact that the circulation of *Consumer Reports* has approximately doubled in the past half decade.

Choices for Business & Government

Business. In recent years, leading business organizations have made careful studies of consumerism and have proposed voluntary action codes that acknowledge business responsibility to protect the health and safety of consumers, improve quality standards, simplify warranties, improve repair and servicing quality, self-police fraud and deception, improve information provided consumers, make sound value comparisons easier, and provide effective channels for consumer complaints.

Business also is responding to changes in values and tastes of consumers. Leading business firms are hard at work studying the prospects for the changing business environment, and including in their analyses surveys of changing consumer values and tastes, and the demands of the consumerism movement.

Business responsibilities (in a rapidly changing environment) are likely to expand as a result of certain long-range trends in the consumer protection movement. Higher standards of quality, integrity, and social performance will probably be expected. Unfair and arbitrary business performance will probably be more forcefully questioned by both the public and the courts. Business will likely operate more and more under scrutiny of government, press, and other groups. Mass-production industries in particular will be affected by this trend. The credibility of the existing organizational and ethical assumptions of business will likely come under public evaluation with more forcefulness. This means that public opinion will question internal business value systems as they affect individuals, possibly changing the philosophy and practice of management in many ways.

The relationship of mass media to the consumer, for example, is likely to undergo increasing scrutiny. Increasingly, the public questions the value assumptions of advertising messages, as well as the news and public affairs content of TV broadcasting. Articulate portions of the public are demanding higher standards of performance, whether or not TV is "a vast wasteland." If government and business do not share responsibility for improving the educational and cultural level of programing, the demand for regulation and government intervention may become irresistible.

Government. Under pressure from the consumer movement, U.S. Congressmen, State legislators, and local officials are offering legislation on every phase of consumerism. The Nixon Administration has endorsed increased regulatory powers for Federal agencies, the establishment of an Office of Consumer Affairs, and bills fortifying warranties and further requirements for product testing and labeling. With truth-in-lending and truth-in-packaging laws already on the books, there now is discussion of truth-in-pricing, truth-in-warranties, and other measures dealing with producer honesty.

At the same time, government must exercise its responsibility to the consumer in a way that will preserve a favorable business environment. Much of what is being done or proposed in the consumer field is not contrary to the interests of business. If an undesirable practice is prohibited and everybody has to obey, standards of business conduct can be raised, and the competitive energy that was formerly channeled into a practice that did not serve consumer interests can be rechanneled. In the case of truth-in-lending, for example, seldom has a consumer-oriented law been so vigorously opposed. The basic argument of the credit industry initially was: "If we have to reveal everything about our credit terms we shall lose our credit customers." This has not happened. The law, and the regulations under it, have been well planned, with the ultimate cooperation of the credit industry; it appears to be fairly simple to enforce and it is effective. The result seems to have been a high degree of compliance—the disappearance of most of the questionable credit advertising practices and development of more meaningful forms of competition in the credit industry. This instance, however, does not negate the need for vigilance in making sure that regulation does not impose restrictions that will serve neither business nor the consumer.

Clearly the business community can help shape an appropriate governmental role in consumer affairs through constructive comment. The business community itself will benefit from engaging government in open dialog within which some of the problems of an evolving society can be discussed and resolved without resorting to defiance on the one hand and the threat of legislation on the other.

The Government as a large-scale purchaser can set standards directly. The Government can and does set specifications for the products which it buys. Since Government purchases are so large, it frequently is more convenient or economical for a firm to produce all of its run of products according to government specifications rather than produce essentially two different models.

For a technology-based economy to survive and grow requires a vast system of both mandatory and voluntary standards. The Federal Government has important and unique roles with respect to these standards. In cooperation with other governments of the world, it prescribes the basic standards of time, temperature, mass, and length. From these, in turn, are derived the many standards and measurements required for the Nation's scientific, industrial, and commercial activities. Where health and safety are involved, the Government assumes a strong prescriptive, standard-setting role. By far the largest area of standard setting is on a voluntary and cooperative basis in the private sector; e.g., by business and trade associations. In this private sector standard setting the government acts at times as a catalyst, sparking the standard-setting process without having a position of its own. In other instances, the government may argue a position, while being only one of the parties to reaching an agreement.

Meanwhile, Congress and other legislative bodies face problems which have particular reference to desirable and needed standard setting for consumer goods and environmental quality. Legislative standard setting also, to some extent, shifts the focus of expectations of consumers from manufacturer to marketer to government itself. To the extent that government does move toward more widespread standard setting, all parties—producers, consumers, and the scientific and technological community—have a common interest in improving the process by which law reflects current scientific understanding and methodology. Meanwhile, a meaningful goal for informational content in consumer affairs would appear to be to keep the consuming task within the consumer's capabilities, consistent with other economic and social goals.

Finally, government is continually challenged to renew its own institutions and processes to deal with change in ways that would improve the quality of life for all consumers. Thus, the government policy that fosters outmoded or misguided activities positively wastes resources, to the detriment of the consumer, his living standards and his environment.

It seems clear that the American people and their representatives in the Federal, State, and local legislatures have rejected the choice of accepting the full scope of imperfections of the market mechanisms which have stemmed in part from long-standing business practices, and which have been greatly sharpened by circumstances surrounding our recent economic growth.

It is not clear, however, how far they can, will, or should go in the opposite direction.

Today's consumer, while scarcely impotent, seems to need help, but the virtues of the market mechanism, where it works, are well documented. The situation seems to call for a closely reasoned dialogue that will enable society to protect the consumer without interfering so much with the market process that the true growth in the public welfare is impeded.

The central features of the current consumer movement are intrinsically a function of the way the American economy, population, and society have grown over the past few decades. Despite much legislation and changes in many business practices, spokesmen for the consumer continue to assert that his problem of choosing wisely in the marketplace still lies beyond his individual capacities and will continue to do so unless more changes occur. Nevertheless, it remains true that American labor, American business and the consumer himself have jointly created an economy which produces a fabulous array of goods and services for the well-being of everyone. We must keep this in mind when we strive to correct those instances in which things have not gone as well as we might have hoped.

Summary

American business prides itself in its ability to develop, produce, and deliver a great flow of new technologically sophisticated products of a wide variety. Yet, its very success in this has produced a wave of complaints. There have been consumer movements in the past based on issues of product safety and quality, deceptive practices, monopolistic practices, aesthetics, and so on. However, what marks the new consumer movement as distinctive is that it features resentment that the stream of new products is so large and the differences among products so small that choice among them is said to have been made difficult. Furthermore, it is argued that the technical complexity of many of them is such that the untrained individual cannot evaluate them.

CONSUMERISM

The result has been the evolution of a system of consumer protection which, since 1964, has featured commissions and special assistants at the highest levels of Government, increased activity in the regulatory agencies, and, finally in 1969, a Presidential enunciation of a "Buyer's Bill of Rights." Laws have been passed and new standards set. Testing procedures have been tightened. Consumer information services have grown.

The anomaly of the present consumerism market is that a highly market-oriented economy has produced a situation, in which it is said by at least an influential minority, that the doctrine of consumer sovereignty—the notion that the consumer can regulate business by his free choices—is no longer tenable for some undefinable but sizable segment of the marketplace. Some extreme manifestations of this position would have a considerable impact on the way our economy runs. Already, the consumerism movement has had an important and probably beneficial influence on business practice. This movement consists of a myriad of small issues, but the large one confronting us is that of developing a proper policy posture that will give the desirable amount and kind of protection to the consumer and, at the same time, preserve a business environment in which the economy can continue to grow.

The consumerism movement has been regarded by some as a fad. It is important to note that the complaints which stimulate the present consumer concerns are an integral part of a technologically sophisticated, market-oriented economy such as we have so deliberately developed in recent decades and which seems certain to continue.

Guide Against Deceptive Advertising

> *Many of the deceptive practices used widely in advertising and selling were described by the Gas Appliance Manufacturers Association, Inc. in a brochure that it published as a guide for its members against such deception. The contents of this brochure, entitled "A Guide Against Deceptive Advertising of Gas Ranges," are reproduced below.*

Deceptive advertising comes within the prohibitions of Section 5 of the Federal Trade Commission Act against unfair or deceptive acts or practices in commerce among the States, with foreign nations, and within any territory or the District of Columbia. These prohibitions are enforced by the Federal Trade Commission as part of its prescribed duties. In addition, many States have their own laws against false or deceptive advertising.

Reflecting the unending resourcefulness and wily imagination of the marketplace, deceptive advertising includes a vast number of acts or practices. Many of these are obviously and intentionally false or misleading. Many others are of the sort into which the businessman may unwittingly and unintentionally stumble. It is with concern for the latter group that we offer this brochure for the use of our members, reminding them that the principles set out herein can be only very general ones and that the best protection against inadvertent involvement is advance consultation with their own legal counsel.

In addition to the lessons to be learned from the numerous decisions in the courts or in proceedings within the Commission itself, the Federal Trade Commission has published a series of Guides designed to point out to the businessman certain of the prohibited practices and danger areas. Among these are the Guides Against Deceptive Pricing, Guides Against Bait Advertising and Guides Against Deceptive Advertising of Guarantees. Much of the material in this brochure is drawn from those Guides.

The basic rules are simple. If an advertisement can lead a purchaser to believe that he is getting something that he is not actually getting, it is subject to being considered deceptive. And the person who is really the advertiser is the one apt to be in trouble. An attempt to shift the blame to the advertising agency did not succeed.

Apart from involvement with Federal or State agencies, an advertisement may get the seller into troubles with his customer. Representations made in the advertisement may turn out to be express warranties and may come back to haunt the seller in a later product liability suit or other litigation involving the article.

This brochure is limited to the area of possibly misleading or deceptive advertising. Members are reminded that advertising may involve numerous other questions, including the particular rules for cooperative advertising laid down in the Federal Trade Commission Guides for Advertising Allowances and Other Merchandising Payments and Services.

PRICE COMPARISONS

1. *If the advertiser offers a reduction from his own former price, such former price must have been a genuine one.*

    The former price must have been one at which the article was actually offered for sale to the public for a reasonably substantial period in the recent, regular course of business. If the seller creates a price for the purpose of later offering a reduction from it, the comparison and the advertisement containing it are deceptive. Example: The seller sells his Brand X gas ranges at $150. He raises the price to $175 for two days, then drops the price back to $150, and advertises a drastic reduction in the price of Brand X gas ranges—each reduced $25.

2. *Any advertised reduction must be sufficiently large that the customer, if he knew all the facts, would consider that a genuine bargain was being offered.*

    Customers who are informed of a "sale" or a reduction or a bargain have a right to believe it is significant. If the seller advertises his Brand X gas range as "Reduced to $149.75" when the former price was $150, there is nothing significant to the customer, who is merely misled.

3. *If the seller advertises his merchandise at a price lower than that charged by others for the same goods, the higher (competitors') price must be genuine.*

    A genuine price is a real one, established by actual sales in representative locations. The advertiser should be prepared to back up his claim. Prices charged by "others" do not mean isolated or unsubstantial sales in suburban or distant locations but rather the prevailing price of larger outlets in the main shopping area. "Price Elsewhere $200," or "Retail Value $200," means that if the customer wants to look in the larger stores in the principal shopping area, he will find the prevailing price for the Brand X gas range is $200. If this is not true, the customer is being deceived.

4. *If the seller advertises a reduction from the price being charged for other merchandise of like grade and quality, he must (a) be sure that the customer clearly understands that a comparison is being made with other merchandise which is actually of essentially similar grade and quality and being sold in the area, and (b) be sure that the price represented for such merchandise is a genuine one. (See 3, above.)*

    The purchaser must be fully aware of the details of the transaction, the kind of comparison being made and that the comparable value represents the price at which merchandise of like grade and quality is being offered by a reasonable number of representative outlets in the area.

5. *If a reduction is offered from a manufacturer's list, suggested retail, preticketed or other similarly established price, such price—no matter how "established"—must reasonably correspond to the actual price at which substantial sales are being made in the principal retail outlets in the advertiser's area.*

It is well recognized that many consumers believe that the manufacturer's list or suggested retail price, or the price appearing on the tag, is the price at which the article is generally sold or at which it must be sold. It is equally well recognized that such list or suggested prices are widely disregarded by many dealers, who sell at the price they think they can get. Thus the manufacturer's list or suggested retail price may have no relation or resemblance to the current "going" price, making it in effect fictitious. A "reduction" from a price which is not actually in use is meaningless except as a deception.

6. *In setting manufacturer's list, suggested retail or similar prices the seller must act in good faith and with knowledge of the approximate "going" price to avoid establishing the basis for a deceptive or misleading comparison.*

   A manufacturer must exercise caution to establish his list or suggested prices on the basis of actual prices, in order to avoid being guilty of deception himself (e.g. in his national advertising) or lending himself to improper advertising by others.

7. *Bargain offers requiring the purchase of other merchandise (for example, "Buy One—Get One Free," "2-for-1 Sale") require a full disclosure at the outset of the advertisement of all the terms and conditions to avoid deception.*

   Many of these offers are simply not true, since the purchaser must purchase one article in order to get the "free" one. Similarly, where a seller making such an offer increases his price, deception may result unless there is full disclosure.

BAIT ADVERTISING

8. *An advertisement which, instead of being a bona fide offer to sell the product advertised, is part of a scheme to make contact with the purchaser for the purpose of switching him from the advertised product to another is prohibited.*

   Whether the advertisement is genuine or "bait" may be determined by acts occurring after the customer has responded. Among these are refusal to show or sell the article as offered, disparagement of the product, attempts to discourage the customer from buying the advertised product, etc. Even if the customer buys the article, attempts to get him to take something else in its place are part of the prohibited scheme.

WARRANTIES

9. *If an advertisement discloses that an article is warranted or guaranteed* it must also disclose the essential terms of the warranty, namely:*

   The product or part thereof covered.
   The characteristics or properties covered or excluded.
   Duration.

---

* "Warranty" and "guarantee" have identical meaning herein and are used interchangeably.

What the purchaser must do. For example, return the product to the factory, pay labor charges, etc.

What the warrantor will do. For example, repair, replace, refund and at whose option, if any.

Who is the warrantor. Who is to fulfill the warranty—the manufacturer or the dealer.

Many consumers feel that if an article is warranted it must be in some way superior and that the warranty is a valuable adjunct to the purchase. The position taken by the Federal Trade Commission—with the support of the courts—is that saying an article is guaranteed is simply meaningless until the terms of the guarantee are made known. For this reason, if the advertisement mentions the guarantee, all the terms must be disclosed. They may be condensed, provided the essential elements are present and clear. Many manufacturers have found it convenient to reproduce the entire warranty in the advertisement where space permits. This has the advantage of avoiding any arguments about the adequacy of the condensation. Of course, if the advertisement does not mention the warranty, this requirement does not apply.

10. *If the warranty is one which is to be adjusted on a pro rata basis, the advertisement should clearly show the basis of proration (time and manner) and if the adjustment is on the basis of a price other than that paid by the purchaser (but under no circumstances a fictitious list price), the adjusting price should be disclosed.*

    Again, this problem would be solved by reproducing the warranty in the advertisement. Otherwise all pertinent details of the proration or "mileage" must be disclosed.

11. *Special types of warranties ("Satisfaction or Money Back," "Lifetime" and "Savings") require particular disclosures.*

    These warranties are, of course, quite different from the usual ones accompanying an article sold. "Satisfaction or Your Money Back" or "Free Trial" representations are construed as a guarantee that the purchaser can have the full price back at his option. If there are conditions, they must be disclosed.

    "Guaranteed to save you 50%" and "Guaranteed lowest price in town" and other guarantees of this type should clearly disclose what the guarantor will do if the savings are not realized, and what the limitations are. "Life" or "lifetime" guarantees mentioned in an advertisement make it necessary to disclose whose life is meant, e.g., the original purchaser, the original user or the life of the product. And an "unconditional" guarantee means just exactly that, i.e., there are no conditions whatsoever attached.

12. *Warranties—and consequently the advertising of them—may constitute material representations and, if untrue, may constitute deceptions, particularly where the warranty exceeds normal and reasonable expectations or intentions.*

    Warranting an article for a duration or performance which cannot be reasonably expected is deceptive, since the purchaser is led to believe that the warranty bears relation to what may be expected. Thus a warranty of 20 years on an article having an expected useful life of 10 years is a deception. Likewise, warranties which the warrantor has no intention of fulfilling are deceptive.

MISCELLANEOUS

13. *An advertisement should not directly or by implication misrepresent the seller, his status, scope or capacities.*

    The advertiser should not represent himself as a manufacturer if in fact he is not; nor should he use phrases implying that he is a manufacturer, such as "factory to you" or "direct to consumer," unless such be true. Similarly, he should not misrepresent the extent of his activity by using such words as "nationwide," "international" or "national headquarters" to mislead. And a seller should not represent that he maintains a laboratory or a staff of engineers when such is not the fact.

14. *Any picture used in an advertisement and purporting to show the product offered should be an accurate and faithful representation, or the difference should be clearly disclosed.*

    Pictures of more expensive models shown in conjunction with prices of cheaper models may be deceptive unless the potential customer is adequately informed of the fact. The same is true where the model illustrated has optional equipment not included in the advertised price. These practices have been unfavorably regarded by the Federal Trade Commission.

15. *Claims or implications of affiliation with another should be avoided unless true.*

    In a number of instances advertisers have been required to discontinue claiming affiliation or connection with another when such was not true. This includes discontinuance of a claim that the advertiser did repair work for certain organizations.

16. *Any credit arrangement advertised should be fully disclosed.*

    Care should be taken to observe the requirements of any applicable "truth-in-lending" law and Federal Reserve Regulation Z. The potential customer should be able to determine from the advertisement exactly what financing or credit is offered and how much it will cost him. If trade-ins are to be accepted, the exact terms should be disclosed.

17. *If the article offered has undergone any use or other treatment whereby it is no longer in new and unused condition, such fact should be disclosed.*

    A customer has the right to believe that he is buying a new (unused) article and in unused condition. If, by reason of having been a "demonstration" model or equivalent, the article is no longer in unused condition, such should be disclosed.

18. *If the customer will be obliged to pay to the seller anything in addition to the advertised price (such as transportation or installation charges) such should be disclosed.*

> The customer has a right to believe that the advertised price is all he must pay (except sales tax) to purchase the article. In the case of a heavy article, such as a range, which the customer would not normally take home with him, he may well have the right to assume the seller will deliver, at least within the local area. If delivery will be an extra charge, such should be made clear.

19. *If the advertised article is in limited supply, or is an obsolete or discontinued model, such should be disclosed.*

> The customer has a right to believe that the advertising seller has a sufficient supply on hand to meet reasonably anticipated needs and that the article is of current model, unless otherwise advised.

Abbreviations

ABC—American Broadcasting Co.
AMA—American Medical Association
AMC—American Motors Corp.
BNDD—Bureau of Narcotics & Dangerous Drugs
CoC—Chamber of Commerce
CAB—Civil Aeronautics Board
CPSC—Consumer Product Safety Commission
DDT—dicholordiphenyl-trichloroethane
DES—diethylstilbesterol
DBS—Division of Biologics Standards
DEA—Drug Enforcement Administration (of Department of Justice)
FAA—Federal Aviation Administration
FCC—Federal Communications Commission
FEA—Federal Energy Agency
FHA—Federal Highway Administration
FHA—Federal Housing Administration
FTC—Federal Trade Commission
GAO—General Accounting Office
GM & GMC—General Motors Corp.
GRAS—generally regarded as safe
GSA—General Services Administration
HEW—Department of Health, Education & Welfare
HUD—Department of Housing & Urban Development
IUD—intrauterine (contraceptive) device
L-dopa—levo-dihydroxyphenylanine

NAB—National Association of Broadcasters
NBC—National Broadcasting Co.
NCA—National Canners Association
MSG—monosodium glutamate
NHTSA—National Highway Traffic Safety Administration
NIH—National Institutes of Health
OTA—Office of Technology Assessment
OTC—over the counter
ppm—parts per million
PCB—polychlorinated biphenyls
PHS—Public Health Service
RDA—recommended daily allowance
TV—television
USDA—U.S. Department of Agriculture

Index

A

ABBOTT Laboratories—49–50, 61
ACCIDENTS—2, 9, 104–6, 133
ADRIANI, Dr. John—49, 67
ADVERTISING—1–2, 8–9, 11, 13, 66, 99, 114–22, 145–50
    Appliances—155–60. Automobiles—31, 33, 42, 44, 117
    Computer schools—116. Cosmetics—115
    Detergents—117, 199–20. Drugs—50–2, 54–5
    Federal guidelines—114, 117–8. Food & nutrition—9, 94–8; Pet foods—117
    Sales & promotional practices—118–21, 134–5; contests—120–1; 'free' merchandise—114, 122, 157; 'pyramid' sales—119
    Tires—116–7. Tobacco industry—74–7; See also company names
AEROSOL Sprays—66, 110–1
AGRICULTURAL Marketing Act of 1946—79
AGRICULTURE, Department of—85–6, 92–4, 99, 110
AIRLINES—132–3
AIR Pollution—27, 39, 43, 113
ALLEGHENY Airlines—132
ALLEN-Bradley Co. (Milwaukee)—124, 127
ALLIED Chemical Corp.—129
ALLIED Van Lines, Inc.—132
ALLIS-Chalmers Manufacturing Co.—124

ALVORD & Alvord (law firm)—26
AMALGAMATED Sugar Co.—101
AMERICAN Academy of Pediatrics—106
AMERADA-Hess Corp.—128
AMERICAN Bar Association (ABA)—15–6, 21
AMERICAN Brands, Inc.—77
AMERICAN Broadcasting Co. (ABC)—77
AMERICAN Can Co.—87
AMERICAN Color & Chemical Corp.—129
AMERICAN Crystal Sugar Co.—101
AMERICAN Cyanamid Co.—54, 129
AMERICAN Home Products Corp. (N.Y.)—50, 54
AMERICAN Medical Association (AMA)—51–2, 54, 59, 66–8. Journal—50, 74
AMERICAN Motors Corp.—27–8, 41
AMERICAN Physicians & Surgeons, Association of—67
AMERICAN Telephone & Telegraph Co. (AT&T)—127, 135–6
AMERICAN Tobacco Co.—76
AMERICAN Trial Lawyers Association—26
AMOCO Oil Corp.—128
AMREP Corp. (N.Y.)—134
ANDERSON, Jack—107
ANDREADIS, John—51
ANNIS, Dr. Edward R.—51–2
ANTITRUST Actions—27, 31, 42–5, 53, 99–101, 123–30, 135–6. See also specific companies & industries

ANTACIDS—62-3
APPLIANCES—155-60
ARIZONA—101, 134
ARMOUR & Co. (Chicago)—80
ARMSTRONG Rubber Co.—32
ARMY: Corps of Engineers—33
ASPIRIN—50-1, 66
ASSOCIATED Dry Goods Corp.—123
ATLANTIC-Richfield Co.—128
ATLAS Supply Co.—128
ATRAL Laboratories (Lisbon, Portugal)—48
AUERBACH, Dr. Oscar—74
AUTOMOBILE Importers of America—41
AUTOMOBILES & Auto Industry—145. See also specific companies—66
    Advertising practices—31, 33, 42-4, 116-8; car rentals—131; warranties—12. Antitrust actions—27, 31, 42-5
      Gas mileage—43-4, 116-8
      Pollution standards—27, 39, 43
      Safety & defects—25, 33-8; accidents—9; brake defects—32, 41; crash protection & tests—26, 32, 34-5, 50-2; federal standards—9, 28-31, 40-5; recalls—2, 28, 31-3, 36-9; seatbelts—26, 30, 40-1; tires—32, 35, 44-5, 116-7
AUTO Safety, Center for—37-9
AVIS Rent-A-Car System, Inc.—131
AYERST Laboratories—60
AZARNOFF, Dr. Daniel L.—67

B

BANKS & Banking Practices—122-4
BASF Wyandotte Corp.—129
BATES & Co., Inc., Ted—95, 114
BATES Laboratories Inc. (Chicago)—48
BAYH, Sen. Birch (D, Ind.)—2
BEECH Aircraft Corp.—132
BEECHNUT Co.—91
BEEF—73, 79-81, 88-94, 97-8, 100
BELL Telephone System—127, 135-6
BENNETT, Norman—31
BERGDORF Goodman—130
BERLINER, Robert W.—63
BEVERAGES—90-1, 94-5, 97-8, 129
BICYCLES—103, 105
BIRTH Control: IUD—70, 73-4. Pill safety & control—70-3
BLACK, Justice Hugo L.—99
BLACKS—106
BLAIR Corp., D. L. (N.Y.)—121
BOLT Beranek & Newman, Inc.—117

BON Vivant Soups, Inc. (Newark, N.J.)—86-7
BORDEN Co. (Columbus, Ohio)—99, 110
BORNEMEIER, Dr. Walter C.—66
BOSTICK, Dr. Mary Jane—2-3
BOTULISM—86, 88, 93-4. See also 'Contamination' under FOOD & Food Industry
BOYD, Virgil—42
BP Oil Corp.—121
BREAD—95-6, 100
BRENNAN Jr., Justice William J.—22
BRIDWELL, Lowell K.—30-1
BRISTOL-Myers Co. (N.Y.)—50, 54
BRITISH Medical Journal—71
BROOKER, Robert E.—13-4
BROWN, Gov. Edmund G. (D, Calif.)—6
BROWN & Williamson Tobacco Corp.—76-7
BROWNELL, Herbert—136
BRUCE, James T.—132
BRUNER, D. L.—7
BRYANT, Judge William—62
BUGAS, John S.—27, 29
BUREAU of Narcotics & Dangerous Drugs—64
BURENS, George E.—125, 127
BURGER, Chief Justice Warren E.—130
BURKE, Clarence—125
BURNEY, Dr. Leroy E.—74
BURROUGHS Wellcome & Co., Inc. (Tuckahoe, N.Y.)—47
BUSES—35-6
BUSINESS & Industry—5-6, 12, 14-5, 27-8, 31-2, 41-5, 47-8, 50, 54, 60, 76-7, 80, 87, 100-1, 124-30, 135-6, 149-51. See also ANTITRUST Actions, CONSUMERISM & Consumer Protection, CREDIT & Credit Abuses, STOCKS & Bonds, specific department & agencies, companies & industries
BUSINESS Council for Consumer Affairs, National—14-5
BUTTERFIELD, Alexander P.—132-3
BUTZ, Earl L.—92

C

CAHILL, Gov. William T.—122
CALIFORNIA—86, 101
CALIFORNIA & Hawaiian Sugar Co.—101
CAMPBELL Soup Co.—85, 87
CANADA—6, 84
CANCER Control Bureau—73
CAPLOVITZ, David—2, 143
CARRIER Corp.—124
CARROLL, Sen. John A. (D, Colo.)—53

INDEX

CARSON, Rachel—143
CELEBREZZE, Anthony J.—7
CEREALS & Cereal Industry—94, 98-100
CHAMBER Of Commerce of the U.S.—22
CHANCE Co., A. B.—124
CHAPMAN, Bernard A.—27
CHARLES, Dr. Seymour—28
CHARTER Oil Co.—128
CHAVEZ, Cesar—86
CHEMICALS—66, 73, 82-84, 105-11, 133. See also specific chemical
CHEMWAY Corp.—69
CHESEBROUGH, Harry—27
CHICAGO—101, 104
CHILD Health & Safety—8-9, 91-2, 94-5, 103-10, 114, 142
CHILD Protection & Toy Safety Act (1969)—103-4
CHILD Safety Act—8
CHOATE Jr., Robert B.—94
CHRYSLER Corp.—28, 30, 42, 117-8, 121, 131
CIBA-GEIGY Corp.—129
CIBA Pharmaceutical Co. (Summit, N.J.)—52
CIGARETTES & Cigarette Smoking—9, 74-7
CIVIL Aeronautics Board (CAB)—132
CIVIL Readers Club, Inc.—119
CITY-Wide Coalition Against Childhood Lead Paint Poisoning—106
CLARK, Justice Tom C.—99
CLARK Controller Co.—124
CLOTHING—130-1
COAL Mine Health & Safety Act of 1969—25
COBURN Corp. of America—21
COCA-Cola Co.—94, 120, 129
COCHRAN Jr., Samuel—86
COHEN, Dr. Sidney—64
COLE, Edward N.—34, 42
COLGATE Palmolive Co.—107, 114, 119-20
COLUMBIA Broadcasting System, Inc. (CBS)—77
COMMERCE, Department of—29, 105
COMMONER, Dr. Barry—83
COMPREHENSIVE Occupational Safety & Health Act of 1970—25
CONCERNED Engineering, Center for —110
CONNECTICUT Citizens' Action Group —132
CONSOLIDATED Foods Corp.—101
CONSUMER Federation of America —93

CONSUMERISM & Consumer Protection—139-53
  Advertising—5-9, 13, 94-8, 108, 115-21; see also ADVERTISING. Antitrust actions—27, 31, 42-5, 53, 99-101, 123-30, 135-6
  Beverages—90-1, 94-5, 97-8. Birth control—70-4. 'Buyer's Bill of Rights'—143-4
  Carpet standards—137. Cigarette smoking—9, 74-7. Class-action suits—21-2, 32-3, 100, 120. Competition & monopoly—5-6. Consumer product information—94-8, 113-4. Consumer safety—7-10, 13, 103-4, 108, 110; aerosol sprays—66, 110-1; bicycles—103, 105; chemicals—66, 73, 82, 94, 105-11; child health & safety—8-10, 13, 91-2, 94-5, 103-10, 114; cosmetics—2, 5, 7-8, 13, 79, 92, 109, 115, 131, 133-4; fire hazards —9-10, 13, 103, 105, 111-2; food—3, 5, 6-8, 19-20, 33, 47-50, 55-63, 68-73, 79-98, 100-1, 103-9, 113-4, 133-4, 141 (see also FOOD & Food Industry, specific types and companies); household products—9, 111-2; plane safety—132-3; poisons—86-7, 105-6; radiation hazards—111-2; soaps & detergents—103, 106-7, 109. Credit—5, 7-11, 117, 121-4, 143, 159
  Drugs—See under Medicine & Health
  Funeral prices—136-7
  Labeling & Packaging reform —94-8, 143. Land & real estate sales—134-5
  Pricing practices—1-2, 99-101, 115
  Shipping & moving companies —112, 131-2
  Warranties & refunds—12, 134, 157-9
CONSUMER Federation of America—133
CONSUMER Finance, National Committee on—123
CONSUMER Product Safety Commission (CPSC)—103-5, 110
CONSUMER Protection Agency—13, 23
CONSUMER Reports (magazine)—38-9
CONSUMERS' League—2, 142
CONSUMERS' Research, Inc.—142
CONSUMERS Union—93, 123
CONTRACTS & Leases—134-5
CONTROL Data Corp. (South Bloomington, Minn.)—116
CONTROLLED Substances Act—64-5

COOPER Tire & Rubber Co.—45
CORDI Corp. (Miami, Fla.)—69
CORDINER, Ralph J.—125-6
CORD Laboratories—60
CORNELL-Dubilier Electric Corp.—124
COSMETICS—2, 5, 7-8, 79, 92, 109, 115, 131, 134-4
COURTS & Court Actions—18, 21-2, 31, 38, 40-3, 44, 48, 53-6, 67, 93, 99-101, 114, 120, 130-1
COWLES Communications, Inc.—119
CREDIT & Credit Abuses—5, 7-11, 117, 121-4, 143, 159. Credit cards—121-2. Installment plans—122-3. Interest rates—123
CREDIT Disclosure Act (1968)—143
CRESAP Jr., Mark W.—125-6
CROMPTON & Knowles Corp.—129
CROUT, Dr. Richard—50
CRUSH International, Ltd. (Canada)—129
CUNNINGHAM, Rep. Glenn (R, Neb.)—27
CUTLER-Hammer, Inc.—124
CYCLAMATES—89-90

D

DAIRY Products—88, 99-100, 108
DANCER-Fitzgerald-Sample, Inc.—50
D'ARCY Advertising Co. (St. Louis)—121
DAVIS, Dr. Hugh J.—72
DAVIS-Edwards Pharmacal Corp. (N.Y.)—48
DDT (dichlorodiphenyl-trichloroethane)—84-5, 108
DEATHS—105-6, 108
DeBUTTS, John D.—136
DEFENSE, Department of—131
DELANEY Clause (of the Food & Drug Act)—89
DELTA Refining Co.—128
DEMOCRATIC Party—14-5
DENTAL Products—69, 109
DEODORANTS—109
DES (diethylstilbesterol)—73, 92-3
DETERGENTS & Soaps—103, 106-7, 109, 117, 119-20
DIABETES—59-60
DIELDRIN—86
DIRKSEN, Sen. Everett M. (R, Ill.)—53
DIXON, Paul Rand—6, 15-6, 33, 75, 100
DLOUHY, Jan—68
DODD, Sen. Thomas J. (D, Conn.)—53
DOLCIN Corp. (N.Y.)—50
DOLE, Sen. Robert (R, Kan.)—51-2
DOUGLAS, Justice William O.—22
DOUGLAS Oil Co. (Calif.)—129

DOW Corning Corp. (Midland, Mich.)—60
DRAPER, John B.—132
Dr. PEPPER Co. (Dallas)—129
DRUG Enforcement Administration (DEA)—65
DRUG Research Corp.—51
DRUGS—See under MEDICINE & Health
DULUTH Clearing House Association—124
DULUTH National Bank (Minn.)—124
DUNLOP Tire & Rubber Corp.—44
Du PONT de Nemours & Co., E. I.—90, 114, 129
DUROVIC, Marko—48
DuVAL, Dr. Merlin K.—106

E

EAST Coast Terminal, Inc. (Wilmington, N.C.)—85
EASTLAND, Sen. James O. (D, Miss.)—6
EASTWOOD, General Corp. (Los Angeles, Calif.)—69
ECKHARDT, Rep. Bob (D, Tex.)—21
EDUCATION—116, 143
EDUCATIONAL Book Club, Inc.—119
EDWARDS, Dr. Charles C.—6, 19, 55-8, 60-3, 65, 69, 71, 81-3, 89-92, 106, 108-9
EGEBERG, Dr. Roger O.—49
EGGS—88
EISEN, Morton—22
ELECTRICITY & Electrical Equipment—9-10, 124-7
ELECTRONIC Computer Programming Institute, Inc. (N.Y.)—116
ELKIND, Arnold B.—112
ELMAN, Philip—16-7
ENGMAN, Lewis A.—18, 53
ENVIRONMENTAL Defense Fund—93
ENVIRONMENTAL Protection Agency (EPA)—14, 39, 84-6, 106
ERBEN, Henry V.—125-6
EXXON Corp.—128-9
EYEGLASSES—69

F

FAIR Labeling & Packaging Act (1966)—143
FEDDERS Corp.—117
FEDERAL Aviation Administration (FAA)—132-3
FEDERAL Communications Commission (FCC)—76, 119, 127, 136
FEDERAL Deposit Insurance Corp.

INDEX

(FDIC)—124
FEDERAL Energy Administration (FEA)—128–9
FEDERAL Highway Administration (FHA)—31–3
FEDERAL Home Loan Bank Board—124
FEDERAL Housing Administration (FHA)—137
FEDERAL Pacific Electric Co. (Newark, N.J.)—124
FEDERAL Power Commission Act (1914)—141
FEDERAL Reserve Board—123–4
FEDERAL Trade Commission (FTC)—5, 12, 15–19, 21, 32–3, 42, 44–5, 50–2, 66, 75–7, 94–6, 98–101, 107, 114–21, 129–37, 141, 155, 159
FEDERAL Trade Act (1914)—141
FEDERATION of American Societies for Experimental Biology—89
FEIKENS, Judge John—43
FELLMETH, Robert—19
FINCH, Robert H.—84, 89–90
FIRE Safety—9–10, 103–5, 111–2
FIRESTONE Tire & Rubber Co.—17, 32, 44–5, 117
FIRST American National Bank (Duluth, Minn.)—124
FIRST Bank Stock Corp. (St. Paul, Minn.)—124
FIRST Grand Avenue State Bank (St. Paul, Minn.)—124
FIRST National Bank (Minneapolis)—124
FIRST National Bank (St. Paul, Minn.)—124
FIRST Security State Bank (St. Paul, Minn.)—124
FISH—79, 82–5, 87–8, 108. See also specific types
FLAMMABLE Fabrics Act of 1967—10, 103, 105
FLEMMING, Dr. Arthur S.—93
FLETCHER Oil & Refining Co. (Calif.)—129
FLINTKOTE Co.—130
FLORIDA—134
FOOD & Drug Act of 1906—47, 141. Delaney clause—89
FOOD & Drug Administration (FDA)—6–7, 19–20, 47–50, 55–63, 65–6, 68–72, 79–96, 103–9, 113–4, 133–4
FOOD, Drug & Cosmetic Act—3, 8, 79, 92
FOOD & Food Industry—3, 5, 6–8, 19–20, 33, 47–50, 55–63, 68–72, 79–96, 100–1, 103–9, 113–4, 133–4, 141;

see also specific types and companies
Additives—73, 88–94, 108–9; coloring—93–4; MSG—91–2; preservatives—89; sugar substitutes—89–91; cyclamates—89–90. Animal feeds—73, 88–94, 108–9
Contamination—82–8; bottled water—89; chemicals—84–6, 88; federal standards—79–83, 86–8; fish—82–5, 88; poisoning—86–8
Inspection standards—79–83; meat—5, 7, 9–10, 79–83; plants—80–1, 86–7
Nutrition labeling & reform—94–8
Prices & price fixing—99–100
FORD 2d, Henry—28–9
FORD Motor Co.—27–9, 33, 35–7, 39, 41–3, 117–8, 131
FOUNTAIN, Rep. L. H. (D, N.C.)—60, 87, 90, 92
FOX, Judge Noel P.—80
FREEDOM of Information Act—123
FREEMAN, Orville—100
FREEMAN, Dr. Roger D.—50
FRIEDMAN, Milton—55
FRUIT Drinks—94–5, 97
FULLER, Landon—126
FURNESS, Betty—23, 143

G

GAC Corp.—134
GAF Corp.—129
GANEY, Judge J. Cullen—124
GARDNER, John W.—76
GAS, Natural—10
GAS Appliance Manufacturers Association, Inc.—155
GASCH, Judge Oliver—33
GASOLINE Stations—127–9, 133. See also PETROLEUM & Petroleum Industry
GENERAL Accounting Office (GAO)—39, 80–2
GENERAL Electric Co.—69, 124–7
GENERAL Foods Corp.—100
GENERAL Mills, Inc.—100
GENERAL Motors Corp. (GM and GMC)—25–6, 30, 32–8, 42–3, 117–8
GENERAL Services Administration (GSA)—28, 113
GENERAL Tire & Rubber Co.—32, 44–5
GENESCO, Inc.—123, 130
GERBER, Daniel F.—91
GERBER Products Co.—91
GERMICIDES—109–10
GESELL, Gerhard A.—125, 127
GETTY Oil Co.—128
GEZON, L. B.—125

GIANT Food, Inc.—114–5
GIKAS, Dr. Paul W.—26
GILLEN, Vincent—26
GIMBAL Brothers, Inc.—123
GINN, William S.—126
GLENDINNING Cos.—120
GOLDBERG, Justice, Arthur J.—99
GOLDEN Eagle Refining Co., Inc. (Calif.)—129
GOLDFARB, Lewis—130
GOLDFARB, Ruth—130
GOODMAN, Julian—76–7
GOODRICH, William W.—90
GOODRICH Co., B. F.—32, 44–5
GOODYEAR Tire & Rubber Co.—32, 44–5, 110
GORTON, Slade—119
GOSSETT, William T.—15
GOVERNMENT Policy & Regulations—1–2, 5–23, 51, 65–6, 69, 72, 74–7, 87, 90–4, 99–101, 103–6, 117–8, 121–2, 124–7, 134–5, 141–2, 150–2
    Advertising claims—117–8. Animal feed—92–3
    Birth control—72
    Cigarette smoking—74–7. Competition & monopoly—5–6. Credit abuses—5, 7–11, 121–2
    Drugs—5–8, 13, 65–6
    Fire safety—9–10. Food—5, 87, 90–2, 94, 100–1
    Land sales—134–5
    Poisons & other dangerous chemicals—13–4. Pricing practices—1–2, 99–101. Product safety—7–10, 13
GRACE & Co., W. R.—107
GRANT Co., W. T.—117
GRAS ('generally recognized as safe')—89
GRAY, Judge William P.—68–9
GREAT Atlantic & Pacific Tea Co. (A&P)—100, 117
GREAT Western Sugar Co.—101
GREENWALD, Dr. Peter—73
GRISWOLD, Erwin N.—126
GROLIER, Inc. (N.Y.)—119
GROLIER Interstate, Inc.—119
GRUBER, Lewis—74
GULF Oil Corp.—128–9

H

HADDON Jr., Dr. William—29–30, 41–2
HALVERSON, Fred S.—107
HALVERSON, James T.—131
HALVERSTANDT, Albert N.—6
HARDIN, Clifford M.—84
HARDIN, Dale W.—19

HART, Sen. Philip A. (D, Mich.)—6, 32, 53
HARTIG, Paul—125
HARTKE, Sen. Vance (D, Ind.)—27
HAWLEY Hale Stores, Inc., Carter—123
HAZARDOUS Substances Act—108
HEALTH, Education & Welfare (HEW), Department of—6, 49, 53–4, 104, 106–7
HEALTH & Medicine—See MEDICINE & Health
HEALTH Devices—47, 68–71, 73–4, 115. See also specific types
HEARING Aids—113, 115
HEARST Corp.—119
HEIMANN, Robert K.—75
HEINZ, H.J.—91
HELLMAN, Dr. Louis M.—70–1
HENTSCHEL, H. Frank—125
HERDMAN, Dr. Roger C.—84
HERTZ, Dr. Roy—72
HERTZ Corp.—131
HEXACHLOROPHENE—109–10
HIGHWAYS—9, 34–6
HIGHWAY Safety Act of 1966—27
HODNETTE, John K.—126–7
HOGE, James F.—7
HOLIFIELD, Rep. Chet (D, Calif.)—22
HOLLY Farms, Inc.—85
HOLLY Sugar Corp.—101
HOME Readers Service, Inc.—119
HOME Reference Library, Inc.—119
HORIZON Corp. (Tucson, Ariz.)—134
HORMEL & Co., George A. (Austin, Minn.)—80
HOUSEHOLD Finance Corp.—131
HOUSING & Urban Development (HUD), Department of—106, 134–5, 137
HRUSKA, Sen. Roman L. (R, Neb.)—53
HUBBARD Co.—124
HUELKE, Donald F.—26

I

ICI America, Inc.—62
IDEKA, Dr. Kikunae—92
IMPORTS—105–6
'INFO-Tag' System—9
INGERSOLL-Rand Corp.—124
INGRAHAM, Dr. Hollis S.—61
INSURANCE—1–2, 11, 132
INTERSTATE Commerce Commission (ICC)—19, 131–2
INVESTMENTS—9
I-T-E Circuit Breaker Co.—124, 127
ITT CONTINENTAL Baking Co., Inc.—95, 100–1

INDEX

IUD—71, 73-4
IVY, Dr. Andrew C.—48

J

JAPAN—83-4
JENKINS, Donald Ray—125
JENSEN, Malcolm W.—108
JOHNSON, Lyndon B.—7-11, 80
JOHNSON, Nicholas—127
JOHNSON & Johnson—70
JONES, Mary Gardiner—100
JOSLYN Manufacturing & Supply Co.—124
JOURNAL of the American Medical Association—50, 74
JUNGLE, The (book)—2, 142
JUSTICE, Department of—27, 31, 43, 52, 101, 123-9, 135-6

K

KAISER Gypsum Co., Inc.—130
KANSAS—128
KANSAS City, Mo.—99
KAPLAN, Dr. A. D. H.—126
KASSOUF, Dr. Edmond—72
KASTOR, Hilton, Chesley, Clifford & Atherton, Inc.—51
KAUPER, Thomas A.—53
KEELY, Louise T.—67
KEFAUVER, Sen. Estes (D, Tenn.)—3, 7, 48-9, 53, 125-6
KELLOGG Co.—100
KELSEY, Dr. Frances Oldham—6-7
KELSEY-Hayes Co.—32-3
KENNEDY, Dr. Carol—50
KENNEDY, Sen. Edward M. (D, Mass.)—16, 63, 67-8, 92
KENNEDY, John F.—1, 5-7, 143
KENNEDY, Sen. Robert F. (D, N.Y.)—28
KERR-McGee Corp.—128
KIRKPATRICK, Miles W.—15-6, 100, 115-6
KISTNER, Dr. Robert W.—72
KLEBER, Dan—85
KNAUER, Mrs. Virginia H.—3, 11-3, 17, 35, 143
KORVETTE, Inc., E.J.—117
KREBIOZEN—48
KRIEGEL, Glen F.—32
KROGER Co.—100
KUHLMANN Electric Co.—124

L

LABELING—See PACKAGING & Labeling
LAM, Mimi—67
LAND Sales—134-5
LAPP Insulator Co.—124
LARRICK, George P.—6
LARUS & Brother Co., Inc.—76
LATHAM, Prof. Michael C.—94
L-DOPA—60-1
LEAD & Lead Poisoning—88, 105-6
LEAGUE of Women Voters—142
LEAR Siegler, Inc. (Santa Monica, Calif.)—116
LEDERLE Laboratories (Pearl River, N.Y.)—56
LEMMON Pharmacal Co. (Sellersville, Pa.)—56, 64
LENZ, Dr. Widukind—6
LEVER Brothers Co., Inc.—107, 120
LEVIN, Judge Gerald S.—120
LEY Jr., Dr. Herbert L.—84, 114
LIGGETT & Myers Tobacco Co., Inc.—76-7
LILLY & Co., Eli—70
LINDE, Victor van der—50
LINDEN Laboratories—60
LIPTON, Inc., Thomas J.—82
LIVESTOCK—73, 80, 85-6, 88-94, 100
LOEWS Corp.—77
LONG, Sen. Russell B. (D, La.)—49
LOOCK, Fred—127
LORILLARD Co., P.—74, 77
LYNG, Richard E.—81

M

MacINTYRE, Everette—100
MacMILLAN Ring-Free Co. (N.Y.)—129
MAGNUSON, Sen. Warren G. (D, Wash.)—9, 28, 76
MALONEY Electric Co.—124
MANN, Thomas C.—31
MANSFIELD Tire & Rubber Co.—45
MARQUETTE National Bank (Minneapolis)—124
MARSCHALK Co.—94
MARTIN, Joseph—115
MATSUSHITA Electric Corp.—112
MATTEL, Inc.—114
MAYER, Dr. Jean—94
McCARRAN-Ferguson Act (1945)—132
McCLEERY, Dr. Robert S.—67
McDONALD'S Corp.—121
McDUFFE, Dr. Bruce—82
McGOVERN, Sen. George S. (D, S.D.)—91
McGRAW-Edison Co.—124
McKESSON Laboratories (Bridgport, Conn.)—48

MEAD Johnson & Co.—70
MEAT—5, 7, 9-10, 73, 79-83, 86-94, 97-8, 100. Animal feed—73, 88-94, 108-9. Federal inspection—79-83. Labeling reform—97-8. Pricing practices—100
MEAT Inspection Act (1906)—79, 142
MEDICARE & Medicaid—67
MEDICINE & Health:
    Advertising claims—50-2. Aspirin—66
    Beauty aids—115. Birth control—70-3
    Cigarette smoking—9, 74-7
    Diet pills—51, 64. Drug industry & physicians—51-3, 66-8. Drugs—47-73; diabetes drugs—59-60
    Federal control—7, 48, 51, 55-9, 64, 66
    Generic labeling—49
    Health Care—66-9; Clinical laboratories—10; Malpractice insurance—1-2. Health devices—1, 8, 10, 47, 68-71, 73-4, 113, 115; See also specific types
    Intravenous fluids—61
    Krebiozen—48
    L-dopa—60-1
    Misuse—57-9, 63-5
    'Mood' drug & pep pills—63-5
    Prescription & over-the-counter drugs—49-54, 63, 65-8. Prices & pricing practices—49, 52-4
    Safety & effectiveness—5-8, 10, 47-52, 55-66, 68. Sleep aids—65-6
    Thalidomide—5-7
    Vaccines & biologic products—20. Vitamins—52, 58-9
MEDI-Hair International (Sacramento, Calif.)—115
MELAMED, Dr. Myron R.—71
MELCHER, Rep. John (D, Mont.)—81
MENTHOLATUM Co., Inc. (Buffalo, N.Y.)—50
MERCK & Co. (West Point, Pa.)—56
MERCURY—82-5, 88, 133
MERRELL Co., William S.—6
MIDLAND National Bank (Minneapolis)—124
MILES Laboratories—58
MILK—88, 99-100
MILLER, Jerome—69
MINNESOTA—123-4
MISSOURI—134
MOBIL Oil Corp.—128-9
MONSANTO Co.—107, 109
MONTEITH, A. C.—125

MONTGOMERY Ward & Co., Inc.—122
MURPHY Oil Corp.—128
MORRIS, Dr. Ruby Turner—6
MORRIS, Inc., Philip—76-7
MOSS, Sen. Frank E. (D, Utah)—76-7, 94, 105
MOSS, Rep. John E. (D, Calif.)—14
MOTORCYCLES—41
MOTOR Vehicles—See specific type; e.g. AUTOMOBILES
MSG (monosodium glutamate)—91-2
MURRAY, Arthur, Inc.—114
MUSHROOM Co., Inc., Fran (Ravena, N.Y.)—88
MUSHROOM Products Co., Fred (South Lebanon, Ohio)—88
MUTUAL Readers League, Inc.—119

N

NADER, Ralph—2, 19-20, 22-3, 25-6, 29-38, 43-4, 66-8, 92, 103, 113, 132-3
NARCOTICS & Dangerous Drugs, Bureau of—64
NATIONAL Academy of Science—90-1, 94, 97
NATIONAL Association of Broadcasters (NAB)—52
NATIONAL Automobile Dealers Association—43
NATIONAL Biscuit Co.—82
NATIONAL Broadcasting Co. (NBC)—76-7
NATIONAL Canners' Association (NCA)—20, 86-7
NATIONAL Car Rental System, Inc.—131
NATIONAL Child Labor Association—142
NATIONAL Commission on Product Safety—2
NATIONAL Consumers' League—2
NATIONAL Dairy Products Co.—99
NATIONAL Electric Manufacturing Association—126
NATIONAL Highway Safety Bureau—32-6, 41-2, 44
NATIONAL Industries, Inc. (Louisville)—129
NATIONAL Institute for Consumer Justice—21
NATIONAL Institute of Environmental Health Science—107
NATIONAL Marine Fisheries Service—79
NATIONAL Recovery Act (1933)—142
NATIONAL Society of Professional Engineers—129

INDEX

NATIONAL Sugar Beet Growers Federation—101
NATIONAL Traffic & Motor Vehicle Safety Act of 1966—25
NATIONAL Traffic Safety Agency—29–30, 107
NATIONAL Transportation Safety Board—112
NATURAL Gas Pipeline Safety Act of 1968—25
NELSON, Sen. Gaylord (D, Wis.)—20–1, 49, 51, 55, 72, 89
NELSON, Mrs. Helen Ewing—6
NEUBERGER, Maurine—143
NEW Jersey—86
NEW Mexico—134
NEW York—128, 130
NEW York Stock Exchange—22
NICHOLS, Byron J.—42
NISSAN Motor Corp.—42
NITRATES & Nitrites—93–4
NIXON, Richard M.—11–3, 77, 143–4, 150
NORTH American Chemical Corp. (Paterson, N.J.)—107
NORTH Carolina—86
NORTHERN City National Bank (Duluth, Minn.)—124
NORTHWESTERN National Bank (St. Paul, Minn.)—124
NTA (nitrilotriacetic acid)—106
NUTRITION—94–8

O

OBSTETRICS & Gynecology, Committee on—71
OCEAN Spray Cranberries, Inc.—95
OFFICE of Technology Assessment (OTA)—63
OLNEY, Dr. John W.—91
OMEGA Chemical Co., Inc. (N.J.)—50
100,000,000 Guinea Pigs (book)—2, 142
OPPENHEIM, Prof. S. Chesterfield—126
ORAL Contraception—See BIRTH Control
ORTHO Pharmaceutical Corp.—70
OUIRIN, Terrence M.—67

P

PACKAGING & Labeling—2, 6–9, 13, 94–8, 107–10, 143
PACKARD, Vance—143
PAINTS—106
PARKE, Davis & Co.—51–2, 70
PARKSON Advertising Agency, Inc.—52
PARROTT, Dr. Max H.—67
PAXTON, Robert—125–6
PCB (polychlorinated biphenyls)—85–6, 108–9
PEDIATRICS, American Academy of—106
PENNSYLVANIA—81
PEPSICo, Inc. (Purchase, N.Y.)—129
PERFECT Film & Chemical Corp.—119
PESTICIDES & Germicides—8, 84–6, 109–10, 117
PETERS, John—125
PETERSON, Mrs. Esther—7, 143
PETERSON, Howell & Heather, Inc.—43
PETROLEUM & Petroleum Industry—43–4, 116–8, 120–1, 127–9, 132
PFIZER & Co. Inc., Charles (N.Y.)—47, 52, 54, 56
PHARMACEUTICAL Manufacturers Association (PMA)—53, 63, 67
PHILIP Morris, Inc.—108
PHILLIPS, Russell E.—67
PHILLIPS, William F. P.—48
PHILLIPS Petroleum Co.—128
PHOSPHATES—107
PITOFSKY, Robert—51
PLANNED Parenthood Foundation—71, 74
PLOUGH, Inc.(Memphis, Tenn.)—50, 62
POISONS—13–4, 73, 84–8, 104–8. See also specific poison
POOR Pay More, The (book)—2
POPEIL Brothers, Inc. (Chicago, Ill.)—115
PORCELAIN Insulator Co.—124
PORTER Co., H.K.—124
POSNER, Richard A.—15–6
POTTERY—105–6
POULTRY—79–80, 85–6, 93, 108
POULTRY Products Inspection Act—79
POWELL Jr., Justice Lewis F.—22
POWERLINE Oil Co. (Calif.)—129
PRESCRIPTIONS—52–4, 63, 65–8
PRESERVATIVES—89
PRICES & Price Fixing—50–4, 59, 99–101, 114–5, 119, 124–31, 136–7, 156–7
PROCTER & Gamble Co.—107, 119
PRODUCT Safety — 109–10, 112. Bicycles—103, 105. Cosmetics—7, 13, 109. Drugs—See under 'D.' Federal standards—13. Flammable fabrics—9–10, 13. Health devices—69. Household products—9–10, 69. Toys—9, 13, 103–5, 114. Vehicle safety—9, 25–42. See also specific types
PRODUCT Safety, National Commission on—10, 112

PRODUCT Safety Act, Consumer—13
PROFESSIONAL Standards Review Act—67
PRO-Ter Laboratory (Milan, Italy)—48
PUBLIC Health Service—104, 112
PUBLIC Interest Research Group (Washington)—105
PUBLISHING Industry—118-21
PURE Food & Drug Act (1906)—2

Q

QUAKER Oats Co.—100

R

RADIATION—112
RADIATION Control Act of 1968—25
RAILWAY—112
RAPID American Corp.—123
RASKIN, Winton B.—91
RAUCH, Thomas N.—64
RAUSCHER, Frank J.—92
RCA Corp.—131
RDA—97
READER'S Digest Association, Inc. —120-1
REAL Estate—134-5
RECORDING Industry—118
REGINA Corp.—114
REPUBLICAN Party—15
REVLON, Inc.—131
REYNOLDS Tobacco Co., R.J.—76-7
RELAXACIZOR Sales, Inc.—69
RICHARDSON, Elliot—20
RIBICOFF, Sen. Abraham (D, Conn.)—20, 26, 28, 34, 69
RICHLYN Laboratories (Philadelphia)—48
RICKELS, Dr. Karl—65
ROBBINS, Co., A.H.—73
ROBINSON-Patman Act—99
ROBY, Frank—127
ROCHE, James M.—26
ROCKEFELLER Foundation—71
RONDEX Laboratories (Guttenburg, N.J.)—48
ROONEY, Rep. Fred B. (D, Pa.)—119
ROSENTHAL, Rep. Benjamin S. (D, N.Y.)—9, 21-3
ROSTOW, Eugene V.—126
ROWLAND, W. C.—124
ROYAL Crown Cola Co. (Columbus, Ga.)—129
RUBBER Manufacturers Association (N.Y.)—44
RUCKELSHAUS, William D.—106
RUMBERGER, C. L.—6
RUSSELL, George—27

RYAN, Rep. William F. (D, N.Y.)—85, 108-9

S

SACCHARIN—91-2
SADUSK, Dr. Joseph F.—70
SAFEWAY Stores, Inc.—100
SAKS Fifth Avenue—130
SANDBACH, Walker—42
SANDOZ Pharmaceuticals (Hanover, N.J.)—52
SANGAMO Electric Co.—124
SAYERS, Dorothy—145
SCALISE, Lawrence F.—26
SCHMIDT, Dr. Alexander M.—49-50, 69, 88
SCHMIT, Loren—100
SCHULZ, Prof. John E.—15
SCHWAGER-Wood Corp.—124
SCOTT, Max—127
SCOTT, T. Harold—50
SEARLE & Co., G. D.—70
SEARS, Roebuck & Co.—117
SELLERS, R. B.—125
SEVEN-UP Co. (St. Louis)—129
SHEEP—92
SHELL Chemical Corp.—110
SHELLFISH—82
SHELL Oil Co.—120, 128
SHERMAN Antitrust Act (1890)—129-30, 141
SHIMMERLIK, George—50
SHIPPING & Shipping Safety—112, 131-2
SHIRKEY, Dr. Harry C.—67
SHORELL, Inc., Irma (N.Y.)—115
SIMMONS, Dr. Henry E.—54-5, 59, 61, 64
SIMPSON, Richard O.—103-4
SINCLAIR, Upton—2, 142
SKELLY Oil Co.—128
SKINKER Specialty Food Co. (Alexandria, Va.)—87
SLEEP Products—105
SLOAN-Kettering Institute-Memorial Hospital—71
SMITH, Dr. Austin—53
SMITH Jr., Judge John L.—129-30
SMITH, Raymond W.—125
SMITH, Kline & French Laboratories (Pa.)—56, 60, 64
SOCIAL Security Act—67
SOFT Drink Association—90
SOLOMONS, Dr. Gerald—49
SOUTHERN States Equipment Corp.—124
SPENCER International, Inc.—119
SPERRY & Hutchinson Co.—18

INDEX

SPIEGEL, Inc.—116, 122
SQUARE D Co.—124
SQUIBB Beech-Nut, Inc.—54
STANDARD Oil Co. (Calif.)—116, 118, 128
STANDARD Oil Co. (Ind.)—128
STANDARD Oil Co.(Ohio)—127-9
STANS, Maurice H.—105
STARE, Dr. Frederick J.—94
STAR-Kist Foods—87
STATE Fish Co., Inc. (San Pedro, Calif.)—85
STEHLIK, Frank E.—125
STEINFELD, Dr. Jesse—49, 106-7
STEPHANO Brothers, Inc.—76
STERLING Drug, Inc. (N.Y.)—50, 66, 116
STETLER, C. Joseph—63
STEWART, Justice Potter—99
STIEGLITZ, William I.—30
STILBESTROL (synthetic sex hormone)—93
STOCKS & Bonds—8-9, 22
STOUFFER'S Food Co.—88
STOVER Candies, Inc., Russell—82
SUGAR & Sugar Substitutes—89-91, 96, 101, 115-6
SUGAR Association, Inc.—96, 115
SUGAR Information, Inc.—115
SUN Oil Co—128
SUPREME Court—114, 120, 131-2
SVEDA, Dr. Michael—90
SWARTZ, Edward M.—104
SWORDFISH—82-4
SYMBRA'ETTE Inc. (Calif.)—119
SYNTEX Corp.—70, 72-3

T

TAXES—11
TEITELBAUM, Judge Hubert I.—130
TELECOMMUNICATIONS—135-6
TELEPHONES—127, 135-6
TELEVISION—76-7, 94, 112, 114-5, 117, 150
TELEX Corp.—115
TERRY, Luther L.—74-5
TEXACO Oil Corp.—128
TEXAS—134
THALIDOMIDE—5-7
THELIN, Carl—34
THOMPSON, Rep. Fletcher (R, Ga.)—99
THOMPSON, J. T.—126
3-M Co. (St. Paul, Minn.)—110
THROWER, Randolph W.—20-1
TIME, Inc.—119
TIRE & Rim Association, Inc. (Akron)—44

TIRES & Tire Safety—44-5, 116-7
TIRE Industry Safety Council—44
TOBACCO—9, 74-7
TOBACCO Industry Research Committee—74
TOBACCO Institute—74, 77
TOMS, Douglas W.—35, 37, 41
TOPPER Corp.—114
TOWNSEND, Lynn—42
TOYOTA Motor Co., Ltd.—42-3
TOYOTA Motor Sales of U.S.A., Inc.—38-9, 43
TOYS—8-9, 13, 103-5, 114
TRAFFIC & Motor Vehicle Safety Act of 1966—29
TRAFFIC Safety Act—9
TRAIN, Russell E.—43
TRANQUILIZERS—65
TRANSPORTATION—9, 29, 112, 131-2
TRANSPORTATION, Department of—2, 35-6, 41, 112
TRAVELERS Health Association (Omaha, Neb.)—132
TRUTH in Lending—7, 10-1, 121, 143
TRUTH in Packaging—8-9
TUNA—82-3, 87
TURNER, Donald F.—27

U

ULTRAMAR Co., Ltd. (England)—129
UNIROYAL, Inc.—44
UNITED Canning Corp. (East Palestine, Ohio)—88
UNITED Farm Workers Union—86
UNSAFE at Any Speed (book)—3, 25
UPJOHN Co.—54, 56, 59, 70
U.S. RUBBER Co. (New York)—44
U.S. TOBACCO Co.—76
UTAH-Idaho Sugar Co.—101

V

VACCINES—20
VERONA Corp.—129
VETERANS Administration—113
VINSON, Arthur F.—124, 125-7
VIRGINIA—130
VITAMINS—52, 58-9, 95, 97-8
VOLKSWAGEN of America, Inc. 37-8, 42
VOLPE, John A.—33-4, 36
VOLVO of America Corp.—117

W

WAGNER Electric Co.—124
WALSH, Joseph—87
WANTZ, Albert T.—50

WARNER-Lambert Pharmaceutical Co. (Morris Plains, N.J.)—56
WARRANTIES & Refunds—12, 134, 157-9
WASHINGTON, D.C.—99
WATER Pollution—88
WEINBERGER, Casper W.—17, 49
WELCH, Dr. Henry A.—49
WERKER, Judge Harry F.—130
WESTERN Electric Co.—127, 135
WESTERN Union—127
WESTINGHOUSE Electric Corp.—124-7
WHEELER Manufacturing Co., Foster—124
WHIRLPOOL Corp.—117
WHITE, Justice Byron R.—18
WHITE Jr., Frank B.—36
WHITEHALL Pharmacal Co. (N.Y.)—50
WHOLESALE Meat Act (1967)—25, 81
WHOLESOME Poultry Products Act—80

WILLIAMS, Carla S.—6
WILLIAMS, Tom A.—31
WILLIAMS Co., Inc., J. B.—52
WILSON & Co. (Phoenix, Ariz.)—80
WIRTH Food Products (Lawrence, Mass.)—88
WODICKA, Dr. Virgil O.—80, 82
WOLFE, Dr. Sidney—68
WOMEN—130-1
WORTHINGTON Corp.—124
WRIGHT, Judge Caleb—33
WRIGHT, Dr. Irving S.—70
WYATT, Judge Inzer B.—131

Y

YEUTTER, Clayton—81

Z

ZALE Corp.—121
ZENITH Laboratories (Inglewood, N.J.)—48

DATE DUE